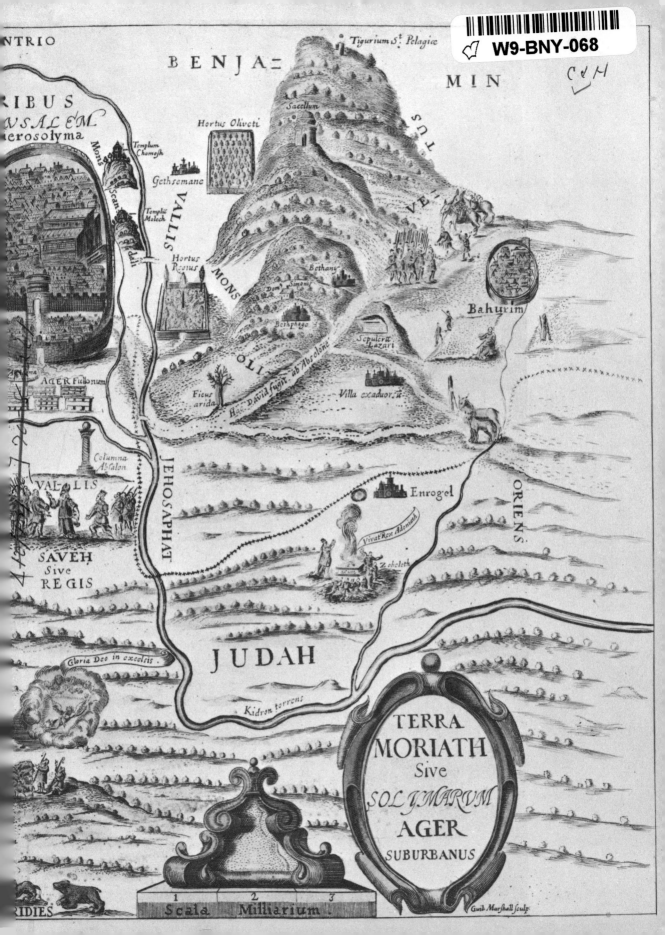

TERRA
MORIATH
Sive
SOLYMARVM
AGER
SUBURBANUS

HOLY PLACES

Endpapers:
Detail of a map of
the Holy Land from a
seventeenth-century
copper engraving.

HOLY PLACES

Jewish, Christian, and Muslim Monuments in the Holy Land

Christopher Hollis and Ronald Brownrigg

FREDERICK A. PRAEGER, Publishers
New York · Washington

BOOKS THAT MATTER

Published in the United States of America in 1969
by Frederick A. Praeger, Inc., Publishers
111 Fourth Avenue, New York, N.Y. 10003

Designed by Shashi Rawal

Printed in Denmark

Contents

List of Maps and Plans

A Canaanite stele from
Hazor of hands uplifted
in prayer, dating from the
fourteenth century BC.
This shrine is thought to
be dedicated to the moon-
god of an earlier pre-
historic religion.

Prologue

IN THE ANCIENT WORLD OF 2000 BC, THE TWO GREAT CENTRES OF civilisation were those of the Nile and of the two rivers, Tigris and Euphrates. Between these two centres flowed a constant stream of military and merchandise, travelling inevitably along one or other of the two main trade routes.

The first, called 'The Way of the Sea', kept to the coast of the Mediterranean until it turned east through the passes of Mount Carmel into the plain of Esdraelon. There it skirted to the north-west of Galilee and turned east again towards Damascus.

The second, called 'The King's Highway', crossed the Sinai Desert to the Gulf of Aqaba and followed the Rift Valley northwards, passing east and west of the Dead Sea and so to Damascus. Both these routes passed through the little land of Canaan, which by the fourth century BC became known as 'Palestine', after its Philistine invaders. This land was thus a bridge between Egypt and Babylon; its people were influenced by both civilisations. It was through the people of this small and insignificant country, that God was progressively revealed to mankind. Yet it was not from the settled and cultured, but from the nomadic and Semite tribes that Abraham was summoned by God, 'to go to a country that I will show you'.

Abraham was the father and founder of not one, but two great Semitic races. Both Arabs and Jews share the *same* grandfather. However, the former are the children of Ishmael, son of Abraham and Hagar the bondswoman, the latter are the children of Isaac, son of Abraham and Sarah, the freewoman. In Genesis the Israelites appear in the role of the children of promise and the Ishmaelites as the children cast out into the desert, of whom God made a 'great nation' also.

Today, the Holy Land is to both Muslim and Jew the land of the twelve patriarchs springing from the call, courage, faith and obedience of Abraham. Today, to the Christian, the Holy Land is the land of the early Church and twelve apostles springing from the call, courage, faith and obedience of the peasant girl, Mary. For the Muslim, the Holy Land is the land where God has spoken through successive prophets, of whom Jesus-ibn-Joseph is mentioned with great respect in the Quran, and of whom Muhammad is the greatest and the last. For the Jew, the Holy

Steps at the foot of Mount Sinai, suggestive of the place where Moses ascended the mountain alone.

9

Land is the land where God has spoken through both the Law and the Prophets, promising the Land to the People on the condition of their keeping the Covenant, and foretelling the coming of their Messiah and Deliverer. For all three faiths it is a land where God continues vividly to speak, to inspire and to invigorate his people.

For the Christian, the Holy Land is the land where God in Jesus 'became human that we might become divine', as summed up by St Athanasius. The Christian acknowledges God's choice of land or people for his great purpose, yet he points to Jesus' claim: 'Before Abraham was, I am!' St Ignatius described the Jewish people as 'the sacred school of the knowledge of God for all mankind.'

This book sets out to describe the Holy Places of these three great monotheistic religions to be found in the Holy Land. It seeks to trace the origin,

Within the lunar landscape of the Judaean wilderness, the Muslim 'Tomb of Moses' is commanded by the graves of the Faithful.

history and importance to the people of these three great world religions of such places as the Cave of Machpelah, the Rock of Calvary and the Dome of the Rock.

The Jews, the Christians and the Muslims base their faiths on historical claims, as well as present experience. These acts of God's providence happened on a particular day and in a particular place. To that extent these three religions have a similarity, but their 'Holy Places' have a very different significance and meaning in the faith and language of each religion. It must be made clear, however, that both Jews and Muslims venerate many places in common, because of their common ancestry and heritage in both Law and Prophets. It is therefore, our intention to examine a selection of places holy to Jews, Christians and Muslims – in that order – because that is the historical order of the emergence of their faiths.

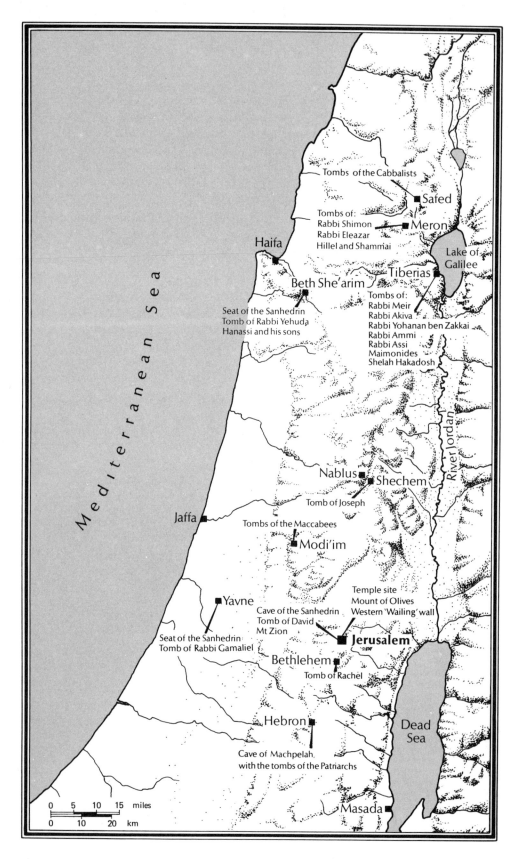

Tombs of the Cabbalists

■ Safed

Tombs of:
Rabbi Shimon
Rabbi Eleazar
Hillel and Shammai

■ Meron

Haifa

Lake of
Galilee

■ Tiberias

Beth She'arim ■

Seat of the Sanhedrin
Tomb of Rabbi Yehuda
Hanassi and his sons

Tombs of:
Rabbi Meir
Rabbi Akiva
Rabbi Yohanan ben Zakkai
Rabbi Ammi
Rabbi Assi
Maimonides
Shelah Hakadosh

M e d i t e r r a n e a n   S e a

River Jordan

Nablus ■
■ Shechem

Tomb of Joseph

Jaffa ■

Tombs of the Maccabees

■ Modi'im

Temple site
Mount of Olives
Western 'Wailing' wall

Yavne ■

Cave of the Sanhedrin
Tomb of David
Mt Zion

Seat of the Sanhedrin
Tomb of Rabbi Gamaliel

■ **Jerusalem**

Bethlehem ■

Tomb of Rachel

Hebron ■

Cave of Machpelah,
with the tombs of the Patriarchs

Dead
Sea

0   5   10   15   miles
0   10   20   km

■ Masada

1 The Jews and the Holy Land

IT IS NOT SO MUCH THAT PALESTINE IS A LAND OF HOLY PLACES, BUT that to the Jews it is *the* Holy Land. Abraham, the father of the Jewish people, was originally an inhabitant of Ur of the Chaldees. According to the excavations of Sir Leonard Woolley, the site of Ur is Al-Mugayyar, the Mound of Bitumen, eleven miles west of the Euphrates, a hundred and fifty miles from the present sea coast. In the time of Abraham, Chaldaea was a reclaimed marsh, as intensively cultivated as is today the delta of the Nile. The Ur known to Abraham was only a hundred miles from the Persian Gulf, but since the gradual silting of the delta the Euphrates has encroached upon the gulf some fifty miles.

Partly from a revulsion against the sophisticated city life of Chaldaea, partly from the motive power of his own 'conversion', Abraham migrated north-west with his father, Terah, to spend the rest of his days among the nomads. They paused at Haran, high up on the middle reaches of the Euphrates, near the present city of Edessa. Thence, after Terah's death, Abraham moved, by divine command, with his flocks and herds round the Fertile Crescent and down to the land of Canaan.

Hebron   It was at Hebron that God made with Abraham a covenant that he would be the father of a chosen people. According to tradition, Abraham lived at the Oak of Mamre, about a mile from the town, at a site now in the possession of the Russian Orthodox Church. It was at Beersheba that Abraham made a treaty with Abimelech, purchasing the right to dig a well, the traditional site of which is still pointed out.

On the death of Sarah his wife, Abraham purchased the Cave of Machpelah from Ephron the Hittite as a burial place, which became the patriarchal vault. This cave has for centuries been preserved beneath a vast shrine, the Haram El-Khalil, in Arabic the Shrine of the Friend of God. Surrounded by an enormous Herodian wall enclosing a mosque of Byzantine, Crusader and more recent masonry, this cave is the focus of both Jewish and Muslim devotion. The impressive catafalques of Abraham and Sarah, Isaac and Rebecca, Jacob and Leah, remind us of their burials below.

The patrimony passed from Abraham to Isaac and from Isaac to Jacob. Jacob's son, Joseph, was hated by his brothers and sold to merchants who took him to Egypt where his brothers subsequently followed him. The

Map showing the Jewish Holy Places.

13

Israelites lived for four hundred and thirty years in Goshen in the land of Egypt, until Moses led them back to the Promised Land, but was not permitted to enter it himself. It was left to Joshua to lead his people into the land flowing with milk and honey.

The chapters of the Old Testament in which these stories are recorded are, of course, filled with the names of places where God wrought marvellously on behalf of his people and preserved them from their enemies, but with the very considerable exception of Jacob's Well, there seems to be little in the way of architectural record. Until the conquest of Canaan by Joshua, the tribes were largely nomadic and utterly dependent on a supply of water for their flocks and herds. Consequently, they camped where they found a well and when it was exhausted, moved on.

There are, however, two major shrines of commemorative rather than contemporary archaeological interest, linked with the patriarchal period. The first is the shrine over the Cave of Machpelah at Hebron, already mentioned. The second is the traditional Tomb of Rachel, outside Bethlehem Ephrata. A less known shrine is Joseph's tomb near Shechem. These shrines and others have been venerated and shared by both Jews and Muslims down the centuries, for their patriarchal associations.

At the same time as Herod the Great enclosed the Temple area at Jerusalem and built the Third Temple, so he enclosed a sacred area over the Cave of Machpelah. In the year 1115 a Crusader church was built on

A nineteenth-century illustration of Hebron showing the mosque which enclosed the cave of Machpelah.

the site, within the Herodian enclosure. Whatever other shrines, Jewish, Christian or Muslim, may have briefly adorned this sanctuary, the present Haram el-Khalil, Shrine of the Friend, is a conversion of the Crusader church into a large Muslim mosque. The outer enclosure is of fine Herodian masonry. From these walls with their alternation of pilaster and recess, one gains a good notion of how the outer walls of the Third Temple must have appeared, with their enormous blocks of stone and the delicate inward sloping of their corner stones. The upper courses of the wall are of Arab construction. Inside the Haram enclosure, with its Crusader nave and aisles, is a magnificent mosque, probably of the thirteenth century.

The cenotaphs of Abraham and Sarah occupy two octagonal chapels to the north and south. Those of Isaac and Rebecca are within the mosque itself, those of Jacob and Leah in chambers to the north. In a separate enclosure is a cenotaph of Joseph. In a corner beside the cenotaph of Abraham is a small window. Inside it, is a stone with a depression in it which is said to be the footstep of Adam. All the catafalques are covered with richly embroidered palls. The pulpit is of splendid Muslim carving, having been presented by Saladin. Yet to the Jews, Hebron, apart from its connection with Abraham, was also the capital of David before his capture of Jerusalem. To them, too, it is holy. After their capture of Hebron in the recent fighting, the Israelis have turned the greater part of it into a museum. Only a small part of it near the entrance is still

The well and enclosure walls at Mamre – the site of Abraham's traditional Oak Tree – constructed by Herod and rebuilt by Hadrian, Constantine, Modestus and later by the Arabs.

carpeted, reserved for the Muslims, labelled 'Holy Place'. The Muslims are admitted there for prayers four times a day and on their holy day, Friday, when Jews are not allowed in. Just a mile away from the centre of Hebron is the traditional Oak of Mamre, in fact, a terebinth, beneath which Abraham showed hospitality to the three angels who visited him on their way to the Cities of the Plain.

The Tomb of Rachel, at Bethlehem, has also had recently a rather chequered history. The Muslim Pasha, Muhammad, of Jerusalem, gave the Jewish community, in 1615, a firman by which he rebuilt the tomb and granted them exclusive use of it. The then Muslim guardian of the tomb handed over the keys to the new Jewish guardian. The Muslims of the neighbourhood, however, seem to have continued to venerate it as a place of prayer and to have entirely enclosed it within their surrounding

The Mosque of Abraham at Hebron is of mixed Crusader and Saracen architecture surrounded by a magnificent Herodian perimeter wall.

right: On the northern outskirts of Bethlehem is the Tomb of Rachel, one of few shrines shared over the centuries by Jew and Muslim alike.

cemetery. The tomb was included among the Tombs of the Prophets and identified with a signboard. Sir Moses Montefiore, at the time of its restoration, especially assigned the antechamber to the Muslims for prayer. Both Jews and Muslims continued to pray there, happily together. In 1912, the Ottoman government allowed the Jews to repair the tomb. After the establishment of the mandatory government, the Jews whitewashed the whole shrine, but when in 1921 the chief rabbinate applied for permission to carry out further repairs, certain Muslims protested. The mandatory government decided to carry out the repairs itself, but was prevented by a Jewish protest. In 1925, however, the government went ahead with essential repairs to the exterior, but the Jews still witheld the keys to the interior. From 1948 the tomb was within Jordanian territory and Jewish access was impracticable. Following the Six Day War, the tomb passed into Irsraeli hands and has now been renovated and rededicated. Today it is a popular and frequently visited reminder to the sons of Jacob of their early ancestry.

The only holy 'building' of the early years of Jewish history was the Tabernacle, a portable sanctuary in which was kept the Ark of the

right: Since the Six Day War in June 1967, Jews are able to return and pray at the catafalque within the Tomb of Rachel.

below left: An early eighteenth-century German representation of the Tabernacle in the wilderness viewed from the rear, its two compartments shown without roof to illustrate the method of boarding and fixing.

below right: The Tabernacle seen from the front with its embroidered entrance and its four covers each turned back.

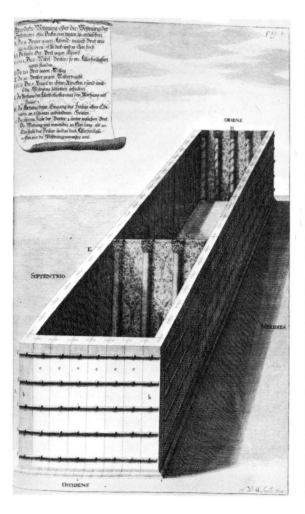

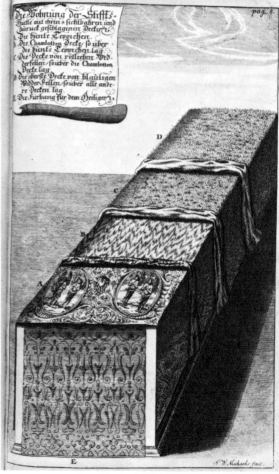

Covenant. The Tabernacle consisted of a rectangular stockade or screen, about fifty metres long by twenty-five metres wide, containing at one end of the enclosure a ridge-pole marquee tent, about fifteen by five metres in area, and about five metres high. Before the tent stood the bronze altar upon which the sacrifices were burned. Nearby was the bronze laver of water for the purification of the priests before sacrifice. The tent roof consisted of four layers or coverings. The first or outer covering was of badger skin, the second of ram's skin dyed red, the third of woven goat's hair, similar to the cloth made by the Bedouin for their tentage today. The last and inner covering was of an embroidered fabric consisting of twined linen with blue, purple and scarlet strands. Within this waterproof and protective covering was assembled the mobile shrine of the Tabernacle proper. This consisted of forty-eight planks or boards of acacia wood plated with gold and stapled with rings, so that they could be quickly assembled into a three-sided sanctuary, open towards the courtyard. The method of fixing was by five long poles passing the whole length of the

A mural painting from Dura (on the Euphrates) of the Ark of the Covenant, as a wheeled shrine drawn by oxen.

20

A stone bas-relief of the Ark of the Covenant, one of the decorative motifs in the second- or third-century synagogue at Capernaum.

structure through the rings in the ends of the acacia boards, the whole assembly forming a wooden room fitting exactly within the tent.

The interior of the wooden tabernacle was divided into two chambers by a veil made from an embroidered fabric of the same kind as that of the innermost layer of the tent roof. The first and outer chamber, known as the Holy Place, contained three articles of furniture: in the centre was the altar of incense, on which incense was burnt twice a day. On the one side was the seven-branch candlestick. There were no candles, but little cups of oil on each branch, in the shape of almonds. The oil lamps burnt continually from the hour of the evening sacrifice to the hour of the morning sacrifice. On the other side was the table of the Show Bread on which were twelve golden trays holding twelve oblong, flat cakes of unleavened bread – representing the twelve tribes of Israel. Only the priests were allowed to enter the Holy Place and only the High Priest to enter beyond the veil into the Holy of Holies, and he only on the Day of Atonement.

Within this inner chamber was one solitary feature facing the veil: the

Ark of the Covenant, a chest of acacia wood covered within and without with gold, standing about three-quarters of a metre high and wide and one and a quarter metres in length. Over the Ark, or either side, were two cherubim of hammered gold whose wings outstretched one towards the other. Between them and resting upon the Ark was the Mercy Seat, a plate of solid gold on which, at the Feast of Atonement, the High Priest sprinkled the blood of the sacrificial victim. It was from here that God 'communed' with Moses 'from above the Mercy Seat'.

Within the Ark were the stone tables of the Decalogue, which God revealed to Moses on Mount Sinai. Such were the Tabernacle and Ark that journeyed from Sinai to Gilgal.

The Ark of the Covenant was thought of as the visible evidence of God's election of the Israelites as his chosen people. It was therefore reasonable that the Ark should be carried about from place to place in the company of his people. When the Israelites had established themselves in the land of Canaan, Joshua pitched the Tabernacle at Shiloh. To offer sacrifices anywhere else than at Shiloh was an act of rebellion against God. Shiloh, identified with Seilun east of the Nablus-Ramallah road, was excavated by the Danish archaeologist, Schmidt, but is now little more than a heap of ruins. After Joshua, religious discipline declined and sacrifices began to be offered in places other than Shiloh. Then, in the early years of Samuel, a great catastrophe occurred. The Philistines captured the Ark of the Covenant in the battle of Aphek. The Ark was put in Dagon's temple at Ashdod, but on both the following morning and the day afterwards Dagon's statue was found lying shattered before the Ark. At the same time the inhabitants of Ashdod were attacked by boils. They moved the Ark to Gath and then to Ekron, both of which cities suffered the same afflictions. The Philistines therefore thought it best to return the Ark to the Israelites, and it was given a new home at Kirjath Jearim. There it remained until the time of King David.

Jews from the time of Abraham until today have always seen in the Land of Israel a Holy Land divinely bestowed upon them, a home without which the Jewish destiny could never properly be fulfilled. In pre-exilic days the Jew felt that he could only practise his religion on Jewish soil. David, threatened with exile, complained that his enemies had driven him from the heritage of the Lord, saying, 'Go, serve other gods!' Naaman, wishing to continue to serve the God of Israel in Damascus, begged 'two mules' burden of [Jewish] earth' from Elisha to take back with him. Chaim Nachman Bialik, the Jewish poet, said in his speech at the opening of the Hebrew University in 1925, 'Without the *land* of Israel – land in the plain meaning of the word – there is neither hope nor promise for a Jewish future in any place, in any time.' Israel was the land in which the Jew should live whenever it was possible to do so and after which he must always yearn, whenever circumstances made it impossible for him to go there. 'Our Rabbis taught,' according to Tractate Kethuboth from the Talmud, 'one should always live in the land of Israel.' The land was to the Jewish prophet almost a person. 'Oh land, land, land, hear the

This Torah cover from the Diaspora, now in the Israel Museum, which is embroidered with a representation of the Western Wall (above which are the Dome of the Rock and the Aqsa Mosque) demonstrates the everlasting spiritual attachment of the Jews for the Holy City of Jerusalem.

word of the Lord', said Jeremiah. The Word of God – the Torah – is translated by the Septuagint into the Greek 'nomos' and by English translators into 'Law'. In reality, however, it has the general meaning of 'God's teaching'. It is far more than a merely legalistic system. To the Jews, the Torah is part of the marriage contract between the Chosen People and the Eternal. By their obedience to His Torah, they must be worthy of their bride – the Promised Land.

In the Jewish liturgy the Torah is solemnly read in its entirety every year in the synagogue. In addition, the faithful are expected to re-read each pericope in Hebrew and Aramaic. Thus, every year, practising Jews read and re-read God's words spoken to Abraham: 'And I will give to you and to your descendants after you the land of your sojournings for an everlasting possession; and I will be their God.' They hear and record God's words to Moses: 'And I will bring you into the land which I swore to give to Abraham, to Isaac and to Jacob. I will give it to you for a possession. I am the Lord', and many other such words of promise from the Scriptures. When the synagogue commemorates the destruction of the two Temples, a text from Deuteronomy is read. This promises exile to the people of Israel when they forget God's commandment but eventual return to their true home when they repent.

God speaks to Abraham

The principal prayer of the final office, Mussaf, at the end of the morning's service on festival days runs:

Our God, God of our fathers, for our sins we were exiled from our country and driven far from dwelling on our land. We cannot go up to it and appear in worship before Thee to fulfil our duty in Thy chosen Temple, Thy great and Holy House called by Thy name, because of the violent hand that was stretched forth against Thy Sanctuary. May it be Thy will, Lord our God, God of our fathers, merciful King, to turn and show pity to us, and in Thy great compassion again show pity to Thy sanctuary. Rebuild it soon and make it great in glory. Our Father, our King, speedily reveal the glory of Thy rule over us in the eyes of all living. Recall our dispersed from among the nations and gather our scattered people from the ends of the earth. Bring us with joyous song to Zion, Thy city, and with joy everlasting to the home of Thy sanctuary, Jerusalem. Only there in Thy presence shall we bring the sacrifices enjoined on us, the regular daily burnt offerings according to their order and the additional sacrifices according to their regulation. Only there shall we prepare and bring before Thee in loving offering the additional sacrifices of this day of the Festival.

The daily morning prayer just before the Shema includes 'O bring us from the four corners of the earth and make us go upright to our own land, for Thou art a God who workest salvation.' The tenth of the Eighteen Blessings is: 'Sound the great horn of freedom, raise the ensign to gather our exiles and gather us from the four corners of the earth. Blessed art Thou, O God, who gatherest the dispersed of Thy People Israel.' The fourteenth blessing is: 'And to Jerusalem, Thy city, return in mercy and

An old olive press at Ein Hod, under the Carmel range, still stands as a symbol of dependence on the land.

24

dwell therein as Thou hast spoken, rebuild it soon in our days as an ever-lasting building and specially set up therein the Throne of David. Blessed are Thou, O Lord who rebuildest Jerusalem.' In the Paschal meal of the Seder, the father of the family says in Aramaic, which bears witness to the great antiquity of the words: 'This is the bread of affliction that our fathers ate in the land of Egypt ... Now are we here, next year we shall be in the Land of Israel; now we are slaves; next year we shall be free men.' And the ceremony ends with the words 'Next year in Jerusalem.'

The Zionist attitude to the Land

The Jewish people felt that by their sins they forfeited their patrimony and God punished them with captivity and exile. But God is a God of loving kindness and they could regain their patrimony if they turned to him again in repentance. During the long years of exile Jews recognised the Land of Israel as their natural home. Jews in eastern Europe even in modern times oriented their houses so as to point them towards Jerusalem. The Jews of the Diaspora saw it as a duty through the contributions of the *Haloukka* to support the poor Jews in Palestine. After the first Zionist congresses the custom even grew up of buying plots of land in Israel. To be buried in the Holy Land was to be in a condition of resurrection, and those who could not live there would be buried with at least a small sod of the Holy Land on their grave.

When the modern Zionist movement was launched there were of course those who demanded that the Jews be permitted to return to Palestine for purely secular reasons. Theodore Herzl was alarmed at the time of the Dreyfus case at the insecurity of the Jew in western Europe. Jews after the First World War desperately demanded a place of refuge from perse-cution in Poland and elsewhere and, finally and overwhelmingly, from Hitler's Germany. Yet such movements must not distract us from the quite independent religious impulse which caused Jews to look for a re-turn to Palestine. Martin Buber in *Israel and Palestine: The History of an Idea,* has noted that the movement was called not Palestinianism, but Zionism. With the building of the Temple, Jerusalem was established in the mind of the Jews as the special home of God. Zion was 'the city of the great King'. In the Cabbala, Zion was equated with the presence of God himself. Though it may have been the Temple which sanctified Jerusalem in the first place, yet throughout the literature of the Captivity and the Diaspora references to Jerusalem and to Zion are incomparably more common than references to the Temple. The prophet Ahijah, who came from Shiloh, is the first man of whom we have record that he spoke of Jerusalem as 'the city which I [God] have chosen'. When the Jewish pilgrim caught his first sight of Jerusalem he rent his clothes and bared his heart. Joseph Caro, the great rabbi from Safed, gave exact instruc-tions how this rending should be accomplished. The Jew should rend his garment standing up, 'With his own hand and until the heart was bare. The rent garment must on no account be ever afterwards mended!'

Since the Six Day War Jews gather daily to worship at the Western 'Wailing' Wall. Facing it they touch and kiss the stones of the lower courses as they recite their prayers.

Jerusalem is still to every Jew unquestionably the Holy City. The hymn of the Zionist movement speaks of the 'eye looking towards Zion' and of the hope of a return to 'the land of Zion and Jerusalem'. Zion symbolises the marriage of a Holy People with a Holy Land. Both people and land were considered holy, not through their own virtues, but because it was ordained of God. As Buber put it in his *Open Letter to Gandhi*:

> What is decisive for us is not the promise of the Land but the commandment whose fulfilment is *bound up* with the Land, with the existence of a free Jewish community in this country. For the Bible tells us, and our inmost knowledge testifies to it, that more than three thousand years ago our entry into this land took place with the consciousness of a mission from above to set up a just way of life that cannot be realised by individuals in the sphere of their private existence, but only by a nation in the establishment of its society: Communal ownership of the land (Leviticus 25:23), regularly recurrent levelling of social distinctions (Leviticus 25:13), guarantees of the independence of each individual (Exodus 21:2), mutual aid (Exodus 23:4ff.), a general Sabbath embracing serf and beast as beings with an equal claim to rest (Exodus 23:12), a sabbatical year in which the soil is allowed to rest and everybody is admitted to free enjoyment of its fruits (Leviticus 25:2-7). These are not practical laws thought out by wise men. They are measures which the leaders of the nation have been convinced are the set task and condition for taking possession of the Land.

So universally is Palestine considered among Jews to be their natural home that even in modern times in Poland, England, America and elsewhere Jews pray for rain at the time of the Feast of Tabernacles in October when in those countries the harvest has already been gathered in, but when in Palestine the first rains come. On the first day of Passover, the synagogue ceases to pray for rain and prays for dew because the dry season in Palestine is beginning. At daily meals they pray: 'Have mercy, O Lord our God, upon thy people Israel, upon Jerusalem thy city, upon Zion, the abiding place of thy glory, upon thine altar and thy temple. Rebuild Jerusalem, the holy city, speedily in our days, lead us up thither and make us rejoice in its rebuilding. May we eat of the fruits of the land and be satisfied with its goodness and bless thee for it in holiness and purity.' The Talmud proclaims: 'The Holy One, blessed be he, gave Israel three precious gifts, and all of these were given only through sufferings. These are the Torah, the Land of Israel and the world to come.'

After the destruction of the Third Temple, the rabbis continued to emphasise under circumstances of great difficulty the importance of permanent settlement in Israel. In the Middle Ages there was a considerable *Aliyyah*, or emigration, to Palestine from England, France and Germany. The main Spanish community did not come to Palestine until later, after the expulsion of the Jews from that country in 1492; but the foundation of the Spanish community was laid by Nachmanides, the famous Torah commentator, in 1267. The Palestinian Talmud continued to urge the importance of emigration to Palestine in spite of all difficulties. 'More beloved is a small school in Eretz Yisrael [the Holy Land], than a large Academy outside it.' 'In your land [Israel] you can sit in safety but you cannot dwell in safety in a strange land.' 'He who resides in Palestine [reads the Shema] and speaks Hebrew, is a son of the world-to-come.'

Emigration to Palestine

The Cabbalists say, 'Happy is he who during his lifetime lives in the Holy Land, for such a one draws down the dew from heaven upon the earth, and whoever is attached to the Holy Land during his life becomes attached ever afterwards to the heavenly Holy Land.'

So, over at least three millennia, it is possible to trace the tradition linking Land and People. Consequently today no one could deny the reality of the feelings of those who equate the state of Israel with the Messianic fulfilment of Judaism. It is possible to lay text to text, through the Law and the Prophets, to support the cause of Zionism. In doing so, however, we should be aware of the tradition of prophecy which confronts us with a constant emphasis on the keeping of the *Covenant*, as the *condition* of the People inheriting the Land.

The Covenant *with God*
The Prophets were motivated by a passionate commitment to a moral God. In the realm of faith or commitment, while they loved their people, over and over again they declared that their people were subject to the moral Covenant. The breaking of their Covenant heralded destruction. The restoration of the Covenant would bring redemption. The Land was Holy *in so far as* the Covenant was *kept*. The Land was subject to the Covenant with God: 'Seek ye ME and live.' The Holy Places, even Zion itself, are holy only when 'the Law of God goes forth from it'. Of the Holy Places, Amos said: 'Seek not Bethel, nor enter into Gilgal and pass not to Beersheba.'

The prophets envisaged a restored state of Israel and a government in a true Zion, as the result of a broadening and deepening of the commitment of the People to the Covenant. 'Let justice well up as waters and righteousness as a mighty stream,' says Amos. The historical restoration of the People to the Land is to be in order that 'all the ends of the earth shall see the salvation of our God'. 'The heaven is my throne and the earth is my footstool. Where is the house that ye may build me? Where is the place that may be my resting place?' It is to be 'a house of prayer for all my peoples'. Thus the prophet Isaiah proclaimed:

> And it shall come to pass in the end of those days,
> That the mountain of the Lord's house shall be established at the top
>   of the mountains,
> And shall be exalted above the hills;
> And all nations shall flow unto it.
> And many peoples shall go and say:
> 'Come ye, and let us go up to the mountain of the Lord,
> To the house of the God of Jacob;
> And he will teach us of His ways,
> And we will walk in His paths.'
> For out of Zion shall go forth the law,
> And the word of the Lord from Jerusalem.

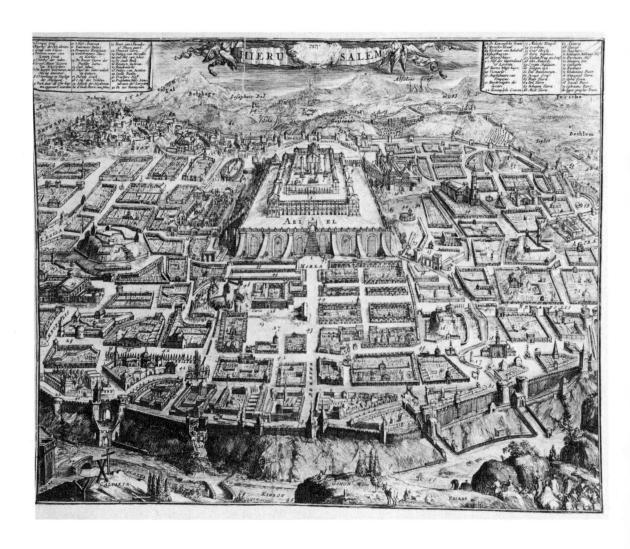

2 The Holy City and the Jews

TO THE JEW IT IS THE LAND, RATHER THAN A SELECTION OF PLACES in it, that is holy. Even if Jerusalem or Zion is especially revered, it is the city as a whole that is holy, rather than particular places in it. If we look through the official list of Holy Places submitted to the United Nations, however, we find in Jerusalem and its environs places holy to the Jewish faith. Beneath the Mount of Olives is a tomb of the Ptolemaic period, possibly that of the prophet Zechariah. Inscriptions show that this and neighbouring tombs had been used as a Christian as well as a Jewish burial place, probably between the fourth and sixth centuries. Many other people have been associated with the four larger tombs, among them Absalom, Hezekiah, Jehoshaphat and James, the brother of Jesus, and first bishop in Jerusalem. The Tombs of the Prophets, as they are loosely called today, overlook the Valley of Jehoshaphat, called after the righteous King of Judah, where according to the prophet Joel the Last Trumpet will sound and the Last Judgement be held.

Further down the valley, through which flows the conduit of the Kedron, is the Gihon, or gushing spring, fed from a water shelf in the spur of Ophel, rising steeply to the west of the ravine. The Gihon, known also as the Dragon's Well or the Virgin's Fountain, played a vital part in both David's capture of the city and also in the repulse of the besieging Assyrians in the time of Hezekiah.

David had established his headquarters at Hebron, the burial place of the patriarchs, and suppressed all opposition. After seven years' rule at Hebron in the south, David realised the strategic importance of the more central fortress of Jebus, the old city of Salem, which had never been captured by the Hebrews.

The Jebusites considered it impregnable, surrounded as it was by steep valleys to north and south. The city stood on a sharp spur to the south of Mount Moriah – the traditional high place of sacrifice, where Abraham had been willing to offer his son, Isaac. David, standing on the Mount of Olives, would look down on this great fortress, built up on rising platforms overlooking the Kedron, fortified by an overhanging scarp at the bottom, with an enormous ditch at the top. It was captured through the action of Joab who entered the cave entrance of the water supply in the Kedron Valley and shinned up the water shaft or 'gutter' to emerge

A seventeenth-century Flemish pictorial plan of Jerusalem and its environs, rather more decorative than accurate.

31

within the city and throw open the gates. Thereafter, David established his capital at Jebus-salem, completed the conquests begun by Saul, consolidated and extended his borders. Having subdued Edom, Moab, Ammon and Damascus, he ruled from the borders of Egypt to the Euphrates, from the Mediterranean to the Red Sea. Only the Philistine foothills and the Phoenician coast remained outside his control.

Having captured Jerusalem, David made it both his military capital and his religious sanctuary too. He brought up the Ark of the Covenant to the city. It was at the Gihon too that David crowned his son, Solomon, king.

Three hundred years later, Hezekiah extended the water conduit to bring water within the city, cutting a tunnel linking Gihon with the Pool of Siloam, sealing the outlet and thus stopping the flow out into the Kedron. This tunnel was a masterpiece of engineering and can still be explored. It is 532 metres long and curiously winding, two metres high at the upper end and nearly twice as high at the lower. Six metres from the Siloam end was found the famous inscription, in pre-exilic Hebrew lettering. It tells how two workmen, starting from either end, at last heard 'pick answering pick' and met near the middle.

Overlooking the Kedron ravine and the spur of Ophel is the village of Siloam on the crags and slopes of the Ras el-Amoud, or Hill of Offence, where Solomon permitted his foreign wives to offer their idolatrous sacrifices, within sight of the Temple Area. At the bottom or southern point of the overhanging rock face of Ophel, there is today a vegetable garden

The Tombs of the Prophets, within the Kedron ravine, and the ancient Jewish burial ground rising up the Mount of Olives.

Hezekiah's Tunnel

Pool of Siloam

32

on the site of the ancient pre-Hezekiah Pool of Siloam. Nearby was the Valley or Fountain Gate, mentioned by Nehemiah on his tour of the walls. Even as late as the first century A D the valley between the upper and lower cities was bridged by viaducts and far too steep for carts or riders. No wonder Nehemiah could not get his horse through the fallen masonry by the ancient King's Pool.

A little further down the valley from the King's Pool is the Fuller's Fountain, sometimes identified with Job's Well. The fullers' basins are still visible in the nearby rock terraces, east of the well (Joshua 15:7-8; 18:16).

Tombs of the Kings

In the northern part of the city, east of St George's Close, the home of the Anglican archbishop, are the so-called Tombs of the Kings. These were in reality the burial vaults of the family of Queen Helena of Adiabene on the Tigris. When a widow, she settled together with her son, Izates, in Jerusalem in the year A D 45. She became a proselyte to Judaism and was renowned for the generosity with which she helped to relieve the victims of a famine, mentioned incidentally in the Acts of the Apostles. The bodies of Helena, Izates, and some twenty of his sons were buried here. A broad staircase leads down into a courtyard thirty metres square, cut out of the rock. A large vestibule leads to the thirty-one tombs, through a low doorway which still has a fine example of a rolling stone.

Jeremiah's Grotto

Returning to the Damascus Gate, to the east of the Nablus road and below the Muslim cemetery, is Jeremiah's Grotto. It is in fact the cave mouth of an ancient quarry, where a sixteenth-century tradition relates that Jeremiah wrote his Lamentations. Just south of this, across the road that circles the north wall of the Old City and set within the rock foundations of the city wall, is the entrance to the so-called Quarries of Solomon.

Solomon's Quarries

These white limestone caverns extend in many galleries towards the Temple Area. Their stone is so soft, until exposed to the open air, that it can easily be broken by hand or sawn to shape. Huge blocks of stone were separated from the rock face by the mere insertion of wooden wedges wetted to make them swell. There is little doubt that these quarries explain how at the building of the First Temple 'stones were fashioned beneath in the earth ... so that the sound of the hammer was not heard'. The quarries were discovered at the end of the last century by a man who lost his dog down a rock shaft. They are now sealed and closed to the public for security reasons.

The road to the north of the city leads up on to the spine of Judaea. Where the Mount of Olives curls round to the north, not far from the British War Cemetery, is the site of Nob. Behind the suburb of Shaphat towers the ancient fortress of Gibea of Saul. Across the valley to the west is the ridge of Mizpah, where Saul and Samuel rallied the tribes for the relief of Jabesh Gilead and similar emergencies. The Tomb of Samuel, within a little mosque, stands sentinel on the skyline. Nebi Samwil, as the Muslim calls it, was to the Crusaders the Mons Gaudii, the first place from which it was possible to get a glimpse of Jerusalem. There Richard Coeur de Lion held up his shield before his eyes, thinking the sight too holy to be seen. As the road continues north, within two miles, signposts to the east point: to Anathoth, home of Abiathar the priest and Jeremiah the prophet – to Michmash and Geba, scenes of the valour of Jonathan and his armour bearer – to Rama of Samuel.

The road to the south leads across the Plain of Rephaim, indicated today by a street of that name, known to Joshua as 'the Valley of the Giants' (Joshua 15: 8). Just before the ridge which gives a view of Bethlehem, there is a cistern on the left of the road, beside which there is a block from the aqueduct built to bring water from Solomon's Pools to the Temple. To the left also the ridge is crowned by the Monastery of Mar Elias, where tradition claims that Elijah rested on his way from Carmel to Horeb (1 Kings 19). Once over the ridge, Bethlehem of Boaz and Ruth, Jesse and David, lies due south, while over to the right is the attractive village of Bethjala, once the home of that unfortunate counsellor, Ahitophel.

South of Bethlehem, at the head of the Vale of Artas, are three large reservoirs known as Solomon's Pools. 'I made me pools of water' (Eccles. 2:6). According to Josephus, Solomon often visited this lovely valley. One aqueduct leads towards the Frank Mountain east of Bethlehem, where Herod had a summer palace. Two other aqueducts lead back towards Jerusalem, which is some twenty-five metres below the level of the Pools. *Solomon's Pools*

If we now return to the city we can examine the history of the Tomb of David, just outside the Zion Gate and perhaps, too, just outside the Upper City of David's time. A strange story is recorded by Benjamin of Tudela, the learned rabbi from Navarre, who visited Jerusalem in 1163.

On Mount Zion are the graves of the House of David and of the kings that came after him. The site, however, cannot be identified in as much as fifteen years ago a wall of the church on Mount Zion fell in and the patriarch commanded the superintendent to restore the church, saying to him, 'Use the stones of the old wall of Zion for the building of the church', and he did so. He hired about twenty workmen at fixed wages who brought the stones from the base of the wall of Zion. Among these men were two friends who were confederates and on a certain day the one entertained the other; after their meal they returned to their work when the superintendent said to them, 'Why have you tarried?' They answered 'Why need you complain? When our mates go to their meal we will do our work.' When the dinner time arrived and their fellow workmen had gone to their meal, they removed the stones and discovered the entrance to the cave. Thereupon one said to the other 'Let us go in and see if any money is to be found there.' They entered the cave and found a chamber resting upon pillars of marble overlaid with silver and gold. In front was a chamber of gold and a sceptre and crown. This was the sepulchre of King David. On the left thereof was the sepulchre of King Solomon in like fashion. And then followed the sepulchres of all the kings who were buried there belonging to the kings of Judah. Closed coffers were also there, the contents of which no man knows. The two men essayed to enter the chamber when a fierce wind came forth from the entrance and smote them. They fell to the ground *The Tomb of David*

A great feat of engineering in the eighth century BC: the water conduit of King Hezekiah, which flows through the Mount of Ophel from the gutter of Gihon to the Pool of Siloam.

34

like dead men and there lay until evening. And there came an
wind crying like a human's voice, 'Arise and come forth from
place'. So the men hastily went forth in terror and they came upo
patriarch and related these facts to him. Thereupon the patriarch sent
for Rabbi Abraham, the pious recluse of Constantine who was one of
the mourners of Jerusalem, and to him related all these things according to the report of the two men who had come from the cave. Then
Rabbi Abraham replied, 'These are the sepulchres of the House of
David belonging to the kings of Judah, and tomorrow let us enter the
cave, I and you and these men, and find out what is to be seen there,'
And on the morrow they sent for the two men and found each of them
lying upon his bed terror-stricken. The men said 'We will not enter
there, for the Lord does not desire that any man should see the place.'
Then the patriarch gave orders that the place should be closed up, and
hidden from the sight of man unto this day.

An older tradition was that recorded by Nehemiah that David's tomb
was near the stairs that went up from Siloam to Ophel. Apparently
St Peter knew of its whereabouts at the time of Pentecost. Josephus tells
us of two attempts to rifle it, one by Hasmonaean prince and high
priest, John Hyrcanus, and the other by Herod. The site of the Tomb of
David was for more than a thousand years enclosed within a series of successive Christian churches commemorating the Last Supper of Jesus with
his disciples. The last and present church, or coenaculum, built in 1310,
is in two storeys, of which the Upper Room commemorates the Supper.
It was not until 1523 that Muslims again brought forward the theory that
the Tomb of David was beneath the Christian church of the Coenaculum.
In 1551 the Franciscan monks were expelled and the lower storey of their
church adapted and venerated as the Tomb of David, Nebi Daoud.

After 1948, although only a few yards outside No Man's Land, it was
in Israel, and was the leading Holy Place in Israeli hands in Jerusalem.

The Temple   Yet, of course, the architectural glory of Jewish Jerusalem was the
Temple. It was because the Jews had now created for themselves a settled
state that David thought that they must now have a settled capital. In the
earlier days of the Judges, the children of Israel had no overall unity of
government. The tribe was the unit of government and the Judge was
called by God to contrive the rescue of his people only in the day of
emergency. The rescue effected, the Jews returned again to their tribal
divisions. Under Saul and after him under David, in face of some protest
from Samuel, Israel formed itself for the first time into a kingdom. If it
was to be a kingdom and at the same time a holy kingdom, then it was
necessary that it should have a religious as well as a political centre, a
centre of ritual and discipline. The Jews by their commandments were
most strictly forbidden to make to themselves any graven image. To the
modern reader it can never be quite clear why this temptation to idolatry
was as desperately strong, as it clearly was, to those early Jews. It was felt,
indeed, even by Solomon, the man who had built the Temple primarily to
combat this temptation; yet he himself in his closing years succumbed to it.

The Tomb of Samuel,
within the Crusader
building which is now in
use as a mosque.

37

SALOMONS TEMPEL.

David had bequeathed to Solomon a site for the Temple, treasures to pay for it, with priests and levites for its service. The site was the threshing floor of Araunah, where David had been permitted to stay the avenging angel that was to bring plague upon Jerusalem and all Israel, for David's sin in ordering a census. It was here on Mount Moriah that, a thousand years before, Abraham had obeyed Yahweh by his willingness to sacrifice his son, Isaac. It is the site where today stands the Muslim shrine of the Dome of the Rock, within the noble sanctuary of the Haram es-Sherif.

Solomon's Temple consisted of a dwelling facing east and its surrounding courts. The dwelling was the House of Yahweh. It was a rectangular building, about thirty metres long, ten metres broad and fifteen metres high, of limestone blocks. The interior walls were covered with cedar wainscotting, the floor with cypress. The walls were adorned with carving. All the woodwork was overlaid with gold.

The House of Yahweh, like the Tabernacle in the wilderness, was divided into two parts, the Holy of Holies and the Holy Place. The Holy Place was about twenty metres long, twenty metres broad and fifteen high. It was thought of as the audience chamber of Yahweh. Through his

priests he received the homage of his people. The Holy of Holies, which was a perfect cube of about ten metres, was Yahweh's own dwelling place. There were above it certain private chambers which brought that part of the building up to the same fifteen metres as the rest. A folding door of two leaves of olive wood guarded the entrance to the Holy of Holies. Before it hung a veil of purple, violet, crimson and fine linen embroidered with the figures of cherubs. The entrance to the Holy Place was a square folding door of cypress wood in an olive wood framework of two leaves, each consisting of two sections. The Holy Place had lattice work windows. The Holy of Holies was in total darkness.

East of, and facing, the Holy Place, was a Porch of the same height as the Holy Place itself. In the Porch were two hollow bronze columns, about nine metres high, each of which was surmounted by a molten bronze capital, curved upwards in the shape of a lily. These columns were known as Jachin and Boaz.

above left: The Altar of Incense within the Holy Place *(above)*; a bronze basin, in the shape of a lily, for the washing of the priests' hands *(below)*.

above right: The Table for the Show Bread, complete with two stacks each of six shelves, to contain one loaf for each tribe.

In the Holy of Holies were two statues of cherubs, each about five metres high, made of olive wood, overlaid with gold. Their wings were outstretched, each with one towards the outer wall on either side, each with one towards the centre, meeting wing to wing, as if hovering over the Ark of the Covenant. In the Holy Place was the Altar of Incense, which was made of cedar wood overlaid with gold, together with tables for the Show Bread, ten golden candlesticks and various other golden vessels.

The House of Yahweh was surrounded by an Inner and Outer Court. The Outer Court was frequented by the laity, and from it steps ran up to the Inner Court. The Inner Court was surrounded by a low wall or parapet of stone, but not high enough to obstruct the vision of those below. Both courts were paved with stone. The Outer Court had gates of wood overlaid with bronze. In the Inner Court, before the entrance to the House of Yahweh, stood the Altar of Sacrifice. Between the Altar and the Porch stood the huge cast bronze basin with a brim shaped like a lily and two rows of gourds below the brim. It was supported on twelve bronze oxen, facing outwards in sets of three to the four cardinal points. The sea was about five metres in diameter and had a capacity of about 16,000 gallons.

Hiram, King of Tyre, furnished all the timber that was used in the Temple, and Solomon paid for it in wheat, barley, oil and wine, also by ceding to him twenty frontier towns. Solomon despatched thirty thousand Israelites to help the Phoenicians in felling the required timber in the mountains of Lebanon. The Temple was seven and a half years in building. Solomon then held a very solemn service of dedication. The Ark of the Covenant was carried in procession to the Holy of Holies and there deposited. According to the story as recorded in Kings, during the subsequent songs and dances, a miraculous cloud descended on the Temple. Solomon knelt before the Altar of Sacrifices and offered a long prayer to God who had thus established the Temple as his dwelling place.

The building of the Temple firmly established Jerusalem as the headquarters of the Jewish faith, the one place where sacrifices could properly be offered. It was not only the headquarters of the Jewish faith; it became, under the Prophets, the headquarters of the service of the one God who made the world. By an act of surrender and sacrifice the Jews made themselves more fitted to serve God. Nor was the sacrifice the mere sacrifice of an individual. The people was a chosen people, each individual embodying the whole people. Thus, even today, in the Passover service, the Jew is bidden to identify himself with the events of the Exodus and to say, 'And thou shalt show thy son in that day, saying, "because of that which the Lord did unto me when I came forth out of Egypt".' The High Priest, when he offered sacrifice on the Day of Atonement, offered sacrifice for the whole people. The Jews were the chosen people, but they were not in their belief chosen for their own personal advantage, but that through their righteousness they might redeem the world. We read in Isaiah:

And also the sons of the stranger that join themselves to the Lord to serve him and to love the name of the Lord, to be his servants, everyone that keepeth the sabbath from polluting it and taketh hold of my covenant, even them will I bring to my holy mountain and make them joyful in my house of prayer. Their burnt offerings and their sacrifices shall be accepted upon mine altar, for mine house shall be called a house of prayer for *all* people. The Lord God which gathereth the outcasts of Israel saith, 'Yet will I gather others to him besides those that are gathered unto him'.

If it was hoped, however, that all irregular religious sacrifices would cease, that hope was not fulfilled. Indeed, seeing that Solomon himself in his old age indulged in illegal sacrifices, a total success for his policy was hardly to be expected.

After Solomon's death the kingdom was divided into the two kingdoms of Judah and Israel. Jerusalem was the capital of Judah. Israel held the northern territory. If the inhabitants of Israel were to continue to go up to Jerusalem for the sacrifices, it was almost inevitable that their political

Solomon's Temple

Samaritan priests with their ancient scroll of the Pentateuch outside their modern synagogue at Nablus.

allegiance to their own kings would be weakened. It was, therefore, hardly surprising when Jeroboam, the King of Israel with his capital at Shechem, set up his own golden calves at Dan and Bethel and bade his people go there to sacrifice. Once the political unity of the nation was broken it was naturally not long before the doctrinal purity of its religion was also impaired. The people soon began to sacrifice at the 'high places' and to indulge in idolatrous habits. The surrounding powers took advantage of their divisions and the Prophets were naturally not slow to point out that the calamities that befell them were the proper punishment, with which God was afflicting them for their wickedness. It was common among their neighbours, as among other peoples all over the world, to believe that their gods fought for them and brought them victory in battle, just as they believed that Yahweh did the same for them. But the genius of the Jewish religion was that its great prophets pronounced that calamity had come, not because God had deserted them but because they had deserted God, and that they were being justly punished for their disloyalty and disobedience.

The Samaritans
In 722 BC the Assyrians invaded and captured Samaria, deported a proportion of the population and imported several alien tribes to take their place. It was commonly said that the intermingling of the aliens and Israelites who remained formed the Samaritan race of later days who were not recognised by the Jews as Jews. The Samaritans repudiated completely any obligation to go up to Jerusalem to worship. They built their own temple on Mount Gerizim above Shechem. This was destroyed by the Hasmonaean prince, John Hyrcanus, in 129 BC. The Samaritans in our time have been reduced to a small community of under two hundred, who live mainly in Nablus. Even this diminished survival they owe in part to the Jews. In 1841, for example, when the Muslims of Nablus threatened to exterminate them, the chief rabbi of Jerusalem saved them by giving a certificate that 'the Samaritan people are a branch of the children of Israel who acknowledge the truth of the Torah'.

The Samaritans continue to observe their ancient separatist rites which they claimed to be purer than those of the regular Jews. They admit the canonical authority only of the Books of the Pentateuch. They wear long hair and beards and in their synagogue is a volume of the Torah written in the Samaritan script, which is similar to ancient Hebrew. They celebrate the Passover on the summit of Mount Gerizim. On the Passover eve, the entire community ascends the mountain. Surrounding their altar, they slaughter seven sheep for an offering, while the High Priest stands on a rock and reads aloud the twelfth chapter of Exodus. When he comes to the sentence 'the congregation of Israel shall kill it', the people kill the sheep. They then pour water over the carcasses and, stripping off the fleece, extract the fat and burn both fat and fleece. The forefoot of each sheep is cut off and given to the priest in accordance with the biblical command. After being cleaned, the sacrifices are thoroughly salted and each sheep is then spitted on a rod and roasted.

Close to the altar is a pit, or tannur, heated by the burning of brushwood. In this primitive and vast oven, the 'carcasses' are roasted. After

The Hellenistic tower at Samaria, with a view of the village of Imrin in the distance which derives its name, perhaps, from Omri the builder of Samaria.

45

prayers and at about midnight they take the roasted sheep out of the pit and put them into huge casseroles. They then all sit round, fully clothed and shod, to eat their sacrificial portions. No bone must be broken nor anything edible left unconsumed. When all is finished they gather up the bones, hooves, horns and also anything, such as the spits, that has come in contact with the sacrifice, and solemnly burn everything.

As a result of the Assyrian invasion the kingdom of Israel was destroyed. The kingdom of Judah with its capital at Jerusalem survived for another one hundred and thirty years. It was the misfortune of the Jews that they inhabited a small country on the high road that connected the empires of Asia with those of Egypt. Humanly speaking it was almost inevitable that sooner or later Judah, like Israel, would fall a victim to one or other of its powerful neighbours. It was in 587 BC that Jerusalem, after prolonged siege, fell to the Babylonians. All the precious vessels of the Temple were sent to Babylon. The Temple itself was burnt down. The people were deported. The fifty years of Jewish exile in Babylon do not directly concern us, but the laments of the exiles are important as evidence of the depth of Jewish belief that Jerusalem was their natural home. Ezekiel and the Psalmists continuously called upon them never to forget their obligation to return to Jerusalem as soon as they could.

In 539 Babylon, then under the rule of Nabonidas, fell to the Persian King Cyrus. Cyrus' wise policy was to build up the strength of his empire by granting freedom to those over whom he ruled. In particular, he thought that if the Jews were freely allowed to return to their own land they would prove loyal subjects and be valuable as defenders of his frontiers against the Egyptians. He therefore allowed them to return and gave back to them the vessels of the Temple, which Nebuchadnezzar had seized. The Jews, returning under their first governor, Zerubbabel, made it their business to rebuild the Temple. They first built the Altar of Sacrifice, and started once more to offer the sacrifices, but the full rebuilding of the Temple was delayed by the hostility of the Samaritans. The Samaritans thought that their Mount Gerizim, where they had continued with their religious observances throughout the Captivity, was as true a centre of religion as Jerusalem. The objection of the Jews to the Samaritans was that they regarded them as schismatics. By 520 BC the prophets Haggai and Zechariah had persuaded the Jews to defy the Samaritans and to begin the work. Zechariah called on all Jews living abroad to return to Jerusalem and announced that it had been revealed to him in a vision that they would receive the blessing of God if they did so. He predicted that Jerusalem would one day be the centre of a universal religion.

The Second Temple was completed and dedicated in the spring of 515. *The Second* The history of the Jews and of the Temple during the immediately suc- *Temple* ceeding years is not very clear. But it is obvious, first, that in spite of their appeal, a large proportion of the Jews preferred to remain in Babylon; secondly, that there was a good deal of corruption in the religious life of Jerusalem at that time. In particular, the priests freely took wives from their non-Jewish neighbours in defiance of the commands of the Mosaic

Samaritan High Priests at prayer before their Passover Sacrifice on the top of Mount Gerizim, above the present city of Nablus.

law. The priest, Ezra, came from Babylon to insist in the name of the Torah on a reform among the Jews in Jerusalem. Ezra obtained the promise that those priests should put away their foreign wives. He had the authority to do this, because he occupied a position previously unknown in Jewish history. David and subsequent kings had exercised a territorial authority, ruling all the inhabitants of their kingdom more or less impartially, whether Hebrews, Canaanites or other races. Ezra, on the other hand, when he was given authority by Artaxerxes, was given it not over a territory but over all Jews wheresoever they might be to the west of the Euphrates. 'And I, even I, Artaxerxes the king, do make a decree to all the treasurers which are beyond the river that whatsoever Ezra, the priest, the scribe of the law of the God of Heaven, shall require of you, it be done speedily. And thou, Ezra, after the wisdom of thy God that is in thine hand set magistrates and judges which may judge all the people that are beyond the river, all such as know the laws of thy God, and teach them that know them not.' (Ezra 7:21,25).

47

In the reign of Artaxerxes, Jewish leaders attempted a rebuilding of the walls of Jerusalem to protect the Jews against their Gentile neighbours. However, the Samaritans objected to this and were for a time able to persuade the king Artaxerxes that there would be a political danger in allowing the Jews to fortify themselves. The king later gave leave to his Jewish cup bearer, Nehemiah, fully to rebuild Jerusalem. Artaxerxes appointed Nehemiah governor of Judaea. In his Book, Nehemiah tells the vivid story of how the Jews rebuilt the walls of Jerusalem, with their tools in one hand and their weapons to repel the Samaritans in the other.

After the fall of the Persian empire Palestine, along with all the other *Alexander's* territories in nearer Asia, fell under the domination of Alexander the *conquest* Great, who wisely granted complete religious toleration to all his subjects. He granted the Jews exemption from taxation in their sabbatical years and allowed those who wished to settle with full civic rights in his new city of Alexandria. According to Josephus, he offered sacrifices himself in the Temple.

Whereas before the Captivity sacrifices had been paid for by the princes, within the Second Temple they were offered by the whole people and paid for out of the Temple revenues. The Temple was supported partly by compulsory levies and partly by voluntary contributions.

The Temple was the ceremonial centre of Jewish life, whether of the Jews of Judaea or of the Diaspora. It was the duty of the pious Jew to go up to Jerusalem and share in its atoning sacrifices three times a year. The High Priest became the effective ruler of the land, but the Temple was not the teaching centre of Judaism. The synagogue was the place of teaching.

The country was divided into twenty-four districts, in each of which there was established a body of priests, levites and laymen, who were responsible in turn for the Temple's services, for a week at a time. On Monday they offered prayers for travellers by sea, on Tuesday for those travelling through the desert, on Wednesday for sick children and on Thursday for nursing mothers. On some days there were in the service two scriptural readings, one from the Pentateuch and one from a historical or prophetic writing. It has been suggested by some scholars that such Books as Nahum, Habbakuk and Joel embody special liturgies and the apocryphal Book of Baruch is claimed to be the liturgy for the Ninth of Ab, the commemoration of the destruction of the First Temple.

A consequence of Alexander's conquest, and the rule of his generals who succeeded him, was that Hellenistic culture was spread over the eastern world. The Jews were faced with the problem as to what extent their religion permitted them to accept the modification of these non-Jewish influences. The Jews of Alexandria translated the Sacred Scripture into the Greek Septuagint. The words 'synagogue' and 'sanhedrin' are evidence of the strength of Greek influence on Jewish life. But later, under Antiochus IV Epiphanes, the Seleucid prince, who ruled the province of Syria from 175, the Hellenising influences became dominant. Traditional Jewish ceremonies were almost completely neglected and the Temple services were abandoned in favour of athletic contests. The people of

Jerusalem eventually rose in rebellion against Antiochus. As a result, he marched on the city, occupied the Temple, took the golden Altar, the golden candlesticks, the table of the Show Bread, cups, bowls, censers, all valuables and hidden treasures that he could find and removed them to his capital at Antioch. All sacrifices according to the Mosaic law were forbidden. The sanctuary was profaned by the offering there of pigs in sacrifice. A heathen altar was erected on the Altar of Sacrifice and the Temple rededicated to the Olympian Zeus. Menelaus, a Jewish Hellenist, who usurped the office of High Priest, sold the Temple vessels to raise money. Against these outrages the orthodox rose in revolt under the leadership of the Maccabees. Their followers were, perhaps, the first in history to offer themselves for martyrdom in the full sense of the word, that they preferred death to the abandonment of their faith. The aged priest, Eleazar, as recorded in the fourth Book of Maccabees, when faced with a martyr's death, prayed: 'Be merciful unto Thy people and let our punishments be a satisfaction on their behalf. Make my blood their purification and take my soul to ransom their souls.'

During the revolt, the first Book of Maccabees tells us that the Syrians:

> put to death certain women that had caused their children to be circumcised. They hanged the infants about their necks and rifled their houses and slew them that had circumcised them. Howbeit, many in Israel were fully resolved and confirmed in themselves not to eat any unclean thing. Wherefore they chose to die that they might not be defiled with meats, and that they might not profane the holy covenant, so then they died. Others fled into the desert, where the Syrians came upon them on the Sabbath day. They refused to defend themselves. Let us die in our innocence, they said. Heaven and earth will testify for us that ye put us to death wrongfully.

Judas Maccabaeus recaptured Jerusalem; on the Feast of the Dedication he purified the Temple.

A hundred years later the Romans came. Pompey first captured Jerusalem in 63 BC. He entered the Holy of Holies, interrupted the sacrifices, executed all those, including the priests, who had opposed him, but did not loot the Temple or attempt permanently to suppress its ceremonies. A few years later, when Crassus came to suppress a subsequent revolt, he was more ruthless, looting the Temple and removing all the valuables on which he could lay his hands. Julius Caesar, when he was victorious had the wisdom, like Alexander, to pursue a policy of tolerance. With his consent, the Hellenised Herod became the ruler of Galilee and later king of the whole province. Herod was suspect in the eyes of orthodox Jews. For that reason and in order to win their favour, he decided to restore the Temple which had suffered so much from these various depredations.

He began the work in 20 BC. The old Temple was, he said, of too small an area. He enlarged the available area by large subterranean structures on the south of the Temple hill. These are what are known as Solomon's Stables beneath the Aqsa mosque. The whole new area was surrounded

by a quadrangular stone court, which in turn was surrounded by battlements to make it defensible. The northern, western and eastern sides had one gate each, the southern side two. Against each of the inner sides of the perimeter walls, a portico or cloister was built of marble columns roofed with cedar. Of these four porticos completely surrounding the enclosure, the finest was that on the south side, the Stoa Basilike, or royal portico, which consisted of one hundred and sixty-two columns with Corinthian capitals, arranged in four rows to form three aisles. Herod was a secularly minded man and the piously orthodox complained that this portico, magnificent as it was, was more a place of business than of worship. It was probably here that the business and the money-changing took place, against which Jesus was to utter his violent protest.

The Antonia Fortress
The eastern portico was known as 'Solomon's Porch'. It was here in all probability that Jesus taught and discussed with the people. It was certainly here that the first Apostles used to meet. The Acts records that 'They were all with one accord in Solomon's Porch' (Acts 5:12). At the north-west corner of this vast area was the Antonia Fortress, built by Herod on the site of an earlier Hasmonaean fort and named after his friend Mark Antony. The Antonia was built with the dual purpose of defending the north-east of the city from without and maintaining internal security and good order within the Temple Area. Consequently, it dominated and towered above the temple courts, its sentry walks leading down by stairs to the courtyard level. This enabled the captain of the guard to rescue St Paul from the angry mob and gave Paul a platform, 'on the steps of the castle' (Acts 21:31-40), from which to harangue them.

This enormous quadrangle which formed the floor, or bottom level, of the Temple Area was the outer courtyard. It was the Court of the Gentiles and surrounded on north, east and south the Inner Temple, from which it was rigidly separated. First, a low stone breastwork called the Sorak rose like a wall from the pavement. On this at intervals were tablets in Greek and Latin warning Gentiles not to proceed into the inner court, on pain of death. Two such warning notices in Greek have been discovered. One is now in the Museum at Istanbul. The second was unearthed when the new road was being built outside St Stephen's Gate. No warning in Latin has yet been found. Secondly, within the stone breastwork, fourteen steps encircled a raised terrace on which a high towered and gated enclosure, like a fortress, protected the Inner Temple. Set within this surrounding wall, some twenty metres high, were nine gates into the Inner Temple, four to the north, four to the south and one facing east.

The inner and walled enclosure was itself divided into two by a wall running north and south. The smaller and outer courtyard to the east was known as the Court of the Women, but open to all ceremonially clean, men or women. Between this and the western courtyard was an impressive bronze gate, at the top of fifteen circular steps. This was the Nicanor Gate, so named after the donor, an Alexandrian Jew. Through this gate was the Court of the Israelites, only entered by male Jews offering or witnessing sacrifices. Within this Court yet again there was an inner quadrangle encircling the walls of the central shrine on three sides. This was the Court

Vaulted substructures of Crusader and Herodian masonry below the pavement at the south-east of the Temple Area, sometimes associated with the Stables of Solomon.

51

of the Priests, in the very centre of which, and in front of a broad porch, stood a vast altar of unhewn stone. The site of this great Altar of Sacrifice one would like to think was identical with the Sacred Rock, 'as-Sakhra', beneath the Dome of the Rock today. Thus would be linked Abraham's sacrifice on Moriah, David's and Solomon's sacrifices on the theshing floor of Araunah the Jebusite, the sacrifices of the Third Temple and the mystical Ascension of Muhammad.

Within the Third Temple, the Altar of Sacrifice was washed clean twice a year, on the Feasts of Passover and of Tabernacles. At the south-west corner of the Altar were two holes, through which it was once believed that the sacrificial blood flowed into a channel leading into the Brook Kedron. On the north side of the Altar were twenty-four rings to which the heads of the sacrificial animals were tethered before they were killed. Beyond them were eight columns supporting cedar boards. On each board there were three rows of hooks on which the carcasses of the animals were hung after sacrifice. At the foot of the altar were two tables: one of marble for the preparation of the victim before the burning; one of silver for the utensils of the sacrifice.

The greatest of the sacrifices was that of the Passover, which in the Crucifixion year took place exactly at the same moment in the afternoon of the same day as that on which Jesus was delivering up His spirit on the cross. It is sometimes said that a million pilgrims came up to Jerusalem for the feast. This is not credible, but certainly a very great crowd came

and they all forced their way into the Temple. A blast of trumpets then rang out, and the people filed through the Temple gates into the Inner Court. The men in charge of the victims advanced. The priests in their white garments with long embroidered sashes stood waiting for them.

The lambs were then killed to the sound of a trumpet, a priest receiving the blood of each one in a basin of precious metal. The vessels containing the blood of the lamb were passed from hand to hand until they were finally given to the officiating priest at the Altar. He tossed all the sacrificial blood against the base of the Altar. Subsequently the lambs were flayed, their intestines and fat were separated, and the fat was burnt. The intestines were cleansed and replaced in the corpse, and then each wrapped in its own skin until it was removed by the men in charge. Throughout the sacrifices the crowd at large conducted a chant of psalms. At the conclusion of the Daily Sacrifice, morning and evening, a priest sprinkled a libation of wine over the Altar.

To the south-west of the Altar of Sacrifice was the bronze laver for the priests' ablutions. To the west or behind the Altar of Sacrifice was the Temple proper. Josephus describes it thus: 'The whole was built of huge blocks of white stone, with plates of gold upon the front, so that from the distance it appeared like a mountain covered with snow'. It was of two parts, the Porch and the Sanctuary. Its roof was flat but covered with spikes, to keep the birds away.

Twelve steps led up from the Court of the Priests to the Porch. Its height

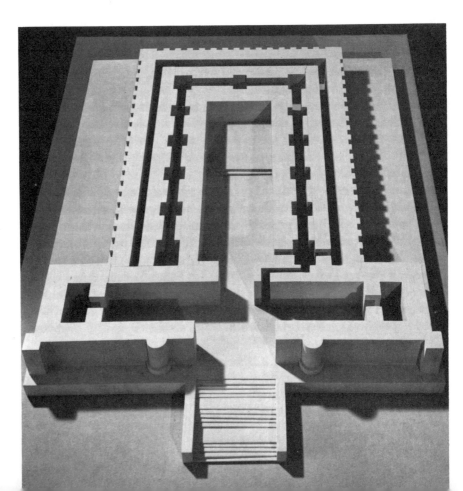

The Temple of Herod dominated by the Antonia Fortress: *(left)* an accurate model to be found in the Franciscan Museum within the Old City of Jerusalem today and *(right)* a model made according to plans by Professor Michael Avi-Yonah.

and breadth, says Josephus, were both about fifty metres. A double door overlaid with gold gave entrance to the Sanctuary. Before the Sanctuary hung a veil in four colours, byssus, purple, scarlet and violet. The door was about ten metres high and five metres broad. Above the door was a golden vine and cluster of golden grapes, the cluster according to Josephus 'as large as a man'. The Sanctuary again was divided into two parts: the Holy Place and the Holy of Holies. The Holy Place, about forty metres long, contained the Altar of the Incense, the Golden Candlestick and the Table for the Show Bread. Josephus tells us that he saw the Altar of the Incense in Rome, after it had been removed to that place at the time of the destruction of the Temple. The seven-branched candlestick was also taken to Rome by Titus.

Two-coloured veils divided the Holy Place from the Holy of Holies. The High Priest alone entered this inmost sanctuary, and he only on the Day of Atonement. The Holy of Holies was bare except for a stone, to mark the former place of the Ark of the Covenant which had been lost during the Babylonian Captivity. Above both the Holy Place and the Holy of Holies were upper chambers from which workmen, who had to do repair work, were let down in boxes which so shut them in that they could only see the part of the structure on which they were called to work.

The Porch and the Sanctuary of Herod's Temple were completed in a year and a half, but much work even after that still remained to be done, and the full structure was not finally finished until the procuratorship of Albinus in AD 62-4. Hence, it was possible for the Pharisees to say to Jesus 'forty and six years was the Temple in building', in reply to his prophecy of his resurrection that he could rebuild the temple of his body within three days. And, with work in progress and stones still lying around, it is easy enough to see how it was possible for them to 'take up stones to cast at him'. The Temple was, as we have seen, a place that in the Jewish view was divinely appointed to be the centre of religious life. When it was destroyed it was at first thought to be the duty of pious Jews to restore it at the first opportunity. Julian the Apostate toyed with the idea of restoring it in order to annoy the Christians, though he did not live long enough to do anything about it.

Successive Roman procurators treated Jewish customs with increasingly blasphemous insolence. Cumanus allowed the Jewish crowds to be enraged by the indecent gesture of a Roman soldier from the battlements of the Antonia and then massacred them. Felix, according to Tacitus, 'exercised the powers of a king with the outlook of a slave' and under him rebellion and murder became endemic. Florus in AD 66 robbed the Temple treasury of seventeen talents. The mob, in defiance of the High Priest, stopped the daily sacrifices for the emperor and war broke out. The Jews revolted against the tyranny of the Roman procurators. After years of siege, Titus captured Jerusalem in AD 70, burnt the Temple to the ground and proclaimed the land a Roman province under the title of Syria-Palestine. The ruins of Masada bear witness to the final Jewish stand against the Romans. Even the unsentimental Romans were a little frightened at their own vandalism. '*Hierosolyma, longe clarissima urbium*

54

A nineteenth-century
photograph of Jewesses in
picturesque Yemeni
costume praying at the
Western Wall.

orientis, non Judaeae modo' ('Jerusalem by far the most famous city, not just of Judaea but of the orient') was Pliny's description of it at a time when it was already no more than a 'bustum' – a heap of ashes.

Following the siege of Titus and the subsequent capture by Hadrian some half a century later, the Jews were banished from their homes and were never again to be the masters there until recent times. The city was destroyed and rebuilt under the name of Aelia Capitolina. Of the Temple all that was left standing was the Western Wall, a portion some fifty metres long and twenty metres high of the western part of the ancient wall surrounding the Temple area. The five lower courses of the wall are of stones which date back to Herod's time. The courses above are of a later date, the lower being of the time of Hadrian, the higher of Arabic times. It was the custom of the Jews in Palestine to pray daily at the Western, or Wailing Wall. In particular, on the anniversary of the destruction of the Temple, they assembled there to recite the lamentations of Jeremiah. Following the Truce of 1948, the Old City of Jerusalem was

left in Jordanian hands and Jews, for the first time since the fifth century, were excluded from the Western Wall. Twenty years of exclusion, in defiance of the Armistice Agreement, coupled with the loss and destruction of all synagogues in the Old City, including the beautiful Hurva and Nisan Bek Ashkenazi synagogues, provoked much grief and frustration among them.

Diggings near the site of the Southern Wall, south of the Aqsa Mosque, are at present going on under the direction of Professor Mazar of the Hebrew University. They have uncovered part of the original stone plaza laid down by Herod. Digging down thirty feet below the existing level, they have uncovered the stone blocks of the lowest course of the original wall. The Southern Wall now stands thirty metres high. Some of the stones had been damaged when the massive stones from the upper wall fell on them, at the time of the destruction by Titus. Along with them were found lamps, potsherds and Jewish coins of the period. These excavations are still continuing.

left: An aerial view of the Zealots' stronghold at Masada from the south showing, to the north, the fortress of Engedi and, to the east, the Dead Sea.

right: A photograph taken in 1937 of the Nisan Bek synagogue later destroyed while the Old City of Jerusalem was in Jordanian hands.

3 The Rabbis and the Synagogue

JEWISH HISTORY CAN BE DIVIDED INTO THREE PERIODS – THE PERIOD before Solomon and the building of the Temple, the period of the Temples, and the subsequent period of rabbinic Judaism. It is not at all certain at what date the Jews first adopted customs of congregational worship and private prayer as a normal activity. By the time of the first century AD such customs were so firmly established that such writers as Philo and Josephus imagined that they had been instituted by Moses, but this was certainly not so. Before the Captivity it was indeed customary for the pious Jew to pay visits to great Prophets at certain stated times. For instance, the man of Shunem could not understand why his wife should wish to visit Elisha, seeing that it was 'neither the new moon nor the sabbath', from which it may be adduced that it would have been understandable for her to visit him on those days. King Jehoshaphat sent out priests and Levites to teach in the cities of Judah, 'having the book of the law of the Lord with them'. But it was during the Captivity that Jews, of necessity divorced from the Temple, developed a habit of congregational worship. It was during the Captivity that Ezekiel, as he records, 'sat in my house with the elders of Judah sitting before me'. It was likewise from Ezekiel that we get the first suggestion that salvation might be a matter of righteousness for the individual rather than of a merely national salvation. 'The righteousness of the righteous shall be upon himself,' said Ezekiel, 'and the wickedness of the wicked shall be upon himself.'

There is no evidence that there were any special buildings for religious worship during the period of the Captivity. Soon after the Return, the Jewish place of common worship became, as it has since remained, the synagogue. If we look at the official list of Jewish Holy Places, we shall find that the greater number among them are synagogues, whether in Judaea or in Galilee, and date from a time after the destruction of the Temple.

The term *synagogue* – in Greek literally 'gathering together' – has, like the term *church* – in Greek literally 'those called out' – a double meaning embracing both the people *and* the building.

Exactly how and when the built synagogue came into existence is not certain. It was, it seems, during the Captivity that a regular system of interpretation of religious duties was developed, interpretation being of

The Ark in the synagogue of Pekin in Galilee, the home of an ancient Jewish community.

59

two kinds, Halakah, or rules of conduct, and Haggadah, or moral rules. It is out of the latter that both the parables of the New Testament and the sermon in the Christian Church have developed. Halakah and Haggadah were included in Midrash, or exegesis. These tasks were, to begin with, as we see from Nehemiah, undertaken by the levitical priests. It was only after the return from Captivity that a special class of non-priestly scribes was formed.

It is usually thought that the prayer, put into the mouth of Solomon at the dedication of the First Temple, was really the composition of an exilic author. Prayers were, of course, offered on special occasions in pre-exilic times, but it is not till the Psalms that we find the reiterated assertion that prayer was more pleasing to God than sacrifice. It was natural,

The outlet of the Wadi Qumran, whose water is channelled through the whole length of the Essene Monastery near the Dead Sea. The caves in the cliff face, on either side, were among those used for the concealment of scrolls.

in the course of time and particularly after the return from Captivity, that special buildings should be erected for prayer and preaching. Both the Christian Church and the Christian Liturgy of the Word are, of course, the direct descendants of the Jewish synagogue.

The function of the synagogue

The general form of the service of prayer and benediction in the synagogue had already fixed itself before the destruction of the Third Temple and was thus able to survive that destruction without great difficulty. There have been throughout the ages constant complaints at the volume of casual chatter that went on through the synagogue services. According to a legend, the Rabbi Eleazar once met Elijah driving four thousand heavily laden camels and on asking him what was their burden received the reply, 'These camels are laden with wrath and fury for those who talk during prayers'. Pious Jews objected to the easy manners of some of their co-religionists because of the scandal that they created. Similarly, there was no rigid regulation as to who might take part in the services of the synagogue. As we learn from the Gospels, there was no objection to Jesus or to St Paul speaking in a synagogue. A hazan, or synagogue official, could intone the liturgy and sometimes was also the schoolmaster and the ritual slaughterer.

The synagogues were generally small and designed only for a small congregation. Ten male adults are sufficient to form a synagogue congregation. Though many of the buildings are of great beauty, they have not therefore the majestic architectural grandeur which the Temple must have had and which the Dome of the Rock or the great Christian basilicas possess. The rabbinic Judaism which they developed was a didactic Judaism, shaped by learned rabbis to teach the faithful the nature of their duties towards God. The notion so commonly held among Gentiles that the teaching of the Pharisees was one of rigid regimentation is very far from true. On the contrary, in many ways it taught the believing Jew a code a great deal more humane and flexible than was to be found until recent years, if indeed it is to be found even now, anywhere else in the world. For instance, at no time did Jewish law permit torture, although it was widely practised everywhere else in the world and throughout every Christian country.

The Tractate Aboth gives a picture of the ideal Jewish scholar:

The possessor of Torah is one who recognises his place, who rejoices in his portion, who makes a fence to his words, who claims no credit for himself, is loved, loves the All Present, loves his fellow creatures, loves righteous ways, welcomes reproofs of himself, loves uprighteousness, keeps himself from honours, lets not his heart become swelled on account of his learning, delights not in giving legal decisions, shares in the bearing of a burden with his colleagues, uses his weight with him on the scale of merit, places him on a groundwork of truth, places him on a groundwork of peace, asks and answers, listens to others and himself adds to his knowledge, learns in order to teach, learns in order to practise, makes his teacher wiser, notes with precision that which he has heard and says a thing in the name of him who says it.

To whatever exact date we attach it, the Jewish moral teaching of the Torah very early established itself as an integral part of the Jewish religion. When, for instance, Mattathias rose in revolt against the desecration of the Temple, he rose, as he proclaimed, 'equally in defence of the Torah'. 'Whoever is zealous for the Torah and maintaineth the Covenant, let him come after me,' he said. The rabbis had, it is true, no powers of compulsion to impose their rulings on the people and there are examples of revolt against and repudiation of their authority, but such incidents were rare.

The Temple was destroyed by the Roman legions under Titus in AD 70. The whole of Jerusalem was destroyed and the city rebuilt on a different plan by Hadrian after the second war in 134. When the Khalif Omar came to explore the site of the Temple in 634, with the intention of building there a mosque, he found nothing but an impenetrable rubble. Jews were never after the days of Titus until recent times to be the masters of Jerusalem. Jewish opinion, however, mindful of the destruction of the earlier Temples, did not at first doubt that before long another Temple would be built. In the Dead Sea Scrolls, for instance, there are records of dimensions of a Temple, which are quite different from those of the actual Temple and which, it is reasonable to believe, were the dimensions of the intended Temple at any rate as the Essenes hoped to see it. As a third-century rabbi put it, with the destruction of the Temple the gates of prayer were locked and the gates of tears were opened.

Yet of course the Fourth Temple was not to be built. Therefore, as a consequence, though the belief that the Temple would one day be rebuilt was never abandoned, in practice there were no more sacrifices. Jewish religious life ceased to be a life ordered by priests and became instead a life ordered by teachers or rabbis. Even while the Temple still survived, it was the synagogue that was the place of teaching. The life of the synagogue and the life of the Temple grew up independently. Pirque Aboth, in the Sayings of the Fathers, describes the college of the Men of the Great Synagogue in whose hands the regulation of rabbinic teaching rested.

In face of persecution, the Essenes had already adopted a policy of retirement from the world into the desert. Such a policy of withdrawal was contrary to the general tradition, according to which it was the duty of the religious man to spread 'righteousness' throughout the world. The Pharisees saw it as their duty to save the people from 'impurity' and the three particular ways in which this 'fence' against corruption was to be defended was 'by ritual dress, by observation of the Sabbath and by obedience to the dietary laws'.

Seeing that the destruction of Jerusalem was inevitable, the Rabbi Yohanan ben Zakkai obtained from Vespasian leave to establish a Jewish Academy of Learning at Yavné, called by Josephus Iamnia. He escaped from Jerusalem, according to the story, by being carried out in a coffin. At Yavné, the modern village of Yíbna where no historical building remains, he established his school of the Torah or Vineyard and set up there the seat of the Sanhedrin. Hadrian, after the Bar Kochbar revolt, decreed the expulsion of all Jews from Jerusalem. This, of course, by no

One of the Dead Sea Scrolls, the Thanksgiving Scroll, showing the hanging Hebrew script. The damage and discolouration to the parchment was one of the hindrances in deciphering the text.

means brought the Jewish community to an end. Long before the destruction of Jerusalem, Judaism had become much more than a geographically national religion. The story of Pentecost in the Acts of the Apostles, along with many other stories, shows us how the Jews were already dispersed widely throughout the Mediterranean world and how Judaism was well on the way to establishing itself as a universal religion, as Zechariah had demanded. The Sibylline oracles of the second century BC speak of every country and sea being inhabited by Jews. Any monotheist religion is compelled by its own logic to find some divine purpose for the creation of those who are not the specially elect. If some Christians thought that the Jews had received their faith in order that they might prepare the way for Jesus, to such a Jewish thinker as Maimonides the task of Christianity was equally to prepare the way for the Messiah who was yet to come.

Thus, for some time after the destruction of the Temple, the intellectual centre of Judaism remained in Palestine but later it moved elsewhere.

Benjamin of Tudela, the famous traveller of the twelfth century, found more Jews by that time in Damascus than in all Palestine. The most ancient synagogue of his day was in Aleppo. The Rabbi Jacob, a visitor from Paris in the thirteenth century, records without any sort of resentment that Muslim mosques had been established over the Altar of Elijah at Carmel, the Tombs of the Patriarchs at Hebron, the Tomb of Jethro at Kefar-Hittim, the Tomb of Jonah at Kefar-Kanna, the Tomb of Samuel outside Jerusalem and the Tomb of Gamaliel at Yavné.

By the next century, the Rabbi Chelo found the Jewish conditions somewhat improved.

> The Jewish community in Jerusalem [he reported], God be gracious to her, is quite numerous. It is composed of fathers of families from all parts of the world, principally from France. Among the different members of the holy congregation at Jerusalem are many who are engaged in handicrafts, such as dyers, tailors, shoemakers, etc. Others carry on a rich commerce in all sorts of goods and have fine shops. Some are devoted to sciences, such as medicine, astronomy and mathematics. But the greater number of their learned men are working day and night at the study of the Holy Law and of the true wisdom, which is the Cabbala.

He recorded that the Tomb of David on Mount Zion was 'no longer known today either to Jews or Muslims', but he praised the Tomb of Huldah, the prophetess, on the Mount of Olives and the Tombs of the Kings which are, he says, 'of ancient and very massive construction, and form a masterpiece of sculpture. All the strangers who come to visit the Holy City say that they have never seen anything so beautiful.'

Jewish community life in the Holy Land

The most important Jewish immigrant to Palestine at the time of the Renaissance was Bertinoro who arrived there in 1487 and lived there till the beginning of the next century. He was able to establish a rabbinical college in Jerusalem and to maintain very friendly relations with the Arabs. He records that 'the Jews are not persecuted by the Arabs. I have travelled the length and breadth of the country and none of them has put an obstacle in my way. They are very kind to strangers, particularly to anyone who does not know the language; and if they see many Jews together they are not annoyed by it.' Bertinoro travelled by way of Hebron where he found that 'neither a Jew nor an Arab may enter the cave itself. The Arabs remain above and let down torches into it through a window, for they keep a light always burning there. All, who come to pray, leave money which they throw into the cave through the window; when they wish to take the money, they let down a young man by a rope.' Rachel's Tomb he found 'a round, vaulted building in the open road'. Jerusalem, writes Bertinoro,

> for the most part is desolated and in ruins. I need not repeat that it is not surrounded by walls. Its inhabitants, I am told, number about four thousand families. As for Jews, about seventy families of the poorest class have remained; there is scarcely a family that is not in want of the commonest necessaries. The synagogue here is built on columns; it is

long, narrow and dark, the light entering only by the door. There is a fountain in the middle of it. In the court of the synagogue, quite close to it stands a mosque. The court of the synagogue is very large and contains many houses, all of them buildings devoted by the Ashkenazim to charitable purposes. The Jews' street and the houses are very large; some of them dwell also on Zion. At one time they had more houses, but these are now heaps of rubble and cannot be rebuilt, for the law of the land is that a Jew may not rebuild his ruined house without permission. There are some excellent regulations here. I have nowhere seen the daily service conducted in a better manner ... Jerusalem, notwithstanding its destruction, still contains four very beautiful long bazaars, such as I have never before seen, at the foot of Zion. They have all dome-shaped roofs and contain wares of every kind. They are divided into different departments, the merchant bazaar, the spice bazaar, the vegetable market and one in which cooked food and bread are sold.

Jewish Holy Cities   The Jews recognised four Jewish Holy Cities in Palestine: Jerusalem, Hebron, Tiberias and Safed. Of these the pre-eminence of Jerusalem is self-evident and Hebron is, of course, a city that was prominent in biblical history, but Tiberias and Safed are not biblical at all. So long as the Temple and Jerusalem were still standing, and in the time of Jesus, Galilee was very much a frontier province of Palestine. The word means no more than 'district', but for that reason its Jewish Holy Places escaped the full rigour of Roman destruction in the time of Hadrian and the school of the Torah was able to move there from Yavné. There are no synagogues extant which were standing in the time of Jesus. One of the most ancient synagogues must have been that at Capernaum, in which in all probability Jesus taught (see p. 112). Some of the stone carvings from this seem to have been incorporated in the building of a synagogue here in the second century. A partial reconstruction of this synagogue is to be seen today. Capernaum was abandoned in the sixth century. Along the Lebanese frontier where the Israelis have in modern times built a strategic road running inland from Ras en-Naqura, there are the remains of synagogues of Roman times at Sasa, Gush-Halav and Kefar-Biram. In Kefar-Biram is the traditional grave of Queen Esther where Jews used to meet to read the Scroll of Esther on the Feast of Purim.

Just off the Haifa-Nazareth road is Beth She'arim, which in the second century AD was the seat of the Sanhedrin. Yehuda Hanassi, the compiler of the Mishnah in that century, lived there. It was destroyed by the Romans in AD 352 but its ruins, recently excavated by the Israel Exploration Society, show its synagogue with its many catacombs to have been one of the most extensive in the country. Tiberias itself was built by Herod Antipas in AD 22 but the builders, in constructing it, came across a cemetery. This made it, according to Jewish belief, a defiled place and pious Jews would not set foot in it. There is no record that Jesus ever went there although it was only a few kilometres from Nazareth or from Capernaum. The only mention of it in the New Testament is St John's comment that boats from Tiberias brought visitors to the Feeding of the Five Thousand.

After the destruction of Jerusalem, Vespasian allowed Jews to settle in Tiberias. It became the seat of the Sanhedrin and the centre of the school of Talmudic law. It was there that the Mishnah was completed in about AD 200, the so-called Jerusalem Talmud produced in the fourth century, and the Tiberian, or Western, Vocalisation of the Jewish Bible in the sixth and seventh centuries.

Tiberias established itself as one of the leading Jewish cities with the coming of Turkish rule under Suleiman the Magnificent in the second part of the sixteenth century. Suleiman made it a semi-independent principality under the rule of the Jewish Don Josef Nassi, and Jews flocked into the town to make of it a Jewish metropolis. It enjoyed semi-independence throughout the eighteenth century but in 1837 was virtually destroyed by an earthquake. The synagogues there are both of the Sephardim, or Spanish, Jews and of the Ashkenazim, or central European, Jews. The town today is mainly notable as a Holy Place for the tombs of famous rabbis, of whom the most distinguished is the great philosopher Maimonides. He lived most of his life in Egypt, but when he died in 1204, his remains were transferred and buried in Tiberias. Near his tomb are the tombs of other famous rabbis: Yohanan ben Zakkai, Rav Ammi and Rav Assi, of the Roman period, also the seventeenth century mystic Rabbi Isaiah Horowitz, often named after his most well known work, Shelah Hakadosh. A little less than two miles to the south of Tiberias down the lake is the Tomb of Rabbi Meir, a rabbi of the second century who is much regarded by the Orthodox and credited with the working of miracles. His tomb is shared by the Sephardim and the Ashkenazim. When a pious Jew is facing danger, he vows to donate money for the purchase of candles to be lit to commemorate the soul of Rabbi Meir, and he prays: 'O God of Rabbi Meir, answer me. May it please thee, O lord God of our Fathers, as Thou didst hear the prayer of thy servant Meir of blessed memory and didst perform for him miracles and wonders, so likewise do for me and for all thy people Israel, who are in need of public and private miracles. Amen. Selah.'

Safed was the great intellectual centre of the Jewish revival. Today the town circles a hilltop eight hundred and fifty metres above the Mediterranean and well north of the Sea of Galilee. Both these seas can be seen simultaneously from the top of the town. In AD 66 the priest Flavius Josephus, who led the Jewish rebels of Galilee against the Romans, fortified the town of Zef (or Seph). The surrounding hills acted as beacons, to signal to the Jewish people. During the Crusader occupation, Fulke, King of Anjou, built a citadel here in 1140, which was destroyed by Saladin, rebuilt by the Knights Templars and again destroyed by the Sultan Beybars in 1266. The Muslims made the town the capital of the northern district of Palestine. Here a Jewish community gathered and reached the height of its fame in the sixteenth century. Together with Tiberias, Safed became the centre of Jewish study of the Scriptures, mysticism and symbolism, based upon the Mishnah and Talmud.

'In Safed,' it was said, 'is the purest air of the Holy Land and there is not a place where they understand better the profundities and the secrets

A menorah carved in the rock in the Catacombs, containing some two hundred sarcophagi, at Beth She'arim.

of the Holy Torah.' In the sixteenth century the first printing press in Asia was established in Safed. The great exponent of its Cabbalist learning was Haari, in whose name there are two synagogues in Safed today. When it was destroyed by earthquake in 1738, it was said that 'since the destruction of the Temple we have not known such disaster in Israel'. Safed was said to contain in the cave of Shem va' Ever the place where Shem, the son of Noah, expounded the secrets of the Torah to his grandson. Seven kilometres to the west at Meron are the tombs of Rabbi Shimon and his son Rabbi Eleazar. The Rabbi Shimon lived in the second century AD. He was one of the leading exponents of the Talmudic literature. Shimon had to take refuge from the Romans in a cave at Pekin, where he composed his Cabbalistic treatise on The Brightness, or the Zohar. In the great pilgrimage to Meron the people sing

> In a cave he lay hidden
> By Roman law forbidden
> Our Rabbi bar Yohai
> In the Torah he found his guide
> With spring and carob at his side.

left: Tiberias from the south, showing in the foreground the famous Hot Springs and the Tomb of Rabbi Meir, with the city of Safed on the skyline.

Part of Shimon's tomb projects into the adjoining prayer room and the wooden shelf above it is always covered with a large number of notes of supplications, praying that he will intercede with God to obtain the supplicant's desire. On the holiday of Lag Beomer, about a month after the Passover, a pilgrimage is held to the rabbi's tomb, a pilgrimage which has taken place since the sixteenth century. The pilgrims assemble in Safed bearing the flag-bedecked Scroll of the Law and, singing and dancing, process round the city. Then, towards evening, they ride from Safed to Meron where they dance again in the courtyard of Shimon's Tomb. The two tombs are covered with lighted candles and when darkness falls two bonfires are lighted and kept up all through the night, the pilgrims throwing on them clothes soaked in oil to keep them alight. By a Cabbalistic rule, young children have their hair cut for the first time and the cut hair is cast into the bonfires.

Mount Safed was, in ancient times, the site of one of the bonfires by which the news of the new month was passed from Jerusalem throughout the country. 'They used to take long cedar wood sticks and rushes and oleander wood and flax-tow. A man bound these up with rope, went up to the mountain and set light to them. He waved them to and fro and up and down, until he could see his fellow doing the like on the top of the next mountain; so too on the top of the third mountain.' There are also tombs in Meron which are said to be the tombs of Hillel, the famous rabbi of the years shortly before Jesus, by whose teaching Jesus is thought to have been influenced, also that of his rival, Shammai. In Shammai's Tomb is the traditional Tomb of the Messiah, a rock on which the

below: Prayers at the Tombs of Shimon bar Yochai and his son Eleazar, sages of Meron in the highlands of Galilee.

right: The tomb of Rabbi Shimon is covered with lighted candles at the annual pilgrimage which has taken place at Meron since the sixteenth century.

Messiah will sit at the Last Judgement, after Elijah has blown his trumpet in order to summon all the people to judgement. The synagogue there dates from the second century. Its central doorway consists of huge single stones and the upper lintel is also a monolith. It is the Jewish belief that if the lintel should fall of its own accord this would presage the coming of the Messiah. Once, when the lintel was moved by an earthquake, the people of Safed held a feast of celebration for the coming of the Messiah.

The next chapters are devoted to the presentation of some Christian Holy Places. Christians believe that Messianic prophecy has been fulfilled in the person of the Rabbi Jesus-bar-Joseph. They believe Jesus to have been born at Bethlehem; brought up in Nazareth; fulfilling a brief lakeside ministry in Galilee; crucified, risen and ascended in Jerusalem. Christians see, in the life and teaching of Jesus, the consummation of God's self revelation *through* and *to* the people of the Land.

above: An elated group of Jewish pilgrims dance to the music of flute and drum near the walls of the Old City of Jerusalem, after the Six Day War.

right: Proceeding triumphantly in the Old City these pilgrims carry a scroll of the Torah and the Shofar or ram's horn.

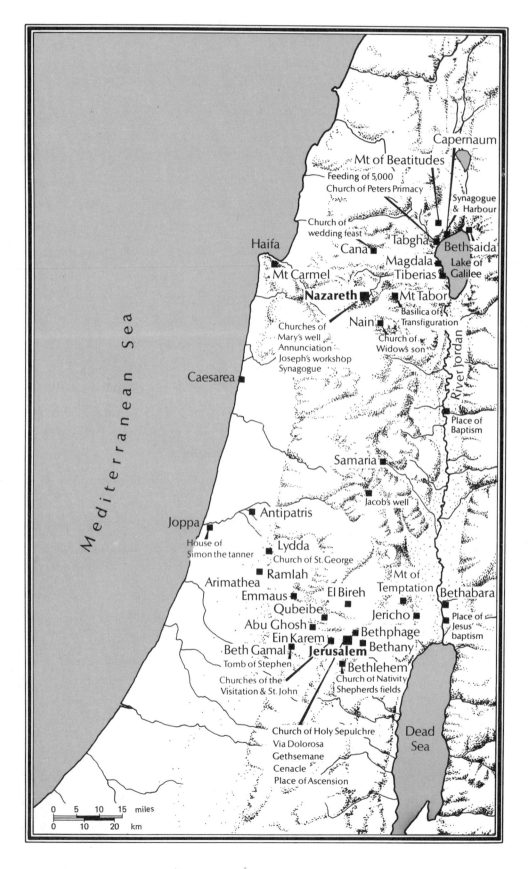

Mt of Beatitudes
Feeding of 5,000
Church of Peters Primacy

Capernaum

Church of
wedding feast

Synagogue
& Harbour

Haifa

Cana

Tabgha

Bethsaida
Lake of
Galilee

Magdala
Tiberias

Mt Carmel

Nazareth

Mt Tabor

Basilica of
Transfiguration

Nain

Churches of
Mary's well
Annunciation
Joseph's workshop
Synagogue

Church of
Widows son

River Jordan

Caesarea

Place of
Baptism

Samaria

Jacob's well

Joppa

Antipatris

House of
Simon the tanner

Lydda

Church of St. George

Ramlah

Arimathea

Mt of
Temptation

Bethabara

Emmaus

El Bireh

Qubeibe

Jericho

Place of
Jesus'
baptism

Abu Ghosh

Ein Karem

Bethphage

Beth Gamal

Jerusalem

Bethany

Tomb of Stephen

Bethlehem

Churches of the
Visitation & St. John

Church of Nativity
Shepherds fields

Church of Holy Sepulchre
Via Dolorosa
Gethsemane
Cenacle
Place of Ascension

Dead
Sea

Mediterranean Sea

0   5   10   15   miles
0   10   20   km

4 The Christian Approach

THE CHRISTIAN INHERITS FROM JUDAISM THE REVELATION OF GOD IN
the Old Testament: The Law, the Prophets, the Psalms and Literature.
He remembers and reverences the great events and scenes of Jewish history. Jesus was a Jewish rabbi steeped in the scriptures and in the story of
the mighty acts of God among his people. His own words and the witness
of his followers indicate a gradual identification of Jesus as the Messiah,
in whom are fulfilled the promises and prophecy of Judaism. Most of the
New Testament was written by Jews, who accepted Jesus as their Christ.
The Christian, therefore, owes an incalculable debt to the spirituality
and vision of Judaism.

In the first century the Jews had insisted that the Temple should be
the only place of sacrifice, in order to avoid the corruption of idolatry.
In the time of Jesus, this danger was no longer present, and he reacted
against the confining of sacrifice to one place. When the woman of
Samaria, at Jacob's Well near Sychar, asked him whether God should
be worshipped in Jerusalem or at her Samaritan shrine on Mount
Gerizim, he replied that 'neither on that mountain nor yet at Jerusalem',
should God be worshipped, but 'in spirit and in truth'. For Jesus, the
ritual of the Jewish Temple was superseded by the spiritual sacrifice of
obedience and penitence, independent of specific times and places. We
recall Samuel's warning: 'To obey is better than sacrifice and to hearken
than the fat of lambs'; also Isaiah's proclamation: 'Thus says the Holy

left: Map showing the
Christian Holy Places.

below: Arab felaheen, in
the hill country of Judaea,
suggest the journey of
Joseph, Mary and the
child Jesus, fleeing from
Herod into Egypt.

One who inhabits Eternity: "Behold I dwell in the high and holy place and with him that is of a humble and contrite heart"'.

So it is that Jesus has left his followers no legal system, but only two commandments: 'Thou shalt love the Lord thy God with all thy heart and with all thy soul, with all thy mind and with all thy strength', and 'Thou shalt love thy neighbour as thyself' (Deut. 6:5 and Levit. 19:18). Nor has he left any ceremonial system, but only simple sacraments to be the vehicles of his love and blessing, including baptism and communion. This last, whether instituted in the context of the Seder Feast or not, is redolent with the atmosphere of Passover. It is the Christian's tryst with God, to *re*present the sacrifice of Jesus, wherever and whenever Christians meet to do so, in remembrance of Jesus who said: 'Wherever two or three are gathered together in my name, there am I in the midst of them'.

This 'gathering together' of Christians was simply the forming of a Christian 'synagogue'. The first Christian synagogue was the Upper Room on Mount Zion, the scene of the Last Supper of Jesus with his followers, and their regular meeting place before and after the event of the Feast of Pentecost. And, wherever the sacrament of communion is celebrated, it is in two parts. The second centres round the actions of the Last Supper, but the first follows exactly the pattern of the synagogue service.

Thus it may be said that Christian faith, scripture, sacrament and liturgy are deeply rooted in Judaism. There is, however, yet another ancient custom which Christians have inherited from Jews. That is the practice of pilgrimage, which from earliest times was a natural expression of the piety and devotion of the Holy People, as they went up to the Holy City to offer sacrifice at the Holy Place to the Holy One.

The prime interest of the Christian must necessarily be in the events connected with the life of Jesus and, to a lesser extent, the followers of Jesus. Perhaps the spirit or philosophy of Christian pilgrimage is most clearly expressed within the Orthodox Church. Dostoievsky wrote: 'When the pious pilgrim comes in sight of the goal of his journey, he climbs down out of his vehicle and takes to the road on foot. There is then a joy mysterious and profound. We enter an unfamiliar world – a realm of joy – a thousand times less known to us and thousand times more profound than the realm of grief, and a thousand times more fruitful.'

St John of Damascus has written about the Holy Places: 'I venerate them, because they are the vessels of God's action. It is thus that I venerate angels and men and all matter which ministers to my salvation, in the purpose of God.' Similarly, Professor Leon Zander has written: 'In saluting these sacred relics of the past, which for ever bear the imprint of Christ, we unite ourselves with the spirit that rests in them. So, we absorb the grace inherent in the material things that have been chosen and exalted by the free acts of God.'

Like the Jews at the Seder, the Christian pilgrim needs to use both his imagination and his memory if he is to recall and to make real the past within the here and now. There is no question of rediscovering a Jesus-in-the-flesh, by the lifting up of old stones, as if to 'seek the living among the dead'. There is, rather, an awakening of an acute awareness to the events that have taken place in such sacred surroundings – an awareness, too, of the presence in spirit of the living Jesus. The Christian pilgrim reconstructs the events of the physical life of Jesus, but with the intention of grasping more fully what happened and what those happenings mean, both for him as an individual and, in the purpose of God, for the world.

Finally, every pilgrim should resemble a bee, not only to be fed by the honey drawn from the sweet flowers of his pilgrimage, but bound to carry back home the pollen, in order to give fresh touches of life in distant places. His visit to the Holy Places should be both passionate and pentecostal.

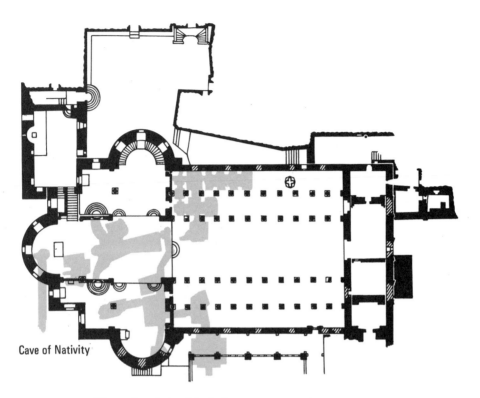

Church of the Nativity, present plan

Cave of Nativity

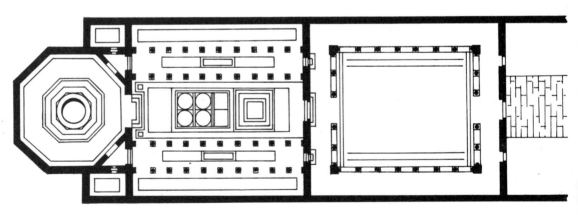

Suggested plan of Constantine's church and atrium

5 Bethlehem and the Birth of Jesus

IN AD 300 BETHLEHEM WAS A VILLAGE IN THE TERRITORY OF AELIA Capitolina, the Roman city that had occupied the site of Jerusalem since its destruction by Hadrian in 135. The village was reached by a track, which left the main road from Aelia to the south, near the fifth milestone from the city. Withdrawn from the main line of traffic, the village probably served as a market for the small farmers and nomads on the fringe of the Judaean wilderness.

Cave of the Nativity
For many years past there had been a local tradition concerning a cave near the village, which was reputed to be the birthplace of Jesus. The cave was of sufficient interest to attract visitors from the outside world, but no church stood there, nor did any Christian ceremonies take place. The cave was in a wood held sacred to the pagan deity Adonis, and was linked with the worship of Adonis. He had been the mythical Syrian paramour of Venus and was also worshipped in another well-known cave at the mouth of the Adonis River.

Referring to the cave in which Jesus was born, St Jerome wrote: 'The earth's most sacred spot was overshadowed by a grove of Adonis; and in the cave where the infant Christ once cried, the paramour of Venus was bewailed!' The first Church of the Nativity was built over this cave on the initiative of Empress Helena, mother of the Emperor Constantine, in 325. From then onwards, there is no real question of the site having been lost. There is a continuous chain of evidence from the building of the first church to the present day. The problem is rather to get back *behind* the year 325.

The history of the site of the nativity at Bethlehem is inevitably linked with that of the crucifixion and resurrection at Jerusalem. In this history, there appear to be two obvious gaps: the first follows the four-year siege and sack of Jerusalem by Titus in AD 70, when for some fifty years the city 'disappeared' from history. A Roman legion was left to complete the destruction of the city against the return of the Jewish inhabitants. A curtain seems to be drawn between the early Jewish Christian Church and the later Gentile Christian Church; and the greater part of the Christian community fled for a time to Pella. The second gap followed the subsequent sack of Jerusalem by Hadrian in AD 135 following the Bar Kochbar revolt. On this occasion a Roman colony of veterans was planted

Plan of the Constantinian and present day Churches of the Nativity at Bethlehem.

in the ruins. The new city of Aelia Capitolina was built rather to the north of the old city. By an edict, which remained in force for two hundred years, the Jewish community were forbidden to re-enter the city.

A number of factors could have combined to bridge these gaps, though many writers assume that there was such a dislocation in the history of the Christian Church in Jerusalem that no continuous tradition could have been possible. As the accuracy of the most important Christian sites are in question, it would seem only right to list the bridging factors, together with any pre-Constantinian documentary evidence.

The common Semitic interest and memory of past history and personalities, together with the veneration of Old Testament sites linked with Old Testament characters, would suggest some early development of a Christian tradition of places, sanctified by the life, death and resurrection of Jesus. Constantine himself certainly respected the early Christian tradition, as rooted in authentic recollection and passed down from father to son. How far were Christians as well as Jews forbidden the city? How far was the destruction of the city as complete as the Roman conquerors claimed, or did they exaggerate? It was the twentieth siege of Jerusalem which, phoenix-like, sprang up from its own ashes. However scattered the Christian community, the line of Christian bishops in Jerusalem is unbroken from James, the brother of Jesus.

Justin Martyr, born in the year 100, described how Christians crept *Early pilgrims* back into the city after AD 70, and did not forget the Christian sites. Certainly, Hadrian had no doubt as to which Christian sites should be desecrated in 135. He built a pagan shrine on the site of the Jewish Temple, but he also smothered the sites of the crucifixion and resurrection with a concrete platform, or podium, on which he erected a statue of Jupiter over the place of crucifixion, and a temple to Venus over that of the resurrection. At Bethlehem he planted a grove, sacred to Adonis, completely surrounding the Cave of the Nativity. This providential desecration of Christian sites only served to mark them indelibly for the future. It was not difficult to point out the correct areas for excavation in 325, though the identification of the particular tomb in Jerusalem or cave at Bethlehem may have been more open to question. There is no doubt, however, that a detailed identification was made, based on local tradition and documentary evidence, to the satisfaction of the Constantinian architects. The great Byzantine basilicas, enclosing slabs of the original rock of the cave concerned, served both to protect and enshrine the places selected, as well as to provide accommodation for prayer, facing the shrine. These Holy Places have been the focus of devotion and pilgrimage for more than sixteen hundred years.

We shall now turn to the documentary evidence of the pre-Constan- *Documentary* tinian period. Both St Matthew and St Luke agree on the birth of Jesus *evidence* in Bethlehem, but do not mention a cave in which he was born. But, then, there is no mention of his being crucified on a hill or knoll! Justin Martyr of Nablus and Rome, in AD 155, wrote: 'Should anyone desire other proof for the birth of Jesus in Bethlehem, according to Micah's prophecy and the history described by the disciples in the gospels, let him consider that,

The threefold doorway of the Church of the Nativity: the Justinian portico, the Crusader arch and the wicket gate of Turkish times.

in harmony with the gospel story of his birth, a cave is shown in Bethlehem where he was born and a manger in the cave where he lay wrapped in swaddling clothes'. So, too, the early Apocryphal Gospel of St James referred to the cave. This means that a 'cave' tradition was current in Judaeo-Christian circles by AD 150.

Origen, in 215, quoted Justin (above) and refers to a *specific* cave as shown to visitors: 'They still show the cave in Bethlehem where he was born. And this which is shown is well known in the district, even amongst strangers to the faith – namely, that in this cave he who is worshipped and reverenced by Christians, namely Jesus, was born.' He, Origen, had 'been at the Places for investigation of the footsteps of Jesus and his disciples'. Melito of Sardis, in 150, 'reached the Places where the gospel history was acted out'. Alexander of Cappadocia visited Jerusalem in circa 180, 'for the sake of prayer and investigation of the Places'. Firmilian of Cappadocian Caesarea visited Origen in 215, 'for the purpose of the Holy Places'. So, by 200, the 'Places' or 'Holy Places' had become a technical term in the language of pilgrimage. At the close of the third century, Eusebius, Bishop of Caesarea, writes: 'The inhabitants of the place bear witness of the story that has come down to them from their fathers, and they confirm the truth of it and point out the cave in which the Virgin brought forth and laid her child.'

The site of the Cave of the Nativity was selected by Empress Helena in 325 for the building of the church. That was, after all, 125 years after the local recognition of the specific cave. Constantine was particularly interested in the Bethlehem church, as a memorial to his mother's piety. The Bordeaux Pilgrim visited the basilica in 333, 'two miles from Rachel's Tomb, built by order of Constantine'. Other anonymous pilgrims of the fourth century describe the church furnishings, mosaics and marbles – also the silver manger. They describe the felling of the trees surrounding the cave and the levelling of the rock on the site with the purpose of sheltering and glorifying the cave, and also of providing a space for worship.

R. W. Hamilton, of the British Mandatory Department of Antiquities, describes the Constantinian church thus: *The Constantinian church*

> The eastern end of the building, directly above the cave, was a self-contained octagonal structure, in the centre of which two octagonal steps led up to the rim of a circular opening cut in the roof of the cave, large enough to expose to view the place of the nativity itself and a good part of the rest of the cave. The rim of the opening was fitted with slots to take the uprights of a railing or canopy. The surrounding floor was paved with mosaics [still to be seen]. This part of the church was probably covered with a conical timber roof of octagonal plan. It was clearly designed to enable the worshippers to inspect the sacred cave from above, or without entering the cave itself to pray kneeling on the steps with the place of the nativity in view.
>
> The congregational part of the church stretched away to the west. It was built in the form of a basilica, divided into a nave and four aisles by four rows of columns. The length and width of this part of the church were almost exactly equal. A wide opening with three steps leading upwards at the east end of the nave connected the basilica with the octagon; and from the two inner side aisles two doors led to small rooms filling the triangular spaces between the octagonal and basilical parts of the church, and to two rectangular chambers beyond them. All of these rooms, as well as the basilica, were paved with mosaic floors, and the walls, as described by early visitors, were lined with marble slabs and more mosaics or painted plaster.
>
> One question left uncertain by the discoveries is where the entrance to the cave was located at that time. The two existing stairways cannot in their present form have existed in Constantine's church; they would have obtruded too awkwardly on the floor of the octagon, which must have been left clear for people to approach the central steps from any direction or pass round them in procession. If the present stairs did not exist, it follows that the entrance must either have lain outside the church altogether or have been located near the entrance to the octagon at the east end of the nave.
>
> The second alternative is the one suggested by the existing remains. The excavations of 1934 revealed, in the middle of the wide steps which

connected the floor of the central nave with the slightly higher floor of the octagon, a narrower flight of steps leading down to a blocked-up doorway in the western end of the cave.

The church was entered from the west by three doors. Between it and the street there was a long atrium or forecourt, surrounded by colonnades and paved partly with stone flags and partly with mosaics.

It is hardly possible to recover today an idea of the internal appearance of Constantine's church, which impressed its visitors with a brilliance of decoration and wealth of furnishing very different from the present dingy interior. Seen from outside it was probably more austere, with walls of cream-coloured limestone, and red-tiled or leaden roofs. The church of Constantine and Helena stood for two hundred years. Then a disaster, of which history has strangely left no record, caused its complete demolition and reconstruction in the form it retains today.

In the year 386, St Jerome, a Dalmatian priest, travelled from Rome to Bethlehem with two ladies of a wealthy Roman family: the Lady Paula, a widow, and her daughter Eustochia. Living in a neighbouring cave

Constantinian mosaics cover a large area some two feet below the present floor level.

on the same hillside, Jerome made his translation of the Vulgate. His tomb and those of the women are within the church, and very near the Cave of the Nativity. During this period innumerable pilgrims flocked to Bethlehem from all parts of the world, from Britain and India, Pontus and Ethiopia. As St Jerome put it: 'The whole Church of the Nativity in nocturnal vigils rang with the name of Christ the Lord. With the tongues of diverse races, one spirit sang in chorus the praises of God.' By the sixth century it was clear that the Church of St Helena was too small, with too little space, for the number of pilgrims and the ceremonial processions.

The Justinian church

Over the years between 527 and 565 the first church was demolished and a new one built at the orders of the emperor, Justinian. This was destroyed by the Samaritans in 529 with much looting and burning. The mosaic floors of the early church were found to be covered with a thick layer of ashes and broken tiles. The patriarch Eutychius, writing in the tenth century, described the roles of both the Samaritans and of Justinian (the king) in the following passage:

Peter the patriarch of the Holy City asked St Saba to go to Constantinople and ask the king to lighten the revenues from the people of Palestine, because of the destruction wrought by the Samaritans. So St Saba set off for Constantinople. And the king was pleased with him and accepted the patriarch's letter from him and asked him his needs. And St Saba said to him, 'I ask you to lighten the revenue from Palestine, for the Samaritans have slain its people and ruined the country.' And the king ordered the churches which the Samaritans had burned to be built again ... and he sent with him an envoy for that purpose and supplied him with a great sum, and wrote to his agent in Palestine to pay the revenue of Palestine to the envoy, to build what the king had ordered him. And the king also ordered his envoy to pull down the church of Bethlehem, which was a small one, and to build it again of such splendour, size and beauty that none even in the Holy City should surpass it. And when the envoy reached Jerusalem he built a hospice for pilgrims, finished the new church, and built the churches that the Samaritans had burned and also a number of monasteries. And he pulled down the church of Bethlehem and built it as it is now.

Opposite above: A distant view of Bethlehem over the hill country of Judaea, with the Herodium on the left skyline.

Opposite below: The complex of buildings which form the Church of the Nativity on the Tell of ancient Bethlehem, whose natural rock terraces form cave basements for the houses.

Justinian's reconstruction to a large extent followed the lines of the old church of Constantine. The nave of the church was extended by one bay to the west and a narthex porch was added. The octagon over the cave was replaced by the existing choir. Instead of an opening through which pilgrims could look down into the cave, two entrances were now provided, one on each side of the altar, so that pilgrims could walk down into the cave. The cave was lined with marble slabs and the internal walls of the church with mosaics and marbles. Outside, on the west wall above the triple doorways, was a mosaic of the Magi, and this was to prove a piece of great good fortune for the church. This story, relating events which took place in the year 614, was told at a church conference at Jerusalem in the ninth century:

Overleaf: The traditional site of the baptism of Jesus in the River Jordan, seen from the east bank.

At Bethlehem St Helena built the great Church of the Mother of God, and on the west, outside, she caused to be made a representation in mosaic of the birth of Christ, with the Mother of God bearing on her breast the Child who bringeth life, and the adoration of the Magi. When the impious Persians had laid waste the cities of the Roman Empire and Syria, burnt Jerusalem and imprisoned the patriarch Zacharias ... on their arrival at Bethlehem they were amazed at the picture of the Persian Magi, the astrologers, their fellow countrymen. In respect and affection for their ancestors, whom they venerated as if they had been alive, they spared the church.

Visit of the Khalif Omar

A few years later the Persians were expelled and soon afterwards the country was conquered by the Muslim invaders. The first of their khalifs, the tolerant and enlightened Khalif Omar, because of his reverence for Jesus as a great prophet and his belief as a pious Muslim in the Virgin Birth, insisted that the church be spared, just as he had insisted that the Church of the Holy Sepulchre be spared. He came to pray in the south apse of the basilica, which conveniently faced towards Mecca. Omar made an agreement with the patriarch Sophronius, by which in return for their promise not to make a call to prayer there, nor to ask for any structural alterations, nor to associate in a group, Muslims should always be allowed to pray singly in the apse. Omar's agreement was kept during his lifetime. After his death it was broken by Muslims who destroyed the mosaics in the south apse, setting up in their place a Muslim inscription, and in defiance of Omar's promise making a call to prayer from there. Even so, in 951 a Muslim writer refers to the great reverence in which the Church of the Nativity was held for its association with both Jesus and David, by Muslims and by Christians alike. When the fanatical Khalif Hakim attacked all other Christian churches in Bethlehem and destroyed them, he left the Church of the Nativity undamaged. Relations between Muslims and Christians in those first days of Muslim invasion were good, indeed they were very different from what they were afterwards to become during the period of Turkish rule, and after the invasion of the Crusaders.

Arculf, a monk from Gaul, visited Bethlehem in 670, and gives a description of the cave of Jesus's nativity as a 'natural half cave', which shows that it was much the same then as it is today. But the Christian community there was in a decline. In Justinian's day there had been at least four monasteries in or near Bethlehem. By Charlemagne's time there were, it was reported, only fifteen monks and two anchorites. When in 1099 the

Crusader occupation

Crusaders were approaching, the Christians in Bethlehem were in some danger, but Godfrey de Bouillon sent a hundred and fifty knights under Tancred to defend them. With the establishment of the Latin Kingdom a community of Augustinian monks was established there and they lived in happy relations with the Greek ecclesiastics of the city.

In 1101 Baldwin I was crowned, in the basilica at Bethlehem, the King of Jerusalem, having refused to be crowned with a gold crown in the city in which the Saviour had been crowned with thorns. His successor Baldwin II was also crowned there in 1109. The third King of Jerusalem,

View of the Lake of Galilee from the basilica on the Mount of the Beatitudes.

Baldwin III, married the daughter of the Byzantine Emperor Manuel Comnenus, and under his successor, Amaury, the great work of the church's restoration was carried through as an act of cooperation between West and East.

In the early seventeenth century, Quaeresmius, the Franciscan *custos* of the Holy Land, wrote a description of the Church of the Nativity as it then was. He is able to give us a detailed account of the decorative plans of the Latin Kings. On the western wall, above the nave, was an elaborate Tree of Jesse. Out of the side of the sleeping Jesse came three stems, each ultimately leading to Mary, the Mother and Jesus, who appeared at the top of the central and highest stems. Each of the stems in its course passed through all the major prophets, the prophets marked by name and holding in their hands scrolls summarising their prophecies. All this Jesse mosaic has perished. On the south wall was a row of half life-size figures representing the descent of Jesus from Abraham, as enumerated by St Matthew. Of these figures seven remain. Above them was a series of architectural devices representing the first seven General Councils of the Church. Of these devices two have perished. The other five have survived, in whole or in part. Above them, in the clerestory windows, were figures of angels which have also perished. On the south wall was a row of figures which represented the genealogy of Jesus according to St Luke. All these figures, too, have perished. Above them were symbolical representations of the six Provincial Councils, of which three have survived and three have perished. Above them were six angels, of which five survive. The walls of the apses were decorated with scenes from the life of Jesus. On the south apse was the Nativity and the Adoration of the Magi. On the west wall were scenes from the Passion, Jesus conversing with the Samaritan woman, the Transfiguration, and the Entry of Jesus into Jerusalem on Palm Sunday. Parts of the Transfiguration and the Palm Sunday scenes remain. Above these scenes were the four evangelists, to the east of them Joachim and to the west St Anne. Of the mosaics in the north transept nothing remained by the seventeenth century when Quaeresmius wrote, except the Ascension, of which part still exists, and the Incredulity of St Thomas, the most beautiful mosaic in the church, which survives entire. On the south side of the choir was the Presentation in the Temple and on the north side Pentecost and the Burial of Mary, the Mother of Jesus. In the eastern apse was the Annunciation. In the centre of the great arch was Mary, the Mother of Jesus, and in the spandrels on each side Abraham and David with their names, the spaces between them being filled with the words 'Ave Maria gratia tecum ... Ecce ancilla domini fiat mihi secundum verbum tuum'. 'Hail Mary full of grace, the Lord be with you ... Behold the handmaid of the Lord, be it unto me according to thy word'. Beneath them were mosaics of Ephrem, the artist, of King Amaury, of the Emperor Manuel Comnenus, and of Raoul, the Bishop of Jerusalem. The church was thus a beautiful picture book of the Christian doctrine of the Incarnation extending around the whole of the interior. Even on the Byzantine columns, today, are faint representations of saints, including St George, King Canute and King Olaf of Norway.

Crusader decoration

Crusader steps lead down, from either side of the crossing, into the natural limestone strata cave which formed the focal shrine of the Constantinian church.

The entrance to the Grotto of the Nativity was also of twelfth-century work. The floors and walls were covered with marble slabs. Outside the church to the north was the convent of the canons regular, of which remains can still be seen. The lower front of the bell tower still stands in a court to the south.

Towards the end of the twelfth century, Bethlehem fell to Saladin a few days before the fall of Jerusalem. Saladin did Bethlehem no damage. In 1192 he gave permission for the re-establishment of the Latin rite and in 1227 the Muslim authorities allowed the erection of the great double door entrance to the nave, parts of which still remain and show interesting Persian and Armenian influences. After the fall of the Latin Kingdom Saladin allowed two Latin priests and two deacons to return to Bethlehem and in 1247 the Bishop of Bethlehem came to England to beg for money. The Sheriff of London founded in Bishopsgate a hostel for the visiting clergy of St. Mary's, Bethlehem. This was later turned into a home for lunatics and the name of Bethlehem corrupted into Bedlam. Various treaties with the Muslims throughout the thirteenth century confirmed the ownership of the Latins, on condition that the Muslims were allowed to go there on pilgrimage and pray there. A Tartar invasion in 1244 threatened and impoverished the church and in 1266 Beybars expelled all western Christians from Bethlehem. The church survived, however, and there are accounts, both from the late thirteenth and early fourteenth centuries, of large pilgrimages to it. Jacques de Verone, writing in 1335, describes a pilgrimage of more than five thousand persons to the cave three days before the Feast of the Assumption:

> We celebrated matins [he writes], each nation according to its custom in different parts of the church. In the morning, each nation took the altar to which it had a right. The main altar of the inner church belongs to the Greeks; the Frank Christians have the altar in the crypt near the manger where I sang a solemn mass, for we were more than a hundred French Christians. There were present two friars preachers, two minors and several secular clergy and priests. To the left of the church (in the

Within the Cave of the Nativity, many pilgrims of Byzantine and Crusader times have left crosses carved in the masonry.

north transept) are three altars and a cistern near which the Virgin Mary is said to have drunk water at the time of her accouchement. At each of the three altars the Syrians, the Abyssinians and Nestorians celebrated. On the opposite side (in the south transept) there is an altar where are buried twenty-four of the Innocents and it is there that the Jacobites celebrate. The Georgians and the Maronites use altars that are outside.

In the fifteenth century, Ignatius of Smolensk records that the Franks officiated alone and that the Franciscans lived in the monastery to the north of the church. 'The basilica itself was under the Franciscans', records the Russian Grethenius, 'but the Greeks held the great altar', and the old sacristy was transformed into a chapel of St George. Up till the end of the fourteenth century, there is every reason to think that the basilica retained intact all the splendour with which it had been adorned under the Latin kings. It was only with the fifteenth century that dilapidation began. Some of the mosaics began to decay and some of the marble slabs were removed. The early Muslim rulers of Palestine, such as Omar and Saladin, had accepted with all seriousness the obligation of their religion to honour all those who were 'of the book' (that is to say, Jews and Christians who accepted the Bible), and to respect their Holy Places. They offered to those who were of these faiths a generosity and tolerance very far in excess of any that was found in the Christian Europe of their *Turkish* day. Even in later years, the Turks certainly permitted in Palestine a *occupation* wider religious freedom than their contemporary Christians permitted in their lands to other Christians, let alone to those who were not Christians at all. But it can hardly be pretended that Turkish tolerance sprang entirely from a spirit of generosity. On the contrary, the Turkish principle was that all religious buildings belonged technically to the Sultan of Turkey as Khalif. Out of his goodness he permitted non-Muslims to worship in their religious buildings. The principle was, in fact, not theological, but economic. The Turkish government did nothing at all to develop the country. The revenue that it received from the country was derived mainly from the money that Christian pilgrims brought into it. If a wide variety of Christian bodies were admitted together in the churches of Bethlehem and Jerusalem, that was not out of any ecumenical spirit but simply because the more sects that could be crowded in, the more bodies there were from whom fees could be collected and, if on the whole in this strange division of spoils, the Latins tended to come out better than the Greeks, that was not merely because the Crusaders had Latin rulers and Latin architecture, but because after the decline of the Eastern Empire and the fall of Constantinople, Eastern Christianity had lost its prestige. In architecture the Byzantine influence always remained strong. The reason for Latin success was a more crude one. It was simply that with Western Christendom behind them the Latins had generally more money to offer.

As soon as the Turks occupied Bethlehem in 1516, they took the marble from the aisle walls for use in the Haram es-Sherif in Jerusalem. The process was repeated until by the end of the seventeenth century there was little marble left in the upper parts of the wall. Today it has all disappeared. In the sixteenth century the mosaics of the nave and the choir also suffered because of the condition of the roof. What attempts at rescue or restoration were made in the fifteenth century were, it seems, of little use. In 1435 there were some repairs to the roof. In 1448 Philippe le Bon, Duke of Burgundy, offered to repair the basilica at his own expense. Nothing much seems to have been allowed. In 1461 Louis de Rochechouart wrote: 'Elle s'affaise de jour en jour surtout au desus de choeur. Les Sarrasains refusent d'en permettre la restauration.' In 1479 total collapse was only prevented by supporting the roof with struts from the floor. A few years later the minimum of repairs needed to save the whole structure from collapse was permitted and carried out. Edward IV of England supplied the lead for the roof. In 1620 Quaeresmius, foreseeing further depredations, made his inventory of the church's possessions. His foresight was justified; by the 1670s all the lead had been removed from the roof. A writer reported: 'Ce bel edifice tomboit tout en ruine, il n'y a que trois ou quatre ans. Le plomb qui le couvroit avant este dérobé en plusieur lieus par les ennemis de notre sainte religion, la pluve avoit corrompu le boi et gastoit tout.' In 1672 the Patriarch of Jerusalem imported workmen from Mitylene to rescue the fabric. *The Church falls into disrepair*

In the post-Reformation world, rivalry between the Christian denominations concerning their ownership of the various Christian Holy Places raged so violently that the Ottoman government in 1757 attempted to settle all disputes by a *modus vivendi* which came to be described as the *Status Quo*. As many of the Greek Christians were subjects of the Ottoman government on whom the government could bring pressure, it tended to favour them as against the Latins, subjects of foreign powers with whom it might well be at issue, and the settlement of 1757 deprived the Latins of a number of Holy Places that had formerly belonged to them. The French and other European powers protested, but without very much effect, over the course of a hundred years. In 1852 the Sultan Abdul Majid reaffirmed the *Status Quo* of 1757. In 1853 an undertaking to maintain its provisions was accepted by all the powers as one of the clauses of the Treaty of Paris which ended the Crimean War. When with the mandate Palestine passed under the control of Britain after the First World War, the British government accepted an obligation to preserve 'existing rights', that is to say, the *Status Quo*, in the Holy Places. Certain suggestions were made during the mandatory regime for revision of the system, but none of them met with general acceptance. Therefore, in 1924, the British government accepted the *Status Quo* as promulgated in 1757 and reaffirmed in 1852 and, on the abandonment of the mandate in 1947, the United Nations Special Committee affirmed the protection of all Holy Places 'in accordance with existing rights'. *The Status Quo and the repair problem*

According to the arrangement of the *Status Quo*, the denomination which can show that it was the last restorer of any religious building has the right to do any repairs in the future. Where a building has in the past been under joint occupation, then repairs shall only be carried out by the agreement of all the occupiers. In virtue of the repairs of 1672 the Greeks claimed possession of the church. The work then done cost one hundred thousand écus, of which twenty thousand six hundred went in bribing the authorities to permit work to be done at all. Nothing was restored, and the work was only designed to shore up the fabric and to prevent its collapse. It remained in this condition throughout the eighteenth century. In 1809 a fire damaged the Grotto of the Nativity and completed the destruction of its ancient decorations. In 1834, a disastrous earthquake threatened it with total collapse. The Greeks obtained leave to carry out necessary repairs. This work was carried out ten years later when the roof was mended, the choir paved with marble and the nave with stone flags. The remaining mosaics were surrounded by plastering.

In 1852, Napoleon III, claiming, as the successor of St Louis, that France was the eldest daughter of the Church and the traditional defender of all Christians in the Middle East, laid his claim to the Church of the Nativity, and this dispute of the East and West about 'a key and a star' was one of the causes, or pretexts, of the Crimean War. Napoleon did not succeed in winning the Church of the Nativity, but he was able to establish his case for a Church of St Catherine adjoining it. The *raison d'être* for this was the legendary appearance of Jesus to St Catherine, when he told her of her forthcoming martyrdom. In 1874 Marshal MacMahon, then President of the French Republic, presented the hangings that still cover the walls of the cave. In 1888, the present Church of St Catherine was reconstructed from the older building by the Franciscans. It was a worthy work and includes some of the remains of the old twelfth-century church of the Augustinian canons, which came to light during the course of its building. The Church of St Catherine has, of course, none of the interest of the ancient Church of the Nativity next door. No further repairs to the Church of the Nativity were carried out during the nineteenth century, and the basilica thus remained in this usable but dilapidated condition until the end of the Turkish rule and the establishment of the mandate. In the 1930s considerable excavations and repairs were carried out under the direction of the Palestine government's Department of Antiquities.

The Church of St Catherine

The Church of the Nativity today

The basilica stands on the mound of ancient Bethlehem. To the west of the church are some vestiges of the former atrium, or forecourt. To the south of this is the Armenian Convent. The part of the forecourt which has not been built over is stone-paved. To the east of this forecourt is the narthex or ante-nave, through which it is possible to enter the main church. The narthex had originally three monumental doorways. Of these the northern and southern are now completely blocked. Even the central doorway is largely blocked, first by a small Crusader arch; now entry to the narthex is only possible through a small gate built to keep out animals on market days some two hundred years ago. The narthex used to be lit by two square-headed windows, one of which is now blocked.

Beyond the narthex, to the east, is the central nave. The nave is flanked by double aisles with avenues of monolithic columns. A clerestory wall rises above the level of the aisle roof in the nave, transepts and chancel. In it are the windows which light the church. The square-headed windows which originally provided light for the aisles are now all blocked.

95

Beyond the nave are the north and south transepts, both of which terminate in apses, each provided with three round-headed windows. Those in the north transept are blocked. Between the transepts and the church are chapels. The crossing which leads to the church and the choir itself are on a higher level from that of the nave or the transepts. The cave of the nativity is underneath the crossing and is entered a little to the east of it. Steps lead down to the grotto from each of the chapels to the north and south of it. The narthex and the apses have flat roofs. The rest of the basilica is covered by a trussed timber roof. The rock upon which the building rests is of a poor quality limestone. The rock under the western half of the church is solid, but under the eastern half there is an extensive system of caves. Thus the northern central column of the north transept stands over an easterly extension of the Cave of the Innocents, and the colonnade of the southern aisle stands over other caves as do the northern column of the chancel and one of the columns of the north aisle. As a result of this weight upon it the roof of the Cave of the Innocents is badly cracked, and fragments of stone fell down from it in the earthquake of 1927. Arches had to be constructed in the caves under the south aisle to prevent them from falling in. There are plenty of cracks in the roofs, and even though the danger of collapse may not appear imminent, the land is subject to earthquakes and no one can be sure what would be the effect of a serious earthquake shock. The north-west pier of the crossing, for instance, does not stand directly over the Cave of St Joseph, but it has clearly been affected by some disturbance of the rock out of which that cave has been formed.

The Crusaders built a vault on top of the narthex and this extra weight has over the years had the effect of pushing out the west wall to an alarming degree. The stonework is badly dislocated and many of the stones are cracked. The Armenian convent serves as a gigantic buttress to the southern part of the original entrance. Had it not been for this buttress, the front wall of the narthex would most certainly have collapsed.

When the Ottoman Empire came to an end, the Church of the Nativity was in no happy state. This was partly because under the Ottoman rule, with its lethargy and corruption, there was no encouragement to indulge in energetic action in any field. Partly it was due to the rule of the *Status Quo*, the workings of which far too often meant that it was difficult to get anything done. The Greeks, being a great deal less wealthy than either the Latins or the Armenians, had every motive to impede repair work, fearing that otherwise their more wealthy rivals would show up to advantage. With the coming of the mandatory government the Department of Antiquities appointed Mr William Harvey to report on the condition of the church. His report in 1935 was a sombre one. He found everywhere cracks in the walls, decaying timber and new timber that was almost as faulty as that which it was supposed to replace, and mortar which time had reduced to dust and which trickled out from its crannies. In defiance of the *Status Quo*, the mandatory authorities boldly pulled down the ugly fence that separated nave from choir. But by then, the political condition first of Palestine and soon afterwards of the world be-

British Mandate survey and repair

This shrine of the Nativity, covered and preserved by tapestry and marble, has been the focus of Christian pilgrimage for eighteen hundred years: the shrine is marked by a silver star set within the marble floor and surrounded by lamps, which symbolise the prayers of the many different branches of the Christian Church.

Jordanian control came such that it was not easy to find money for the repairing of a church. However, when in 1948 Bethlehem passed into the domain of the Jordanian government, that government showed itself considerably more energetic than ever the Turks had been to meet its responsibilities. Today Bethlehem has, as a result of the fighting of June 1967, passed from the Jordanians to the Israelis. A few shots aimed at the police station behind it hit the church during the fighting, but happily did it no serious damage. Nothing could be less favourable for the work of restoration than unsettled frontiers. Yet for all that, if one goes to the Church of the Nativity one finds, as elsewhere in Palestine, plenty of scaffolding about, but it is no longer the minimal work of shoring up that is required to prevent the church from collapse. A serious attempt is at last being made worthily to restore it according to the intentions of its designers, and whatever may be said of the condition of the church, its proportions are those of a very noble and magnificent basilica.

In the choir, stairways lead down into the cave below, from both the north and south transepts. The traditional Holy Place of the nativity is a niche at the east end of the cave which is, in fact, linked up with quite a

97

warren of caves. On the floor within the niche is a silver star, surrounded by many votive lamps, each belonging to and representing the prayers of the different branches of the Christian Church, Greeks, Armenians, Catholics, Copts, Syrians, Russians, Abyssinians and others. The star acts as a focus of devotion for pilgrims. We are reminded of the ecstatic description of the sixth-century patriarch Sophronius: 'Subduing the excessive fervour of sacred love which would burn in my heart, I would go straightway to that little village of Bethlehem, wherein the Lord of all was born. Passing through the noble portico of four columns into the midst of that most splendid triple-vaulted building, I would dance for very joy. Then I would view the cave wherein the Virgin Queen of all brought forth the Saviour of all mortal men. There, upon the famous floor whereon the Christ God was placed, I would press my eyes, my mouth and my forehead that I might bear away from thence a blessing.' And the Christian pilgrim still does so today, gazing wonderingly and lovingly at the inscription on the star: 'Hic de Virgine Maria Jesus Christus natus est'.

The Herodium, or summer palace of Herod, on the hills to the east of Bethlehem. The four corner towers and courtyard are here clearly visible.

Behind him, on the south side of the cave, is the chapel of the manger. Set within the floor, beneath the limestone wall of the cave is a marble token for the manger, which replaced a predecessor long since taken to Rome. Behind the grille and the candles is a painting of the shepherds in the cave by night, worshipping the Christ Child lying in the straw of his manger. The walls are covered with marble, asbestos or tapestry, partly for protection, partly from an oriental devotion, which the westerner does not always appreciate. Together with the more Protestant pilgrims, he would do well to remember just how much he owes to the spirituality and devoted tenacity of the oriental Christian.

Kneeling between the nativity and the manger, reaching up through the tapestry to touch the actual limestone ceiling of the cave, the Christian might well recall Justin Martyr's early second-century description of *two* shrines extant in his day: 'The cave in which he was born *and* the manger in the cave wherein he was laid'. He might, too, remember the seventh-century Bishop Arculf's detailed statement of 'a kind of half-cave, whose *inner* part is called the manger of the Lord, where the Mother laid her new-born Son – while another place, adjoining the manger nearer the entrance, is said to have been the true place of the nativity.' That is exactly the same arrangement as today. Arculf also described another cave down towards the wilderness from the Mound of Ancient Bethlehem. There in the very centre of the traditional Shepherds' Fields was a cave in which the shepherds slept, surrounded by their sheep in the fields of Bethlehem. Even the neighbouring village of Beth Sahur, the Village of the Watching, bears witness to the story. The shepherds' cave came to be incorporated as a crypt within a small Byzantine church, whose ruins still lie scattered among the olive trees. Today, the cave-crypt is in weekly use as a chapel for the local Orthodox congregation.

It is only natural that around an ancient Holy Place, others of lesser and later significance should be linked with different events in the same story. Thus, in the warren of caves below the Church of the Nativity are shown the more doubtful but nevertheless illustrative and stimulating grottoes of the Holy Innocents and of Joseph's Dream, not to mention that of Jerome and his lion. The value of such sites is not so much in their accuracy as in their teaching, enabling the pilgrim to remember and reconstruct the story in his mind. Finally, of course, there neither is, nor can there be actual archaeological proof of the site of the Nativity. Perhaps the whole matter is best summed up in the words of Professor Dalman, in his 'Sacred Sites and Ways':

> The most ancient local tradition out of which the church of Bethlehem grew is, after all, not necessarily authentic, but yet it may well have hit upon the truth. The cave under the church, with its manger, may not be the exact spot where Christ was born. But, at any rate, a hundred years after the Crucifixion it is with Bethlehem, the City of David, that the mystery of Christ's birth was connected. At the same time, it is the oldest firmly-established place of his veneration.

6 Nazareth, the Home of the Holy Family

THE TOWN OF NAZARETH OVERLOOKS THAT GREAT HIGHWAY AND battlefield of history, the Plain of Esdraelon. This fertile plain is the only flat corridor through the mountain ranges between the Mediterranean and the East. Below the hillside town of Nazareth have marched to and fro the armies of Assyria, Babylon, Egypt, Greece and Rome – of Alexander, Richard Coeur de Lion and Napoleon.

Nazareth, the market town of southern Galilee, was also a religious centre. It overlooked 'the Way of the Sea', one of the main trade routes between Damascus and Egypt. Here, caravans of silks and spices passed camels laden with grain and fish. Here, the rough and rustic Galilean peasant mingled with the merchants and travellers of the East in a truly cosmopolitan community.

This town was the divine choice for the youth and apprenticeship of Jesus. There is an ancient Greek proverb, 'the City makes the man'. No doubt the market place of Nazareth was – apart from the synagogue school – his only classroom. There, he might have watched the bargains driven and listened to the stories and gossip of the day. It must have been a rough and ready schooling for the hazards of an itinerant ministry, of open-air preaching and heckling in the years of his public life.

Nazareth ranks with Jerusalem and Bethlehem as one of the three main Christian Holy Cities of Palestine. Yet Nazareth's standing is very different from that of those two other towns. They were from the first marked out as Christianity's most important centres, and as such the victims of hostility towards it. Pagan temples were built over their Holy Places, though these had, in fact, the unintentional consequence of preserving and pinpointing their sites. Nazareth, on the other hand, was in the first centuries of Christianity strangely neglected by its friends and enemies alike. Origen, for instance, in the third century lived for some years at Caesarea – only some thirty miles away – but never, it seems, took the trouble to visit Nazareth.

The reasons are these: in the first place Jerusalem was the centre both of the Jewish and the Christian religions and an easily accessible metropolis. Those who wished to break those religions would naturally deliver their attacks on Jerusalem, and then on Bethlehem which was near to Jerusalem; Nazareth was to the Romans a distant and outlandish place

Nazareth, market town of Galilee and home of the Holy Family, the third city of Christian pilgrimage.

Mosaic floor of the
Constantinian church, to
be seen below the modern
Latin Church of the
Annunciation at Nazareth.

which seemed of lesser importance. Secondly, Nazareth, though it was
the place in which Jesus spent nearly thirty years – very much more time
than he spent in Jerusalem or Bethlehem – was in no way connected with
the birth, the crucifixion, the resurrection or the ascension, on which
Christians build their faith. Nothing supernatural was alleged to have
happened there, except for the annunciation of Jesus' coming birth to
Mary. For these reasons, and also because after the destruction of Jerusalem
and Hadrian's Diaspora Jews established themselves in Galilee in much
greater numbers than ever before, Nazareth became in the years after
Jesus' death a predominantly Jewish town, unlike Bethlehem which became Christian at an early date. When in 614 the Jews joined with the
Persians in attacking the Christians, the Jews of Nazareth provided one
of the largest contingents in that force.

Until recently it used to be thought that there were no Christians at
all in Nazareth in these early years; certainly it was assumed that there
was no Christian church there up to the time of Constantine, when one
was built by Joseph of Tiberias at Constantine's command. Recent excavation, however, has shown that this was not so. In March 1960, when
workmen were preparing to lift a mosaic pavement for preservation from
the south wing of the Byzantine convent which had just then been uncovered, they came upon some bases, columns and a beautifully worked
double arch which were all clearly of pre-Byzantine date. On some of
these were graffiti of which one includes the invocation 'XE MARIA', the
Greek for 'Ave Maria'. There is now no doubt that though the Christians

*The first
Christian
church*

102

in Nazareth in these early years were few, yet they did exist and did erect a Christian church there of a synagogue type. The only member of this community whose name has come down to us is that of Conon, who suffered martyrdom in the middle of the third century. During the persecution of Decius, Conon is reported to have said to his judges in Phrygia: 'I am of Nazareth, a relative of the Lord whom I serve, as did my ancestors'.

The second church   However that may be, this early church perished; the second church at Nazareth was begun in the fourth and completed in the fifth century. The fourth-century building was, according to custom, ascribed to the Empress Helena. Her anonymous biographer tells us that 'the Empress Helena ... turned to Nazareth and having sought the house where the Mother of God, all worthy of praise, received the hail of the Archangel Gabriel, thereat she raised the temple of the Mother of God.' This proves little, except perhaps that a church was erected in that period. There is in fact little doubt that the building there, as in other places in Galilee, was undertaken at Constantine's command by Joseph of Tiberias. The church Joseph built was small, and a mosaic inscription records that it was enlarged in the fifth century by 'the Deacon Conon, a native of Jerusalem' (not to be confused with Conon, the martyr, of earlier date). Some of the floor mosaics have crosses on them, and some are without crosses. This may have been because in 427 the Emperor Theodosius forbade by edict the representation of the Cross on a pavement on the grounds that the symbol was profaned when people walked upon it. It follows that the mosaics with crosses are of an earlier date than those without. Joseph of Tiberias seems to have built most of the central nave of the later Byzantine church which ran from north to south. The Cave of the Annunciation lay below the level of the church and was surmounted by an edicule occupying part of the central nave.

Crusader church   By the end of the eleventh century, when the Crusaders arrived, the Byzantine church was either completely destroyed or in a state of total ruin. It was Tancred who undertook the task of providing a new basilica for the site of the annunciation. The best contemporary description of it comes from the Russian *hegumenos* Daniel, who wrote in 1107: 'Formerly this holy place was devastated and it is the Franks who have renovated the fabric with the greatest care. It is the residence of a Latin bishop who is very rich and who has this place under his dependence.' We can still form a conception of the magnificence of that church from the Crusader capitals that have survived (they are now in the Monastery Museum) which represent, in relief, scenes from the lives and deaths of the apostles. The church, however, was not destined to a long life. In 1263 the fanatical Sultan Beybars sent an expedition to Nazareth to destroy every Christian building in the place and massacre the Christians.

Nazareth was, during the first years of Turkish rule, almost destroyed; the church was reduced to a ruin and only the traditional Cave of the Annunciation was in any way preserved. Friar Francesco Suriano, for instance, in 1485 reported that 'the most holy house at the time of the Christians, upon which house they built a great church, has now been

Figures of the Apostles of Jesus (the figure of Jesus himself distinguished by the cross within his halo) superbly carved in the Crusader capitals of the twelfth-century Church of the Annunciation.

completely destroyed. The church is ruined, except for one aisle in which they keep cattle; but the chapel is honourably held, in which the Christians who live there continually celebrate.'

In 1620 Father Tommaso Obicini, the Franciscan *custos* of the Holy Land, succeeded in getting from the Emir Fakhredin, who then ruled Nazareth from a capital at Sidon, leave for the Franciscans to establish themselves in charge at Nazareth. They wished to reconstruct the Sanctuary of the Annunciation and to build for themselves a convent. They lived there for a hundred insecure years and then, in 1730, were at last able to carry out their task of restoring to Nazareth a suitable church. It was a very modest church, built hastily in six months, but for a hundred and fifty years it was all that they had. Then in 1877 they were able to add to it a facade. The new church lay across the old Byzantine and Crusader basilicas, from south to north, and was divided into three naves by two rows of pillars. In the central nave was the shrine to which one descended by a stair of sixteen steps. Two other flights of steps situated to the right and left of this main stairway led up to the high altar and the choir which stood directly above the shrine. It was tolerable as a functional church, but it was not worthy of a place so great in Christian history as Nazareth, nor, with the increase of pilgrims in modern times, was it large enough for the congregations at great festivals.

In 1907 excavations were begun to find all that could be revealed of the remains of the previous churches about which, up till then, little was known except for the casual notes of earlier pilgrims. It was then that the foundations both of the Crusaders' church and of the earlier church of Joseph of Tiberias and Conon the Deacon were uncovered. Then later in the digging, as we have said, the foundations of the earlier little church, whose very existence had up till then not been suspected, were also unearthed.

Recent excavation In 1955 it was decided to demolish entirely the old church of 1730 and thoroughly to explore the whole terrain. Much interesting material in the way of glasses, lamps, forgotten caves and the foundations of old houses was discovered. When the ground had been finally cleared, Signor Muzio, the Italian architect, was instructed to begin the building of the new church which was to take its place. His problem was that he was narrowly hedged in, by the convent building and by the nearby busy streets of Nazareth. He therefore protected the church from its surroundings by a large square to the west, raised a little on its south side to show the remains of the Byzantine church and the old synagogue, and by a *Modern basilica* high wall to the south with colonnades on its inner side. He decided to build not one but two churches, an upper and a lower. The outer walls followed the lines of the Crusaders' basilica except that they were moved back a few yards at the west end in order to protect the precincts from the surrounding traffic. The churches are both some eighty feet high and a hundred and thirty feet long, not counting the Crusaders' apses which have been preserved and, where necessary, rebuilt. Steps go down from the upper church to the lower and from there descend again to the cave. It is also in the lower church that the surviving relics of the Crusaders' church are preserved. The height of the nave and the apses is about twenty-five feet, except in the centre where it is about thirty feet. There, the level is lowered, so as to drop it to the level of the old Crusaders' church and to preserve its old mosaics. In the centre over the cave entrance there is an opening from the upper church right down to the cave level. The church can be entered either from the west or from the south. Side entrances take one by small stairs to the upper church. The grand stairway from the one church to the other is on the south side. The sanctuaries in the apses join up with the sacristies in the convent.

The height of the upper church is some thirty-five feet with the same above. The centre of it is some hundred and twenty feet above the pavement. There is no bell tower, but there is a magnificent view from the roof at the south-east corner, right out over the whole surrounding valley. The supporting structures are of reinforced concrete, sufficiently strong, it is confidently hoped, to withstand the earthquakes to which the land is so prone.

The west front of the two churches is decorated with statues to illustrate the story of the incarnation, and that to the south, the story of the annun-

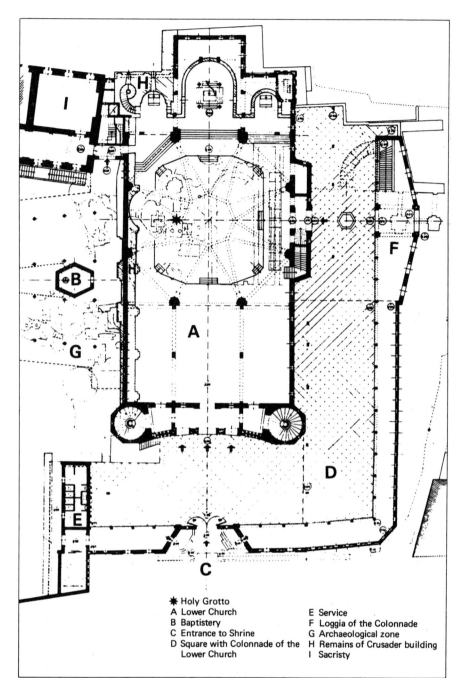

Plan of the modern Latin Church of the Annunciation at Nazareth.

* Holy Grotto
A Lower Church
B Baptistery
C Entrance to Shrine
D Square with Colonnade of the
  Lower Church

E Service
F Loggia of the Colonnade
G Archaeological zone
H Remains of Crusader building
I Sacristy

ciation. The three high altars of the upper church are rich in marble and ornament, those of the lower church simple tables, reminiscent of the catacombs. The Franciscans are often accused of being holy men who are more concerned with the functions than with the beauties of their churches. Certainly at Nazareth they have every justification for saying that the volume of modern pilgrimage made necessary a new and a worthy church. The upper church is used for more populous gatherings, the lower church is designed rather for private devotion and quieter meditation. No one who stands in either of them, who looks at the majesty around him and

The façade of the modern Church of the Annunciation, designed by the Italian architect, Signor Muzio.

meditates on the long history of which this is the culmination, can fail to agree that here the architect has achieved not merely an outstanding functional, but equally an outstanding aesthetic success.

With the discovery of the earliest church of Joseph of Tiberias we now know that we stand, in the present church, on the site of what has been believed to be that of the annunciation for sixteen hundred years.

Some of us who do not perhaps share the easy oriental acceptance of the supernatural will incline to think of the annunciation more as a mental vision than a direct announcement to Mary by another being. If that view is taken, it is not then very easy to say exactly at what moment and at what place the idea came; in fact it would probably not be accurate to pinpoint the annunciation to one single place at all. The Greeks claim that the annunciation took place not only at the site of the present Latin basilica, but at Mary's Well over which they have built their own church. The evidence upon which they base their claim comes from the Apocryphal Gospel of St James, which has of course no sort of canonical authority. In that gospel, we are told: 'One day while the Virgin Mary was found as usual at the fountain to draw water, an angel appeared and saluted her. She was afraid and fled to her house where she started to spin, when suddenly the angel appeared to her again to announce the

divine message.' Without attributing any special authority to the pseudo-James it is indeed likely enough that Mary went to the present well to draw her water, since it was the city's only water supply.

Today the spring still bubbles beneath the altar within the crypt of the Greek church. Between the Crusader arcading of the crypt is the cave entrance from street level down to the well-head. Steep steps cut in the rock wall descend to the water. Today, this same spring water is piped along the street to the modern fountain at the crossroads. However we interpret the appearances of the angel, it is likely enough, as 'she pondered these things in her heart', that she thought of them both at the well and in her own house.

Besides the main Latin and Greek basilicas there are other Holy Places in Nazareth. In the Franciscan monastery is a church, at present, until the final opening of the main basilica, being used as a parish church. It is the so-called Workshop of St Joseph. The altar bears the inscription *Hic erat subditus illi.* The present church is only of 1911, but it is built on the site of a Byzantine church whose baptistry is still to be seen.

Here was the home of the Holy Family: a single-roomed cottage used as a workshop by day and as a bedroom by night. Up above on the flat roof, a booth of green branches gave shade or shelter on summer evenings. Underneath, in a cave-basement, formed between the limestone strata of the rising hillside, was the living-room. Here, in the centre of the cave, a flat raised surface provided the low table. Round this, reclining or

Crusader arcading within the Greek Orthodox Church of St Mary's Well, in whose crypt is the early spring water supply, from which Mary drew water for the Holy Family.

squatting on the floor, the family ate its simple meals. In the centre of the wall above was a small niche, once blackened by the oil lamp for which it was designed. In the floor were the round openings down into the grain silos, carved out of the rock below floor level. Above each silo, carved in the cave wall, are still the staples through which the rope passed to lower a basket or bucket into the silo below.

The Greeks have adapted into a church a building that used to be a synagogue, and which was at one time believed to have enclosed the floor of the synagogue in which Jesus taught. However true this may be, the synagogue in which he taught must have been destroyed in the general destruction of Nazareth by the Romans in AD 67; the present building is some centuries later.

To the south of Nazareth, just off the road to Afule which descends to the Valley of Jezreel, is the so-called 'Hill of Precipitation'. This is the craggy brow of a steep scarp directly overhanging the plain. It is the traditional local place of execution. St Luke describes how Jesus, the rabbi, had returned to his own town and had read from the Prophet Isaiah in the synagogue: 'The Spirit of the Lord is upon me ... to-day is this scripture fulfilled in your ears.' The eyes of all were fastened upon him as they asked: 'Is not this Joseph the carpenter's boy?' And the outraged crowd bustled him out along the hillside to throw him over the cliff. 'But he, passing through their midst, went his way.' The two 'Chapels of the Fright', Latin and Orthodox, on each side of the Precipitation, witness to the tradition that even Mary, seeing the crowd return without him, feared the worst. Truly, 'a prophet is not without honour, except in his own country'.

In many ways the most impressive Holy Place in the neighbourhood of Nazareth is the magnificent basilica which stands on the mountain overlooking Nazareth, majestic in itself and commanding a truly magnificent view. It is the modern chapel of an industrial school, the hilltop Salesian orphanage of 'Jesus Adolescent'. Above the high altar of the orphanage chapel is a statue of the Boy Jesus. It is the figure of a boy of about sixteen years with 'sensitive features and the eyes of a poet, wandering over these very hills, dreaming of the Kingdom of God'.

Within the cave, beneath the traditional site of the carpenter's shop, is the living room of the Holy Family. In the centre of the floor are the remains of a low table. Around the walls are recesses for lamps; in the floor are silos for storing grain.

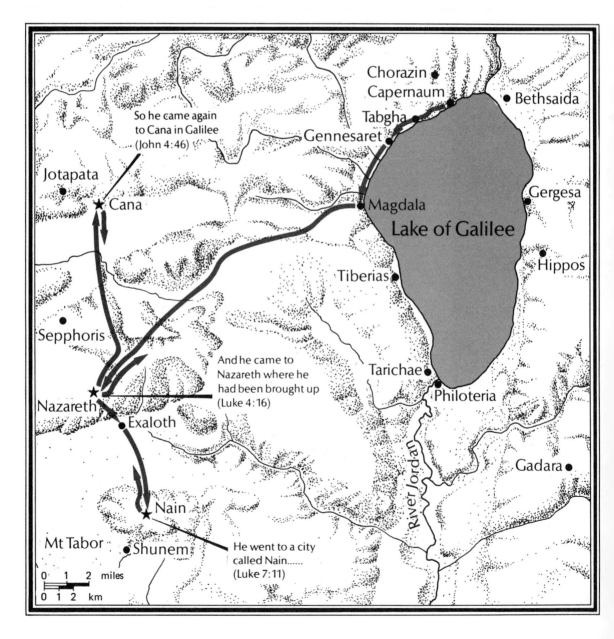

So he came again
to Cana in Galilee
(John 4:46)

And he came to
Nazareth where he
had been brought up
(Luke 4:16)

He went to a city
called Nain......
(Luke 7:11)

Chorazin
Capernaum
Bethsaida
Tabgha
Gennesaret
Jotapata
Cana
Magdala
Gergesa
Lake of Galilee
Hippos
Sepphoris
Tiberias
Nazareth
Exaloth
Tarichae
Philoteria
Gadara
Mt Tabor
Shunem
Nain
River Jordan

0 1 2 miles
0 1 2 km

7 The Lake of Galilee, the Teaching Place of Jesus

TO THE CHRISTIAN THE VERY WORD 'GALILEE' HAS AN EMOTIVE impact. It conveys to him, in a word, the scene of Jesus' lakeside ministry. It conjures up memories of his calling of his disciples, his miracles and his teaching, as does no other word. To most Christians, however, it is the Sea of Galilee rather than the district which they hold in such affection.

The name Galilee, from the Hebrew *Galil* meaning a circuit, is applied to any well-defined region. 'Galilee of the Gentiles', Galil ha-Goim, The Region of the Gentiles, was the name given to the northern province of Israel, because it was surrounded on three sides by foreigners. Following the return from Babylon, the district remained largely Gentile, but by the first century BC was thoroughly Judaised. The words 'of the Gentiles' were dropped from the title of the district, which then became proudly known as 'The Region'.

*Features of
the district*
The main feature of the district is the Jordan Valley, whose waters are fed from the melting snows of Hermon, and descend to two hundred and twelve metres below sea level to form the Lake of Galilee, twelve and a half kilometres wide by twenty-two and a half long. Rising from the valley and running west to the coastal plain are three parallel and rising steps: the Plain of Esdraelon, the Lower Galilee ranges of hills up to six hundred metres and, finally, the plateaux of the Upper Galilee of up to thirteen hundred metres. It is as though the Lebanon has cast her mountainous roots southwards, channelling her snows and rains down the valleys of Galilee. Consequently, Galilee enjoys a great fertility and profusion of flowers, corn, oil and wood – but also hot springs and a tendency to earthquakes.

The most striking feature of Galilee, in the time of Jesus, was the system of roads crossing the district in all directions, from the Levant to Damascus and the East, from Jerusalem to Antioch, from the Nile to the Euphrates. The fertility and the good communications of the district resulted in the growth of a considerable population, engaged in local industry and commerce, concentrated largely upon the lakeside. Unlike Judaea, whose desert borders exerted an austere influence on that province, Galilee was surrounded by pagan and colonial townships, which poured upon Galilee the full influence of Greek life and leisure. All these features – the wealth of water, the extreme fertility, the great highways, the considerable popu-

Map of the Lake of
Galilee, showing the
lakeside towns.

Mount Hermon, seen across the Lake some sixty miles from Tiberias, dominates the scenery of Upper Galilee.

lation, the Greek influences – were crowded into the rift valley, in tropical heat, round a blue and lovely lake. These were the conditions in which Jesus taught and worked – and under which Christianity began to grow. It takes very little imagination, today, as one looks down on the rather sleepy and deserted lakeside, to picture the nine cities round the lake, each of not less than fifteen thousand inhabitants. Of these cities, Tiberias and Magdala were on the western shore, Gadara and Hippos on the eastern hills, Bethsaida, Capernaum and Chorazin to the north, but the remaining two are unlocated.

The Lake

In such crowded surroundings, the lake itself was the redeeming feature. George Adam Smith describes it: 'Sweet water, full of fish, a surface of sparkling blue, tempting down breezes from above, bringing forth breezes of her own. The Lake of Galilee is at once food, drink, and air, a rest to the eye, coolness in the heat, an escape from the crowd, and a facility of travel very welcome in so exhausting a climate.' George Adam Smith goes on: 'Where there are now no trees there were great woods; where there are marshes, there were noble gardens; where there is but one boat, there were fleets of sails.' Only thirty-four years after Jesus' ministry in Galilee, Josephus describes the Plain of Gennesaret as 'the

The hot springs of Tiberias, famous throughout the Roman world, and the reason for Herod's building of the town and the castle there.

ambition of nature ... supplying men with the principal fruits, grapes and figs, continually during ten months of the year, and the rest of the fruits as they ripen together through the whole year.' This plain was the market-garden which supplied the lakeside townships to the west and north of the Lake.

The town of Tiberias is not mentioned in the gospels, probably because the local Jewish population despised the artificial pagan atmosphere of Herod Antipas' oriental court and capital. He had built on the site of the earlier Jewish town of Rakkath of Naphtali, and conveniently near to hot springs, which were already famous throughout the Roman world. His great castle on the hillside dominated the town and harbour. Long after Capernaum, where St Matthew was called from his customs desk, had faded, Tiberias survived as the seat of the government of the province, the only defensible site being both on the lake and on a hill.

North of Tiberias lay Magdala, to-day Migdal, on the south of the Plain of Gennesaret. Here Mary of Magdala lived in a town whose excavated ruins are between the modern road and the water's edge. Across the plain and overlooking the north-west of the lake is a large tell or mound, traversed now by the road to the north from Tiberias. In the past,

this site had been mistakenly identified with Capernaum, but it is more likely to have been one of the Bethsaidas; the word means Fisher-home, or Fishing Town. Peter, the master fisherman, and Andrew his brother, and Philip, perhaps the first followers of Jesus, lived in a lakeside Bethsaida. Immediately above and almost overhanging Magdala is the cliff-face of the 'Gulf of Pigeons'. It was to the caves of this cliff-face that Galilean partisans fled from the Roman legionaries, only to be winkled out by commandos suspended in iron cages from the top of the cliff. Down this gulf blows the Mediterranean west wind to whip up the waves of the lake without warning.

A little further round to the north of the lake and over the ridge is the small Valley of Tabgha. The name is an Arabic contraction of the Greek name for 'the Seven Springs', three of which today still provide an abundance of fresh water. Overlooking Tabgha from the north-east is a conspicuous spur, called the Mount of the Beatitudes, the traditional site of the giving of the Sermon on the Mount, in chapters five, six and seven of St Matthew's gospel. Here, in 1937, was built a fine hospice and octagonal basilica, which command a superb view of the lake. It is not difficult to picture Jesus retreating up the hills from the crowded lakeside in order to select and teach his team of disciples. Indeed, when he wished to speak to the crowds he remained at the level of the lake, speaking often from a boat in one of the little bays along the north shore, with the people surrounding him on the grass. It is thus that the gospel of St Mark describes him: 'There was gathered to him a great multitude, so that he entered into a boat and sat in the sea; and the whole multitude was by the sea on the land.' With the water of the lake as a sounding-board at his back, his voice would carry far up the hillside.

Such a scene could well have been witnessed at Tabgha, below the Mount of the Beatitudes, when he first taught and then fed the five thou-

left: Aerial view of the Mount of the Beatitudes: in the middle distance is the Plain of Gennesaret and market garden of Galilee, beyond which can be seen, through the Gulf of Pigeons, the Horns of Hattim.

right: Byzantine mosaic of the Loaves and Fishes, beneath the altar in the Byzantine Church of the Multiplication at Tabgha.

sand. Indeed, in the year 382, the pilgrim Pelagia visited a basilica built over the site of the Miracle of the Multiplication, as it is called. At Tabgha, in fact, two successive Byzantine churches were built, with slightly varying orientation but with the same position of altar. Their common focus was the traditional altar stone on which Jesus took the five loaves and two small fishes, blessed, broke and gave them to be distributed. Set within that stone is a fifth-century mosaic of a basket of loaves, flanked by two Galilee mullets, sometimes called 'Peter's fish'. Nearby, a sixth-century Greek inscription dedicates the church to the memory of the Patriarch Martyrius. Interesting as the masonry of the successive churches may be, it is the mosaics of the fifth-century church which are really striking. The floor is a magnificent picture guide to the flora and fauna of the lake. Beginning at the entrance and circling the nave or central area from left to right, we find peacocks, flamingoes and snakes, cormorants and lotus flowers, heron and doves, a barnacle goose and an oleander bush, ducks, heron and peacocks. The Byzantine churches and mosaics, only discovered in 1932, are well preserved within a Benedictine chapel, in which Pope Paul VI celebrated mass at the altar of the Multiplication.

Some two hundred metres away, at the water's edge, is the traditional site of Jesus' post-resurrection commission of St Peter, described in the

The Jewish menorah is carved on the top of an acanthus leaf capital within the ruins of the synagogue at Capernaum.

final chapter of St John's gospel. After a fruitless night's fishing, the disciples were bringing their boat to shore, when they were hailed from the beach by Jesus. Following a breakfast of fish, cooked on 'a fire of coals', Jesus gave Peter the pastoral commission to 'feed my sheep'. The column bases of a medieval church are visible in the clear water offshore; they enclose an enormous rock which projects out over the water, as well as into the modern little basalt chapel of the Primacy. This great rock was known to medieval pilgrims as the 'Mensa Christi', the Table of the Lord. It is still, in its striking simplicity, a silent witness to the Galilee resurrection tradition.

Capernaum Three kilometres further still along the lake shore is the site of the frontier town of Capernaum, the headquarters of Jesus' Galilean ministry. Kefar Nahum, the village of Nahum, stands on a site called Tell-Hum. There is no tell or mound, however, and the name Tell-Hum may well be a corruption of the name of a Jewish rabbi called Tanhum buried in this place and mentioned in the Talmud. It has more recently been suggested that Tell-Hum may be a corruption of the Greek word for 'customs house', *telonion*, which links up with the call of the disciple, St Matthew, from the 'receipt of custom'. Certainly, the town lay on the main road to Damascus, within a few kilometres of the Jordan River frontier. It must have had, too, a busy harbour with boats from neighbouring ports loading and off-loading the dried fish and local wares of Galilee, the silks and spices of Damascus, the fruit and produce of Gennesaret. The site fits in well with the gospel references to Capernaum and it has been a resort of Christian pilgrims from the fourth century. Indeed, the ruins of a Byzantine church were discovered here in 1921.

The most important feature of Capernaum is its famous synagogue. Excavations were begun by two German archaeologists, Kohl and Watzinger, in 1905, and were completed in 1926 by the Franciscan fathers who own the site. This synagogue has been fully restored and was well built of white limestone, contrasting vividly with the black lava of the surrounding houses. The prayer hall is rectangular, nearly twenty-four metres long and sixteen metres wide. There are three doorsteps, side by side, facing south towards the lake, complete with recesses on which the double doors hinged, and with doorsteps on to which each pair of doors locked together in the centre. Along the west wall there are stone benches. At the north end of the hall an exterior staircase gave access to a door opening upon the upper storey, the women's gallery. To the east of the prayer hall was an open courtyard, entered by two doors, also on the south side. Both hall and courtyard were colonnaded, the columns in the hall supporting the gallery, those in the courtyard forming a cloister facing a doorway into the hall. Through this doorway, the Gentile 'God-fearers' could listen to the synagogue service.

The whole building was elaborately decorated with carved stone ornament. Its walls may have been covered with frescoes like those of the nearly contemporary Dura synagogue, constructed in AD 244. As Professor Albright has pointed out, the Dura synagogue, the catacombs in Rome and the necropolis at Beth She'arim demonstrate the dependence of early

Christian art upon Jewish frescoes of the Roman period. There remain here some most intriguing representations, carved in relief, upon the square door lintels and elsewhere. What is so striking is the variety of motifs and, particularly, the mixture of both Jewish and Roman symbols. Among the former are the menora (the seven-branched candlestick), the shofar (the ram's horn), the magen David (the shield of David), the Ark of the Covenant, the manna pot, and that old symbol of the land, the palm tree. Among the Roman symbols are two of particular significance for the Christian. The first is the regimental crest of the Tenth Legion, two eagles back to back and beak to beak. The second is the equivalent of the Roman Victoria Cross; it was awarded to a soldier who saved the life of an officer in battle. It is a victor's laurel wreath tied in a circle with a reef-knot and enclosing a round sea-shell. The eagles in the regimental crest are suspending in their beaks the same laurel wreath. What is then the explanation of this combination of symbols?

Although this is a late second- or early third-century building, Professor Albright is certain that it stands on the site of an earlier synagogue. This latter may well have been that in which Jesus worshipped, taught and healed. It may well be, too, that some of the carvings of this earlier synagogue were incorporated in the decoration of its successor. In fact only this explanation, coupled with the story related in St Luke's gospel, chapter seven, can explain why the regimental crest of a Roman legion should adorn the very keystone of a Jewish synagogue. St Luke relates that the servant of a centurion at Capernaum was sick. The Roman wished to

Among the synagogue carvings at Capernaum are the Star of David, together with the Roman laurel wreath *(left)*, and reef knot surrounding a shell *(right)*, this last being the equivalent of a military decoration for valour in battle.

Other carvings at
Capernaum include the
palm tree *(top)*, ancient
symbol of the land, and
the manna pot *(bottom)*,
symbol of God's provision
in the wilderness.

approach Jesus with the request that he, Jesus, heal his servant. It was, however, the elders of the Jews who presented the request to Jesus, saying, 'This man is worthy . . . for he loveth our nation and hath built us a synagogue'. So it is that the Christian venerates the synagogue at Capernaum, for he feels surrounded by the stones which once echoed with the teachings of Jesus. He can well think of Jesus taking his texts from the carvings of that synagogue; for instance, the manna pot: 'Your fathers did eat manna in the wilderness and are dead, I AM the Bread of Life'. Once again, Dalman sums it up: 'Taking all into consideration, we are on safe ground when we regard the synagogue of Tell-Hum as a reconstruction [one might perhaps add 'of a reconstruction'] of that in which Jesus healed . . . and taught . . . There is no spot in the whole of Palestine where memories heap themselves up to such an extent, as in Capernaum.'

Four kilometres north of Capernaum, the ruins of Chorazin include another synagogue, and the ancient Roman road up into the hills from Capernaum is still to be seen.

The first precise statement of the sites and cities we have mentioned meets us in Theodosius (AD 530). Theodosius gives distances that should be exact, and in part are so.

'From Tiberias to Magdala, where the lady Mary was born, is two [Roman] miles. From Magdala to Seven Fountains [Heptapegon], where the Lord Christ baptised the Apostles, is two miles, where he also fed the people with five loaves and two fishes. From Seven Fountains to Capernaum is two miles.'

The other witness is Bishop Arculf (*c.* 685), as reported by Adamnan. What he says is this:

Those who going down from Jerusalem desire to visit Capharnaum, as Arculf told me, go straight through Tiberias; and then pass along Lake

Ginereth, also called the Sea of Tiberias and the Sea of Galilee, and then through the place of the Blessing of the Loaves, from whence at no great distance they reach Capharnaum by the sea in the borders of Zabulun and Naphtali. This city, as I was told by Arculf who saw it from a neighbouring mountain, is without a wall and is confined within a narrow space between the mountain and the lake stretching from east to west for a considerable distance along the shore with the mountain to the north and the lake to the south.

'The Other Side'

In the gospels, the east coast of the lake is known as 'the Other Side'. Here, the identification of sites is rather more difficult. This was the district of the Ten Towns. Gergesa has been identified with the ruins of Khersa, at the only point on the east coast where the steep hills come down to the shore. Hippos was on Mount Sisita which overlooks the kibbutz 'Ein-Gev. Gadara was on the hills south of the Yarmuk River, while Tarichae, 'the pickling places', was between Tiberias and the outlet of the River Jordan. 'Here', as Strabo says, 'the lake supplied the best fish for curing', but there is not a trace of Tarichae to be seen!

The catalogue of towns around the lake conjures up for us an almost unbroken line of buildings. As the Dead Sea is today girdled by a constant hedge of driftwood, so the Sea of Galilee is girdled by a scarcely less continuous belt of ruins. This is all that remains of the city walls, houses, synagogues, wharves and factories; of the castle, temples and theatres of Tiberias, the bath-houses at Hammath, the hippodrome of Tarichae, the amphitheatre and the Greek villas at Gadara. All this was once imposed on the simple open-air life of fields, roads and boats that we see in the gospels.

It is, however, not the buildings so much as the lake itself which is so sacred to the Christian. Jesus drew his disciples from the fishermen of Galilee, whose best fishing grounds were at the north-east of the lake, where the Jordan River deposited her silt. He drew his followers from the hardy men who braved the west wind's sudden squalls, funnelled down through the Gulf of Pigeons above Magdala. In a highly concentrated population, often inflamed by a spirit of nationalism, Jesus, as George Smith writes:

> went to a trade which had no private wrongs. He called men, not from their dreams, but from work they were content to do from day to day, till something higher should touch them. And so it has come to pass that not the jargon of the fanatics and brigands in the highlands of Galilee, but the speech of the fishermen and their simple craft have become the language and symbolism of Christianity.

The head of Jacob's Well within the crypt of the unfinished Orthodox church near Sychar.

How wise was the divine choice of Galilee and how wise was Jesus' choice of his 'fishers of men'!

Ptolemais

0 5 10 15 miles
0 10 20 km

Capernaum
Gennesaret
Lake of Galilee
Hippos

Sepphoris   Tiberias

Nazareth
Mt Tabor
Gadara

River Jordan

Dora

Caesarea

Scythopolis
Pella

Ginae
Salim

After the two days he
departed to Galilee
(John 4:14)

Let us go into
Judea again
(John 11:7)

Meets Samaritan
woman at well

Samaria
(Sebaste)

Vale of Aulon

Neapolis   Sychar

Apollonia

Mt Gerizim

After this there was a feast
of the Jews, and Jesus went
up to Jerusalem
(John 5:1)

Stayed with the
disciples here

SAMARITANS   Ephraim

Joppa

The Passover.....
was at hand, and
Jesus went up to
Jerusalem
(John 2:13)

Lazarus raised
from the dead

Lydda

Jericho

Jamnia

Abila

Healing at pool of Bethesda

Bethabara

Emmaus   Bethany

Jerusalem

Healing of blind beggar

It was the feast of the
Dedication at Jerusalem (John 10:22)

Mediterranean Sea

8 Journeys to Jerusalem

THE PRINCIPAL CHRISTIAN HOLY PLACES ARE NATURALLY TO BE found in those districts where Jesus was born and brought up, where he lived and taught, where he suffered, died and lived again. Broadly speaking, this means Nazareth and the lakeside within Galilee, also Jerusalem and Bethlehem within Judaea. There are, however, a number of places sacred to Christians for their association with the visits of Jesus or his mother, on their travels between Galilee and Judaea.

There are three different roads to be considered. The middle route leads through the highlands of Samaria, the eastern way through the Jordan Valley and the western follows the coastal plain. Josephus describes the middle route as the shortest one, able to be covered on foot in three days, and the usual one for Jewish pilgrims from Galilee to Jerusalem. The main disadvantage of this way was the possible trouble when travelling through Samaritan territory. On the whole, this was outweighed by the greater safety and speed of a shorter route passing always through inhabited localities, in which provisions and lodgings were plentiful. It is very probable that there were sizeable caravansaries at staging posts near El-Lubban and Sanur. On more than one occasion, Jesus is described as needing to spend a night in Samaria (Luke 9:51-5).

The eastern route, via the Jordan Valley, might have taken nearly twice as long, though St John indicates that Jesus and his disciples went from Jericho to Cana in three days (John 2:1). This road may have served Jesus' purpose better than the shorter route on those occasions when he wished to avoid the pilgrim traffic, or when he wished to stay outside Judaean territory as long as possible, or simply when he wished to travel alone with his disciples.

The western route passing through either Emmaus (Amwas) or Antipatris seems to have been little used by Jesus, though Joseph and Mary with the child Jesus would have returned from Egypt to Nazareth by the Via Maris.

It will be well to consider those sites among the glens of Galilee, visited by Jesus on his way to or from the main routes. Six kilometres along the road from Nazareth to Tiberias is the Arab village of Kefar-Kanna, the disputed site of Jesus' first miracle at the Wedding Feast of Cana, when he turned the water into wine. A medieval tradition favoured Khirbet

Map of the routes taken by Jesus through the highlands of Samaria and the Jordan Valley.

Kanna for the site of Cana, but a Byzantine tradition is evident at Kefar-
Kanna. In the Latin church there is an old Hebrew mosaic inscription,
probably of the third or fourth century, which says 'Honoured be the
memory of Yosef, son of Tanhum, son of Buta and his sons who made this
mosaic, may it be a blessing for them. Amen.' This Yosef was probably the
converted Jew, Joseph of Tiberias, of Constantine's period, on whom
Constantine conferred the title of count and who founded many churches
in Galilee. The church possibly stands, therefore, on the site of the old
synagogue. In its early days it still held what were believed to be the relics
of the marriage feast. In 570, Antonius of Piacenza visited Cana where,
as he records, 'Our Lord was at the wedding, and we reclined upon his
very couch upon which I, unworthy that I am, wrote the names of my
parents!' It is customary to condemn the vulgarity of modern tourists who
cover walls with their graffiti, and perhaps in these days of easy travel it
should be condemned, but at Cana, as indeed at Bethlehem and at
Jerusalem, early pilgrims thought it no vulgarity to write up their names
on holy walls, and the inscriptions and crosses of crusading soldiers on the
stairs up from the Chapel of St Helena at the Holy Sepulchre are a moving
memorial.

From the level of the mosaic within the Latin church, steps lead down
into a crypt containing a cistern. Perhaps the synagogue enclosed ritual
washing facilities. There is an old pitcher, with no claim to authenticity
but which serves to illustrate the story. On the opposite side of the village
street is the Orthodox Church of the Marriage Feast in which stands a
large and ancient water jar, again with no pretentions to direct association with the story. Further east along the same street is the Franciscan
Chapel of St Nathaniel Bar-Tolmai, an apostle of Jesus and a native of
Cana.

Almost due south from Nazareth on the north-west slopes of the Hill
of Moreh, the Little Hermon of the Psalms, is the village of Nain, associated with Jesus' raising to life of the widow's only son. Here, according
to St Luke's gospel, chapter seven, was a walled town at the gate of which
Jesus met the funeral procession. Hearing the friends of the young man
extolling him as the only hope and stay of his mother, Jesus halted the
bier and called 'Young man, arise!'. We do not know why Jesus turned
off to Nain, but he was probably on his way to Jerusalem from the Via
Maris. We do know that, in the fourteenth century, Nain was the staging
post between Jenin and Safed.

Some nine kilometres east of Nazareth the Hill of Tabor rises 588 metres
above the Plain of Jezreel. This remarkable hump-backed feature is one
of the possible sites of the transfiguration of Jesus, the spiritual experience
which strengthened him for his final journey to Jerusalem. The other possible site is Mount Hermon, on the Anti-Lebanon range. If this latter site
conforms more to the description of a high snow-clad mountain near
Caesarea Philippi (Banias), it is Tabor which can claim the Byzantine
tradition. There are reasons, however, for believing that this tradition
may have been mistaken. From the times of Barak and Deborah, whose
name is recorded still in that of the village of Daburiyah at the foot of

Tabor, Tabor has been of tactical, if not strategic, importance. In the first book of Chronicles, it is referred to as a Levite settlement and must have been a fortified stronghold. In the year 218 BC Antiochus the Greek captured it, and as late as 100 BC Alexander Jannaeus conquered it. In AD 66, only some thirty-six years after the transfiguration, the whole stretch of hillside, 1,300 metres by 300 metres, was enclosed by Josephus with a still recognisable encircling wall. It seems highly unlikely that the transfiguration, as described in the gospels on a silent, snow-clad mountain, could have taken place on this fortified stronghold, overlooking the great high road through the Plain of Esdraelon.

An early Palestinian tradition linking this remarkable hill with the story of Jesus' transfiguration was universally accepted in the fourth century. On the summit, three churches were built in the sixth century, in memory of the three booths which Peter wished to set up for Jesus, Moses and Elijah. They were visited by the pilgrims Antoninus and Arculf. In the

An aerial view of Mount Tabor rising from the Plain of Esdraelon, famous as the rallying place for the armies of Deborah and Barak, and for the Transfiguration of Jesus.

twelfth century, the Crusaders built a church incorporating a deep-lying apse of Byzantine origin, perhaps as their crypt. On each side of this there was a chapel and one of these is still clearly visible. On the top of the hill there is a long thin plateau; on the eastern end of this are the churches overlooking the Plain of Ahmra and the Lake of Galilee. The modern Franciscan basilica, erected in 1921-3, incorporated portions of the Crusader and Byzantine churches. Nearby is the Greek church of the Holy Elijah, built in 1911, next to a traditional cave of the mysterious Melchizedek. This last church covers the site of a fourth-century basilica, some of whose mosaics are still preserved.

The Route Through the Jordan Valley. Now let us look at the eastern road to the south, passing down the Jordan Valley. It has already been suggested that this was much longer and quieter than the route through the highlands, along the spine of Samaria and Judaea. It is worth noting that the valley route would be very much hotter; in fact in winter and early spring alone would this road be comfortable. Consequently it would be chosen with a particular purpose in mind, such as a visit to John the Baptist's activities at Aenon or Bethabara, a preaching tour of Perea beyond Jordan, or even a call at the Essene monastery at Qumran. Without such a purpose, the traveller from Tiberias to Jerusalem would diverge at Beth Shean, to pass through the Valley of Jezreel and join the highland road at Janin.

The activities of John the Baptist were based on at least two points, one accessible to the people of Samaria, one to the people of Judaea. The former is likely to have been in the area of Salem (John 3:23), Tell er-Ricra, probably at the five wells of Aenon (the place of the spring), located at Ed-Der. The southern Place of Baptism, described by St John as at Bethabara (meaning 'ford-house' or 'ferry-house'), is probably less than a mile from the accepted Place of Baptism to-day. It is unlikely that there was a proper village, but rather a few huts for those operating the ferry, the customs and frontier business between Judaea and Perea. There would probably have been a lodging house or caravansery. The Madeba mosaic shows the ferry above the Place of Baptism, with a house standing on piles presumably designed with a view to floods.

Early tradition, supported by Origen, Eusebius and the Madeba mosaic, has always represented the place where Jesus was baptised by his cousin, John, as being just the spot shown today, the ford at Hajlah. It seems that John lived for some time beyond Jordan, perhaps to avoid the authorities of Judaea and Jerusalem, perhaps because of the regular and clean flow of the Wadi el-Kharrar from the east into the Jordan. It was an ideal place for his purpose, off the road yet easily approached from the ford. At the outlet of the Wadi el-Kharrar, in 1902, two small buildings dating back to Byzantine times, one of these nearly ten metres square, stood on arches, presumably at one time in the water. The pilgrim Theodosius, in the year 530, found a church of John the Baptist built by order of the Emperor Anastasius, at this point on the east bank. This apparently rested on arches out over the water. A cross on a marble pillar

ET TRANSFIGVRATVS EST ANTE EOS

The central mosaic over the altar of the Franciscan basilica of the Transfiguration on Mount Tabor. Jesus is flanked by Moses and Elijah, representing the Law and the Prophets, before the eyes of Peter, James and John.

stood in the river to mark the Place of Baptism. Antoninus, forty years later, only found the pillar. Perhaps floods had carried away the foundations of the little church. The coming of the Persians put an end to other shrines on the east bank.

On the west bank, a monastery of St John had existed since the time of Justinian, if not before. This too appears on the Madeba mosaic and in the writings of Antoninus and Arculf. For centuries this was the focus of Christian pilgrimage from Jerusalem. The present church, erected in 1882 on this site, includes Byzantine remains. Arculf, in 670, describes a small chapel under the monastery and a stone bridge leading out over the water to the cross, at the Place of Baptism. For a variety of reasons, including convenience of approach and the collapse of the west bank in certain places, the present Place of Baptism is slightly below the traditional site.

The gospel descriptions of Jesus' baptism tell of his new-found awareness of his servantship or sonship to God, but they link this with his own association of the Suffering Servant, referred to in the book of the second

129

The traditional Rock of the Temptation of Jesus, within the Greek Orthodox monastery which clings to the cliff face of Jebel Quruntal, the Mount of Temptation.

Isaiah, 'You are my beloved son, *in whom I am well pleased.*' It was to face and test his double vocation of messiahship and suffering that Jesus retreated into the wilderness. There he considered and rejected the various means of winning men's allegiance without first winning their hearts.

For the Place of his Temptation, or Testing, there is a Crusader if not also a Byzantine tradition indicating a mountain some 250 metres high on the edge of the Jordan Valley, and overlooking Ancient Jericho (Tell-es-Sultan). The mountain was named by the Crusaders Mons Quarantana, for the forty days of the temptation, a name still preserved today. The Crusader Theodoric describes the path leading up the mountain, first to a chapel dedicated to Mary the Mother of Jesus, then to an altar in the form of a cross, near to which and halfway up the mountain was shown the rocky place where Jesus sat. On the summit of the mountain was shown the seat of the tempter, which commands today a magnificent view of the Jordan Valley and the land of Moab – if not quite of 'all the kingdoms of the world'.

Neolithic stone tower of the seventh millenium BC, part of a ring of fortifications excavated on Tel es-Sultan, the site of ancient Jericho.

Clinging to the cliff face just below the top is an Orthodox monastery, whose buildings are only a hundred years old but whose site may have been occupied since Byzantine times. The old guestmaster with long white beard and threadbare cassock tells the visitor that once there was a colony of six thousand monks and hermits here. Today there are only seven. They live a life that is to Western understanding rather the life of a hermit than of a monk, three of them quite alone in cells hollowed out of the cliff face. In the chapel, behind a veiled recess are fourteen yellow skulls, reputedly of monks who were murdered by the Persians in the invasion of 614.

There are many theories linking Jesus and his cousin John with the Essene monastery at Qumran but, as yet, they remain theories. It would, perhaps, be surprising if they had not visited Qumran in the months and years which cannot and may never be accounted for. Nor can we say with any certainty that they even knew of the existence of Ancient Jericho beneath the present Tell-es-Sultan. We can, however, be fairly certain that they drank from the ample constant flow of Elisha's fountain beside the

Tell. The Jericho they knew was Herodian Jericho, at the mouth of the Wadi Kelt (Brook Cherith) Gorge. Here, Herod exploited and channelled water from the Wadi Fara, along the whole length of the Kelt Gorge to supply his ornamental water-gardens and palace, overlooked and protected by a citadel upon the crag above. Here was the home and sycamore tree of Zacchareus, also the home of blind Bartimaeus, of the gospel story. By the fourth century, however, there remained little trace of Herod's splendour and the Bordeaux Pilgrim, in 333, was shown only a sycamore, in the area of the present modern Jericho. It was still on exhibition in 570, though by then dried and withered.

The Roman road from Jericho to Jerusalem climbs up the south side of the Kelt Gorge and is still, for several kilometres, passable even for buses. At certain points, this road affords wonderful views down into the gorge, where Elijah was fed by ravens (still to be seen here), and where the Greek Orthodox monastery of St George, still occupied, clings to the cliff face, pitted with hermits' cells and caves.

Half way between Jericho and Jerusalem, the road (at this point surely ancient and modern coincide) is controlled and commanded by the ruins of a Templar fortress, built on the site of its Roman predecessor. Both must have been built to protect a staging post or caravansary on the roadside below. For two thousand years, at least, a succession of similar buildings with the same function have stood on this site, because of the constant water supply, in the centre of a wilderness. The masonry of the well in the middle of the courtyard is Roman; the mosaic floor of a small enclosure is Crusader. The shape of the building is likely to have been the same for centuries: an entrance leading into an open courtyard, surrounded by a covered cloister above which – or part of which – were a row of upper rooms or guest chambers. It is a distinct possibility that this halfway-house has with reason been called the 'Inn of the Good Samaritan'. If the parable of Jesus was, as many others were, taken from life – then this could not be a more appropriate site. From here, the road climbs steadily and steeply though Bethany, over the shoulder of the Mount of Olives, to Jerusalem.

Mary's Journey to Judaea. We have followed Jesus' journey along the Jordan Valley to identify himself with the activities of his cousin, John the Baptist, at the very outset of his own ministry. Nearly thirty years before that, Mary the Mother of Jesus had made another journey, through the hill country of Samaria and Judaea, to visit her cousin Elizabeth, the mother of John the Baptist, in a village four kilometres west of Jerusalem. Together, they exchanged news of their coming first-born children, before Mary returned to Nazareth. When the time came, the two boys were born within three months of each other, in towns within sight of each other. Joseph and Mary had come to Bethlehem for the census; the home of the priest Zacharias and Elizabeth was below Mount Orah in 'Ein-Karem, the 'Gracious Spring'. It was in the time of the Crusader pilgrim Daniel, in 1106, that the birthplace of John was located, within the village, in a cave that is now shown within the Franciscan Church of St John. On the other side of the valley is the Franciscan Church of the Visitation, within the crypt of which is shown the spring that according to a medieval tradition appeared at the meeting place of Mary with Elizabeth. This is the spring which gives a name to the town today. In the wall of the crypt is a hollowed rock in which, according to another medieval legend, the child John was concealed at the time of the Massacre of the Innocents at the order of Herod. An apse of the Crusader Church of the Visitation is to be seen in the upper church today, whose walls are covered in gay mural paintings.

The Russian Convent of Elizabeth, surrounded by little whitewashed cottages, rises among the trees on the slopes of Mount Orah, above the Church of the Visitation. On the Feast of the Visitation, the Russian nuns from the Garden of Gethsemane used (until 1947) to bring ikons, representing Mary, to meet their sisters of 'Ein-Karem with ikons representing Elizabeth. At the village well, called Mary's Spring, they would touch ikons together in a kiss of greeting, before carrying them in procession up the flower-strewn steps to the Convent of Elizabeth.

The Pilgrim Route through the Highlands of Samaria. The central route runs between Galilee and Judaea. It is clear that Jesus returned from Jerusalem by this road several times, as boy and man, among 'his kinsfolk' and acquaintances as well as alone with his disciples. Towards the end of his life, he retired from the bustle of the city to relax in the town of Ephraim, the site of which is probably the Arab hilltop village of Et-Taiyibeh, overlooking the Jordan Valley from the very spine of Judaea.

What a wonderful range of Old Testament history is suggested by the names of the sites just on or off the road to the north: Gibea of Saul, Mizpah of Samuel, Anathoth of Jeremiah, Michmash of Jonathan, Ramah of the Prophets, Bethel of Jacob's dream, Shili of Eli and the child Samuel. The only Christian traditional site within a day's journey of Jerusalem is linked with a return from the Holy City, when the boy Jesus, aged twelve years, was left behind in the Temple. His parents discovered at a caravansary, some fifteen kilometres north of the city and probably at their midday halt, that their boy was not with the party. Crusader tradition locates the place at El-Bireh and Theodoric describes 'a church dedicated to St Mary, with a great cross nearby of hewn stone, raised upon seven steps'. The ruins of this church are still to be seen.

The Woman of Samaria Just south of the Ebal-Gerizim Pass, as St John the Evangelist describes, Jesus rested at Jacob's Well and sent his disciples on to the next village to buy lunch. It was over his midday rest that he had that wonderful conversation with the much-married woman of Samaria, who teased him for his thirsty request for a drink: 'You Jews have no dealings with us Samaritans, besides the well is deep and you have no bucket and rope!' Today the well is still thirty-two metres deep and its identification is unquestioned. A Byzantine cruciform church, with the well beneath the centre of the crossing, was described by Arculf in 679. Antoninus records that the well entrance was in front of the altar rail. Jerome describes the building of a church in the fourth century and the Bordeaux Pilgrim as

early as 333 identified the well by its proximity to Joseph's Tomb. Since then the site has had an unbroken tradition. In Crusader times the well was within a crypt below the high altar of a three-aisled church. Today it still forms the crypt of an unfinished Orthodox church, in exactly the same position and plan. Here, without doubt, was the scene of Jesus' refusal to participate in the Jewish-Samaritan controversy and also of his dictum 'Neither in this mountain, nor yet at Jerusalem . . . God is a Spirit and they that worship him must worship him in spirit and in truth.'

Leaving Jacob's Well and the ancient patriarchal city of Shechem, the road passed between Ebal and Gerizim, skirted Samaria-Sebaste, passed the site of Dothan and entered the Plain of Jezreel at Jenin. A little way off the main road, however, is the climb up to Samaria, the city built by Omri, father of Ahab, on the hill 'bought from Shemer for two talents of silver'.

The history of Samaria is that of five distinct occupations: the Israelite city and royal capital of the Northern Kingdom was destroyed in 721 BC. The Assyrian colonial and administrative centre of Sargon for the next four hundred years left little trace, but some crude walling on the Acropolis. The third occupation was that of Alexander and some six thousand Macedonian veterans. This Greek colonial city was captured

Recent excavations showing both Hebrew and Greco-Roman masonry of the west gate at Samaria-Sebaste, from which the road ran west to link up with the main north-south highway.

A colonnaded street within the Greco-Roman city of Samaria-Sebaste, originally lined on both sides with shops and stalls.

and destroyed by John Hyrcanus in 108 BC. During the Roman occupation, Augustus gave the town to Herod, who renamed it after the emperor to whom also the pagan temple was dedicated. The present name 'Sebaste' is derived from the Greek form of 'Augustus'. Considerable evidence remains of Herod's building achievements, including a long colonnaded street in addition to the temple and forum. Following an early Christian tradition of the burial of John the Baptist here, basilicas were built in his honour during both Byzantine and Crusader periods. There are considerable ruins of the last basilica within the perimeter of the present Arab village. Finally, down below the tell and in what was the Roman hippodrome are two polo posts, left by the Persians in the seventh century.

Pilgrims by this route would enter Galilean territory at the town of Jenin at midday on the third day. Jenin, once called Ain Gannim, 'the gardens', is associated by a fifteenth-century tradition with the village of the Ten Lepers mentioned in St Luke's gospel. Its name indicates an appropriate and refreshing spot for the midday halt. It was also a cross-roads, from which pilgrims would disperse in three different directions, taking the road to Beth Shean for the lakeside, the road through Jezreel for Nazareth and Lower Galilee, the road along the Carmel Range for the coast.

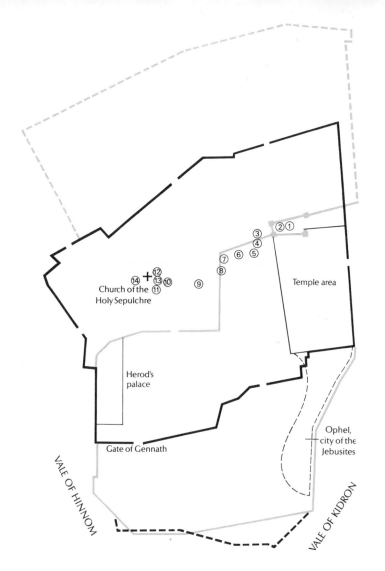

Church of the
Holy Sepulchre

Temple area

Herod's
palace

Gate of Gennath

Ophel,
city of the
Jebusites

VALE OF HINNOM

VALE OF KIDRON

Map of Jerusalem show-
ing the perimeter walls at
different periods and the
Stations of the Cross
along the Via Dolorosa.

A recent aerial view of the
Old City of Jerusalem
from above the Mount of
Olives, showing in the
foreground the Kedron
ravine, and the Temple
Area. To the left Ophel
and the western hill; to
the right, the Holy
Sepulchre.

9 Within and Without the Walls

IN ORDER TO UNDERSTAND THE SITES OF JEWISH, CHRISTIAN AND Muslim Holy Places in Jerusalem it is essential to have some knowledge of the hills and valleys on which the successive cities have been built, and to know something of the walls, fortresses, viaducts and highways which have enclosed, protected and connected these sites down the centuries.

The chief characteristic of Jerusalem is not so much that it is a hill city, whose streets are often steps and whose transport is the ass. Its magic is in the mystery of its valleys, hills and rocks, whether it be the rock of Moriah or that of the empty tomb. A unique history is traced, by these hills and valleys, of a city not three miles in perimeter, set in a triangular basin, between desert and coastline. Indeed, 'the hills stand about Jerusalem', as the Psalmist sang. The city is bounded by two valleys from north to south, the Kedron on the east and the Wadi er-Rababi to the west from the Jaffa Gate, where it curls round the western hill to become the Valley of Hinnom. The two valleys converge below Siloam to become the Wadi en-Nar, the 'Fire Valley', which runs down through the wilderness towards the Dead Sea. Yet a third valley bisects the city from north to south, from the Damascus Gate to the Pool of Siloam. This is the Tyropoean Valley 'of the cheese-makers', once a steep gorge over which viaducts passed thirty metres high, which has been progressively filled in, so that its depression is today hardly noticeable.

Between the first two and separated by the third valley, are two hills. The eastern hill, Mount Moriah, is really on a long spur linking Bezetha, a rise within the north-east of the present Old City, with Ophel, the ridge running down to the Pool of Siloam. The western hill descends steeply to the Valley of Hinnom and overlooks the ridge of Ophel. It is on the Ophel, 'the boil', that the Jebusite city stood in the time of David. This was the original Hill of Zion, a name which may well have meant 'ridge' or 'lump', implying a fortress or citadel.

David built his citadel on the upper part of the ridge, but probably did not extend the Jebusite walls, except perhaps to include the threshing floor of Araunah the Jebusite. Certainly the top of the ridge and Mount Moriah were included in Solomon's time, and two hundred years later, in the time of Uzziah (780-740 BC), the western hill was included within the city, whose north wall ran due west from the Temple. The Kedron and Hinnom Valleys have always prevented further expansion on the east, south or west. Development could only take place northwards. Thus, what is now called the First Wall enclosed both the site of the Jebusite city on Ophel and the western hill. This wall contained the Pool of Siloam to the south and crossed the central Tyropoean Valley to the north, along the line of what is now David Street. It was destroyed by Nebuchadnezzar and restored by Nehemiah, besides being ruined and repaired on several other occasions.

What is called the Second Wall was rebuilt by Herod in about 30 BC. *The walls in* It was this wall that was standing in the time of Jesus. To the east, south *the time of* and west, it seems to have more or less followed the line of the First Wall; *Jesus* but, as is to be expected, there was a development on the north side. Excavations at Herod's citadel, near the present Jaffa Gate, together with recent excavations by Dr Kathleen Kenyon, have shown that this wall did not follow the line of the present wall, turning north-west at the Citadel. This second wall curved eastwards, enclosing a new suburb, before linking up with the north-west corner of the Temple area. Josephus calls this the Second Wall and says that it started from the Gennath (the Garden) Gate, which stood in the First Wall, and that the Second Wall went northwards and eastwards as far as the Antonia fortress.

This would have left an 'L' shaped depression or dart in the north-west part of this Second Wall near the Garden Gate, implying that a garden lay outside the city wall at that point. St John tells us that: 'in the place where he was crucified, there was a garden'. Furthermore, John even mentions that the tomb of Jesus was in a garden 'nearby'. And, indeed, the tombs still to be seen in the rock of the hillside, within the Church of the Holy Sepulchre today, show that this area must have been outside the wall; for no burials took place within the city boundary.

After the crucifixion and resurrection of Jesus; in AD 41 Herod Agrippa built a further wall, which happened to enclose within the city the sites of both Calvary and the tomb. It is, however, unlikely that this unclean area of burial ground was soon built over. Josephus, in fact, relates that this new wall was to protect a weak place in the Second Wall, and he calls it the Third Wall. Considerable traces of this Third Wall have been found in several places, including the Damascus Gate in the present city wall. It is strange to think that the site of Calvary and the tomb of Jesus were enclosed within the city within eight years of the events. And, if they were not built on, they were less likely to have been lost. When Hadrian established a Roman colony in the city following the Bar-Kochbar revolt, he purposefully excluded the Temple area and changed the layout of the city. Whereas the main axis of the Jewish city had linked the Citadel and the Temple, that of Aelia Capitolina ran south from the Damascus Gate. At some time in the fourth century the old line of the wall above Kedron and Hinnom was restored. In the fifth century, the Empress Eudocia repaired *The Monastery of St* it, but after the Persian invasion the line of the south wall contracted to *George within the ravine* something near that of the present south wall. The present walls include *of the Wadi Kelt (Brook* a great deal of Byzantine, Saracen and Crusader masonry, but are mainly *Cherith) which flows* the work of Suleiman the Magnificent, completed in 1541. *through the wilderness of* *Judaea.*

10 On the Way to the Cross

Palm Sunday

The ornate model of the Tomb of Christ within the Church of the Holy Sepulchre, showing the ante-chamber which leads into the inner chamber.

FOR THE PURPOSES OF THIS CHAPTER, THE 'WAY TO THE CROSS' IS THE road of the sufferings of Jesus from his final – sometimes called 'triumphant' – entry into the city of Jerusalem, to his death on the cross. This whole progress, from Bethany to Calvary, is marked by a continuous sequence of shrines commemorating the events of this purposeful journey, 'to give his life as a ransom for many', as Jesus himself interpreted the 53rd chapter of Isaiah. His last journey to Jerusalem followed the Jordan Valley to Jericho, where he gave sight to the blind beggar, Bartimaeus, who called him 'the son of David'. He reached the village of Bethany on the southern slopes of the Mount of Olives, then turned in to his usual lodging in the kindly household of Mary, Martha and Lazarus. This home was to be the base for his operations over the next five days. He needed, perhaps, and here found, the necessary relationships and relaxation to prepare himself for what he knew must lie ahead.

Today the village of El-Azariah (the Arabic form of Lazarion, the House of Lazarus), nestles under the Mount of Olives, facing east towards the wilderness and the Jordan Valley. At a turn in the Jericho-Jerusalem road and at the bottom of a small spur, rising up towards Jerusalem and the Mount of Olives, is the new Church of St Lazarus. It was on the spur that the village of Bethany stood in the time of Jesus and the church stands on the traditional site of the home of Mary, Martha and Lazarus. The tomb of Lazarus, on the north perimeter of the village, was an object of early Christian veneration because, St John records, Jesus had raised him to life at the request of his sisters, Mary and Martha. St Jerome tells us that already at the beginning of the fourth century a church had been built over it. In the sixteenth century the site was covered by a mosque and a little later the Latin *custos* of the Holy Land obtained permission to open a new entrance into the tomb.

The fine new Orthodox church has lately been built a little higher up the same spur, at the top of which are the ruins of a Crusader fort that once commanded the road up to Jerusalem.

The new Latin church at the bottom of the spur stands on the foundations of three older ones. Of the first, built in the fourth century, the apse and some mosaic pavements are still to be seen. The apse is visible, below trapdoors, within the entrance of the new church. The mosaics are outside in the courtyard. Of the second church, built not long after the first, the apse remains behind the high altar of the new church. Of this second church there is also another section of mosaic pavement, two pilasters in the courtyard and masonry walls on all sides. Of the third, the Crusader church, there are buttresses on the north side and some patches of rather crude mosaic.

To the south of the church are the remains of a large convent, built in 1143 by Queen Melisande, who founded here a Benedictine nunnery and installed her sister, Princess Yvette, as its first abbess. The nunnery was well endowed, being the possessor of the estate near Jericho which, twelve hundred years before, Mark Antony had given to Cleopatra. The convent was destroyed during the Turkish occupation, but the vaulted Crusader ceilings, the intriguing oil press (whose pressure-screw is the carved trunk of a palm tree), other Crusader walls, and a tower, bear witness to the vastness of the twelfth century abbey and convent on this site.

The new Church of St Lazarus, by its isolation and austerity of design, its fine cupola and bronze door, gives the appearance of a cemetery cha-

The track which leads from Bethany over the hill to Bethphage, where the disciples of Jesus collected the donkey on Palm Sunday.

pel. The technique of the architect Barluzzi is to make his buildings expressive of the events which they commemorate. The same theme is maintained within, though the interior is enlivened by four large mosaic lunettes, together with explanatory texts from the gospels beneath them. The two side altars are in the form of sarcophagi with sculptured medallions of Mary and Martha, while that of the central altar depicts two angels indicating the tomb of Lazarus. The whole church, however, is bright with light and, within the cupola, a single all-seeing eye is surrounded by forty-eight panels illuminated with doves, flames and flowers. The gospel story is told in the mosaic lunettes high upon the four sides: on the left, Jesus is with the family at Bethany; in the centre, Jesus says 'I am the Resurrection and the Life'; on the right, Jesus raises Lazarus; over the entrance, Jesus dines with Simon the Leper at Bethany.

This is a truly magnificent church, which sums up the significance of Bethany within the story of Holy Week and proclaims the Christian hope of resurrection, through faith in the events of that week.

On that evening of Jesus' arrival from Jericho, he had supper with his friends and disciples. The next day, traditionally called 'Palm Sunday',

The Latin procession on Palm Sunday entering the Old City by St Stephen's Gate, on the way to St Anne's.

he sent two of his disciples ahead into the next village to collect the donkey on which he was to ride into Jerusalem, in purposeful fulfilment of the prophecy of Zechariah. Today, a track leads up the slope of the Mount of Olives to the hamlet of Bethphage – meaning 'House of Figs'. Jesus had told his disciples that they would find the donkey tied up at the crossroads. Now, as then, the junction of tracks from Bethany and Jerusalem is overlooked by the tell, or mound, of ancient Bethphage. At this junction today stands the Franciscan convent built in the last century over the medieval foundations of a Crusader chapel or tower. The squared stones of the apse indicate considerable strength of construction.

It is probable that the focus of this shrine, if not its *raison d'être*, was a rock associated with the finding or mounting of the donkey. This rock or stele was in Crusader times painted to illustrate the story of Palm Sunday. In 1950 the Italian artist Vagarini restored the illustrations of the Raising of Lazarus, the arrival of the donkey, and the procession of palms. It is from this convent that the Latin procession starts every Palm Sunday and,

The Garden of Gethsemane, on the slope of the Mount of Olives, showing the Russian Church of Mary Magdalen and the Franciscan Church of All Nations, together with the tracks that lead down from the Mount of Olives on the left and right, to join at the crossing of the Kedron ravine.

passing over the Mount of Olives, enters the city at St Stephen's Gate. The Anglican procession starts from Bethany and disperses from the top of the Mount of Olives overlooking the city.

The route of the first Palm Sunday procession must be a matter of conjecture. Either it followed the present road south of the Russian convent property, or it skirted it to the north. Either it crossed the northern saddle of the Mount of Olives and descended that track down into the Kedron, or it crossed the southern saddle and descended the track passing the Pater Noster church and the shrine of the Dominus Flevit. Both these tracks join at Gethsemane before crossing the Valley of the Kedron.

The southernmost track from the crest of the Mount of Olives, down into the Kedron, soon passes the Church of the Pater Noster. There are two traditions concerning this site, linking it with Jesus' teaching of the 'Our Father' to his disciples, and also with their meeting to compose the Apostle's Creed before their final dispersal from Jerusalem. In St Luke's gospel the teaching of the Lord's Prayer immediately follows a visit to Mary and Martha at Bethany, but there is no question of this being on Jesus' Palm Sunday entry into Jerusalem. The Lord's Prayer tradition is Byzantine, going back to the seventh century at least, if not to Constantinian times. Certainly a church on this site was destroyed in the seventh century and a new church built in the twelfth. The present church was built in 1869 by the Princess of Auvergne, a cousin of Napoleon III. Attached to it is a convent of Carmelite nuns, and a cloister adorned with thirty-five or more frames of the Lord's Prayer in as many languages. Halfway down the track into the Kedron Valley is the traditional site where Jesus wept over the city, as he foresaw the catastrophe that was to take place within the lifetime of many who now came out of the city to greet him. 'If only you had known, on this great day, the way that leads to peace! But no; it is hidden from your sight. For a time will come upon you, when your enemies will set up siege-works against you; they will encircle you and hem you in at every point; they will bring you to the ground, you and your children within your walls, and not leave you one stone standing upon another, because you did not recognise God's moment when it came.'

On this site today is the striking little church of 'Dominus Flevit', built in 1955 by Barluzzi. When the Franciscans were excavating an ancient cemetery, they found traces of a hitherto unknown fifth-century church. This they rebuilt, preserving the original mosaics *in situ,* and shaping the roof like a tear. Instead of facing east, the church faces west; through a plate-glass window it commands a truly magnificent view across the whole city of Jerusalem.

For the next three days Jesus was to go into the city, evading arrest, surrounded by the crowds of Passover pilgrims as he taught in the Temple, before returning at dusk to the shelter of the quiet village home at Bethany. Meanwhile, the feast approached and the tension, to some extent created by his presence, mounted. On the fourth day he remained in his retreat at Bethany. The following day, Maundy Thursday, perhaps 'the first day of unleavened bread when they sacrificed the passover', but more likely the day *before* the feast, was the day he had chosen for his farewell meal with his disciples. If it was not the actual Seder feast, it was within the context and atmosphere of Passover. He sent two disciples with instructions to enter the city and look out for a man carrying a pitcher of water, surely an unmistakable sign and security measure to ensure the secrecy of the meeting place. The man was to show them an upper room, or guest chamber, where they were to prepare the meal, until Jesus and the others arrived when darkness had come.

At that time, the city walls enclosed the western hill. By a false tradition, however, this western hill has become identified with the Hill of Zion, Ophel, on which David's city once stood. The cenacle, or supper room, according to the strongest tradition, was on the very top of this western

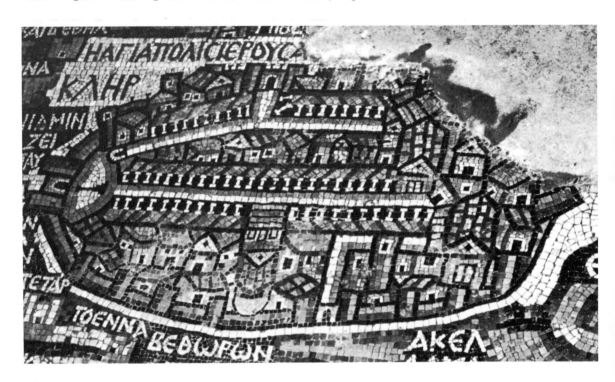

hill and in the immediate vicinity of the Tomb of David. Subsequent Christian monuments and churches in this area are somewhat confusingly referred to, from Byzantine times onwards, as being on 'Mount Zion'. Christians came to regard their fourth-century 'Zion Church' as the 'Mother of all churches', because they cherished on this site memories of the Last Supper, the Washing of the Feet, the many appearances of Jesus to his followers after the resurrection and the outpouring of his spirit, or personality, at Pentecost. Here too, traditionally, had been the house of St John, where Mary, the Mother of Jesus, 'fell asleep'.

The history of this Zion Church is hard to unravel. Bishop Epiphanius, a native of Palestine in the fourth century, referring to documents of the second century, wrote:

The plan of the City of Jerusalem as shown on the Madeba mosaic. The great church on Mount Zion, enclosing the sites of both Cenacle and Dormition is to the right and south, the Holy Sepulchre upside down in the centre, the Gate of the Column to the left and north. These three are linked by a colonnaded street running north and south.

146

Hadrian . . . found the whole city razed to the ground and the Temple of God destroyed and trodden underfoot. There were only a few houses standing and the House of God, a little building in the place where the disciples on their return from the Mount of Olives, after the Saviour's Ascension, assembled in the Upper Room. This [church] was built in the part of Zion which had escaped destruction, together with some buildings round about and seven synagogues that stood alone on Zion like cottages, one of which remained standing down to the time of . . . the Emperor Constantine.

The Zion church
on the western
hill

St Cyril of Jerusalem, in 348, refers to the 'Upper Church of the Apostles where the Holy Spirit descended upon them'. The Spanish nun, Aetheria, in 385, identified the site as the scene of both the Easter appearances of Jesus and the events of Pentecost. She describes the special services held in this church on these great festivals. The pilgrim Theodosius, in 530, adds the fact that the Upper Room was in the house of St Mark, the Evangelist. This was, indeed, the first synagogue of the Christian Church and their headquarters in Jerusalem.

It is interesting to note that this western quarter of the western hill seems to have largely escaped the military operations of the year AD 70, when the main attack of Titus was from the east. It would have been surprising if the Christian community, who had fled to Pella before the siege, had not returned to their headquarters which had been the seat of the first bishop in Jerusalem, St James, the 'brother' of Jesus. It was the 'little building', mentioned by Epiphanius and restored by Massimus, that was transformed into the great basilica called 'Holy Zion' by Archbishop John early in the fifth century. Burned down by the Persians in 614, the 'Mother of all churches' was restored by Modestus, the Christian patriarch of Jerusalem, twenty years later. We know, also, that the patriarchs of the seventh century venerated within the same church a stone, on which tradition relates that the Mother of Jesus 'fell asleep'.

In 685, Bishop Arculf made a drawing or plan of the church on a wax tablet, showing in this one building, facing east, the cenacle or supper room on the south-east side (once within the house of St Mark), and the rock of the dormition on the north-west side (once within the house of St John). This accords exactly with the location of the cenacle and the dormition shrines today. When the Crusaders took Jerusalem, they found (as the pilgrim Saewulf in 1102 relates) the same events – the Last Supper, the resurrection appearances, the descent of the Holy Spirit and the dormition of Mary the Mother of Jesus – still commemorated in what was then called 'The Church of the Holy Spirit, outside the wall on the south of the city'. The Russian Abbot Daniel in 1106 described the church and site in much the same words.

The Crusaders built, over the remains of the earlier church, a large church with three aisles and dedicated it to 'St Mary of Mount Zion'. In the north aisle was a shrine of the dormition, on the south side was the cenacle, a two-storeyed shrine composed of two chapels one on top of the other, linked by a flight of thirty steps. The upper chapel was decorated

The Armenian ceremony
of the feet washing on
Maundy Thursday night,
at which the patriarch
washes the feet of his
clergy and people, in the
Cathedral of St James, on
Mount Zion.

with mosaics of the Last Supper and the Descent of the Holy Spirit. The
lower chapel, called the Galilee, commemorated the Washing of the
Feet and the resurrection appearances.

In 1342, the Franciscans built there a church, of which the cenacle of
today, with its two central columns and pilasters with their bizarre capitals, is the survivor. On the face of it, this Upper Room above the traditional Tomb of David is not an impressive monument of the Institution
of the Christian Eucharist, or communion. The site, however, is based on
as strong and continuous a tradition, preserved clearly and consciously
through the centuries, as any other Christian Holy Place in Jerusalem.
As Doctor Sanday puts it: 'It is the strength of a cord made up of many
strands.' For the Syrian Orthodox Church of St Mark, no comparable
evidence exists to link it with the Upper Room in the house of St Mark.
This church has a great attraction for Christian pilgrims because its
Syrian liturgy is a form of Aramaic, the language spoken by Jesus and his
disciples. The Syrian Orthodox clergy are happy to read to pilgrims Jesus'
words of the Institution of the Eucharist.

Perhaps the most striking reminder today of the Last Supper is in the
Washing of the Feet ceremony in the Maundy Thursday rites of almost
every branch of the Church in Jerusalem. In each cathedral, abbey or
church, the dramatisation of the thirteenth chapter of St John's gospel
presents a vivid lesson in humility, in which the head of each community,
whether Orthodox patriarch, Latin patriarch, Armenian patriarch,

148

Coptic, Syrian or Abyssinian, as the representative of Jesus, washes the feet of twelve men, each ceremony reflecting the devotion and characteristic spirituality of the community concerned. At the Syrian ceremony, which is simple and moving, the bishop gently washes the feet of the choirboys; the Armenian is a majestic and beautiful sequence, in which the Anglican archbishop reads the gospel, and the music is superb; the Orthodox, within the courtyard of the Sepulchre, is at once a serene and realistic dramatisation, in which the only prop is a branch on the convent wall to represent the Mount of Olives: each of the twelve men takes the spoken part of a disciple, and the patriarch strips down to his alb before taking up the basin and sponge; the Abyssinian ceremony, in their tiny chapel on the roof of St Helena's, is a delightfully gay, crowded family affair, with all the devotion and colour of Africa; the Anglican community chooses to make a silent pilgrimage from Mount Zion to Gethsemane, in the darkness, or, it may be, the illumination of the Passover moon. By one means or another, every Christian community relives the events of that night.

The Garden of Gethsemane

The route taken by Jesus and his disciples would probably skirt the Temple Area to the south, leaving the city by the Water Gate above the Gihon and crossing the Kedron ravine over a viaduct or bridge (the Roman masonry of which is still to be seen below the monumental tombs referred to in chapter 2). The old rock level of the ravine was some ten metres below the present level of the Kedron, which contains the rubble of a score of sieges, including that of Titus. Some way up the opposite side, on the lower slopes of the Mount of Olives and very near the junction of tracks leading down from the ridge, was the Garden of Gethsemane. This 'garden' was most probably an orchard of olives or other trees, enclosed within a wall. It probably included the area now covered by both the Russian and Franciscan properties which extend well up the hillside. It is very probable that Jesus and his disciples would have made use of a regular resting and meeting place before they came into the city together, or returned for their night's lodging to Bethany or elsewhere. St Luke's gospel indicates that on occasion they used to spend the night on the Mount of Olives. At any rate, it was not surprising that Judas knew their meeting place, for, as St John says: 'There was a garden there, and he and his disciples went into it. The place was known to Judas, his betrayer, because Jesus often met there with his disciples.'

In the year 390, the Spanish nun Aetheria records this entry in her pilgrimage diary, on a Maundy Thursday night when the congregation came down from a service at the Church of the Ascension on the Mount of Olives,

> to the same place where the Lord had prayed, as it is written in the gospel, 'he withdrew away from them a stone's cast and prayed'. Here is an elegant church into which enter bishop and congregation. A prayer and a hymn appropriate to the occasion are recited; then the passage of the gospel which runs 'Watch and pray that ye enter not into

temptation' is read. Then all reciting psalms go down with the bishop to Gethsemane. Arriving there, a prayer is said, then a hymn, finally is read the passage of the gospel relating the arrest of Jesus.

Later pilgrims confirmed this sequence involving *two* Holy Places, one of the Prayer of Jesus, one of his Arrest, the first being a church, the second being a cave.

Today, the first Holy Place of the Prayer and Agony of Jesus is marked similarly by a modern Church of All Nations, built on the ground plan of, and including sections of, the mosaic floor of the fourth-century church. The focal point of the early and the present churches is part of a rock terrace, one among many on the rising hill-side, but this has since the fourth century symbolised the rock on which Jesus prayed in his agony of apprehension and decision. 'Nevertheless not my will, but thine be done.' The second Holy Place is still a cave, but since the fourteenth century wrongly associated also with the agony rather than with the arrest of Jesus. The cave is of considerable size, seventeen by nine metres, with a height of more than three metres. The remains of twelfth-century frescoes and mosaics were covered by a new pavement when the decorations were restored in 1959. Perhaps the name Gethsemane explains the primitive function of this cave. 'Gat Shemanim' could mean 'oil-press'. The cave has belonged to the Franciscans since 1392, the site of the church and the garden since 1681. Behind and up above the Franciscan property stands the Russian church, built by the Czar Alexander III in 1888 in an avenue of cypresses. But the oldest trees are eight ancient olives in the Franciscan garden which may well be the sons or shoots of olives of the time of Jesus.

If the pilgrim Aetheria could call the fourth-century church 'elegant', modern pilgrims could well describe the present church with the same word. The ground plan of both is the same, even to the Byzantine pattern and the continuity of the lovely mosaics. Here, the Byzantine plan to isolate the focal point of a shrine by cutting out the surrounding rock, can be clearly seen. It is an excellent illustration of the sort of procedure that was followed in the construction of the Constantinian Church of the Holy Sepulchre. One of the features of the modern church, consecrated in 1924, is the purple alabaster used in the windows to give the effect of gloomy darkness. As soon as the lights are lit or the west door opened, the ceiling can be seen to be a mass of mosaic domes, decorated with the coats-of-arms of many nations. Over the high altar and set within the apse is a mosaic of Jesus in prayer on the rock of his agony. Behind him, under the olives, are his sleeping disciples. The mosaic facing the north aisle is of the betrayal: 'Betrayest thou the Son of Man with a kiss?'; that facing the south aisle is of the surrender: 'You seek Jesus of Nazareth, I am he!' While before the central altar, which itself stands upon rock, is the great rock of agony, surrounded by an iron crown of thorns, on which silver doves droop in mourning.

From the Garden of Gethsemane, prisoner and escort returned to the western hill, passing down the Kedron Valley under those monumental

Gethsemane to Gallicantus

150

tombs. Probably entering by the Fountain Gate at the bottom of Ophel, rather than climbing the gorge to the Water Gate, they would be more likely to climb the ancient stairway from the Pool of Siloam directly up to the high priest's palace, 'to Caiaphas, where the scribes and elders were assembled'. It must be admitted that there is a slight conflict of ideas about the exact site, one claim being that covered by the Armenian Church of St Saviour, built in the fifteenth century, the other that covered by the Latin Church of St Peter of the Cock-Crowing, built in 1931. It is one of those occasions when the astounding results of recent excavations seem to contradict much-treasured traditions. Certainly, the evidence of excavations at St Peter of the Cock-crowing, if fully understood and accepted, is not only convincing but provides perhaps the most vivid sequence of illustrations to be seen on any single Jewish site of the period.

Various churches have been built on this site to commemorate the trial and imprisonment of Jesus by Caiaphas, as well as St Peter's denial and repentance. The Pilgrim of Bordeaux in 333, commenting on the ruins of the high priest's palace, wrote: 'In the same Valley of Siloam, you go up to Mount Zion and [in the same valley] you see the spot where the House

The ancient Jewish staircase which constituted the main road from the Valley Gate and the Pool of Siloam, up the western hill to the High Priest's palace, now covered and preserved by the Church of St Peter of the Cock Crowing.

of Caiaphas stood.' In 348, Cyril, Bishop of Jerusalem, recorded much the same evidence. Between 457 and 459, a fine basilica dedicated to St Peter was built on the ruins by the Empress Eudocia. In 530, Theodosius went from the Cenacle to the House of Caiaphas, 'which is now St Peter's church'. In the same century, the writer of the Jerusalem Breviary wrote: 'From here [the Cenacle] you go to the House of Caiaphas, where St Peter denied the Lord: there is the great basilica of St Peter.' In the year 840, the Frankish monk Bernard the Wise wrote in more detail: 'Straight to the east of the Cenacle and to the south of the Temple is St Peter's Church, on the spot where he denied the Lord.' The English Crusader and pilgrim Saewulf, in 1102, said: 'On the slope of Mount Zion is the Church of St Peter-at-the-crowing-of-the-cock.' The twelfth-century monk Epiphanius provided another bearing by stating: 'To the right of St Peter's Church, at three arrow shots, is the Pool of Siloam.' Finally, the Madeba mosaic shows directly to the east of the Mount Zion Church, containing the Cenacle, a small door below a great basilica. This could well be the crypt of the hill-side basilica of St Peter. It was after the Crusaders rebuilt the church in 1100 that it was given the name 'Gallicantus', the cock-crowing, thus only commemorating St Peter's repentance. The Crusader church was destroyed in the early fourteenth century.

The Church of the Cock-Crowing

The present church includes at least three different storeys or levels, being built on to a steep, if not almost sheer, hill-side. Beyond and to the south of it is a superb observation point, commanding a bird's-eye view of the site of the City of David on Ophel, the Tyropoean Valley from the Dung Gate to the Pool of Siloam, the Valley of Hinnom and the Fields of Blood, bought with the thirty pieces of silver for a stranger's cemetery. It is a magnificent place from which to stand and reconstruct in imagination the historical geography of the city, from the Babylonian siege to the Byzantine city of Eudocia. Perhaps the one man-made feature, common to both and still to be seen, is that magnificent rock-hewn staircase ascending the hillside from the Pool of Siloam. It was on to this equivalent of the city highway that the palace of the high priest faced.

The main west doorway of the present church leads into the top level, and from a balcony outside the east end the visitor can look down upon the vast storage chambers below the palace. Staircases lead down into corn stores; oil stores are lined with plaster and have round bottle-necks. There is a complete grinding mill here, with an underground rock-hewn stable for the donkey that operated it. Complete sets of weights and measures, used only by the priests, have been discovered in this 'treasury', also a huge stone door lintel inscribed: 'This is Korban or offering'. Such facilities on such a scale indicate the storage of Temple dues.

Within the church, over the high altar, is an illustration of the trial which was conducted in the rock-hewn courtroom on the next level below the church. The prisoner is standing on a raised platform or dock, in the centre and with his back to the wall, chained by the wrists to escorts seated on either side of him. It is easy to picture this scene on the lower level facing westwards into the hillside in which are cut staircases and galleries. On one of these Peter must have sat with the soldiers, warmed

From the balcony of the Church of St Peter of the Cock Crowing can be seen the storehouse and treasury of the High Priest's palace. This includes wet and dry storage for oil and grain, together with a complete grinding mill and stable for the donkey which operated it.

himself by the fire and denied knowing his master. On either side of the wall, behind the raised rock platform, the corners of the courtroom are cut square to a height of three metres.

In the very centre of the courtroom is the mouth of a bottle-necked prison, into which the condemned prisoner could be lowered after trial. Here the story of Jeremiah's rescue by Ebed-Melech the Ethiopian, during the Babylonian siege, is strangely illustrated and in such detail, even to the rags from the storehouse to protect Jeremiah from the rope, and the fact that Jeremiah, once drawn up out of the dungeon, still remained in the court (Jeremiah: 38).

Descending to a third level there is a complete guardroom, all round the walls of which are still the staples for the prisoners' chains. On one side is a small window opening on to the condemned bottle-neck cell. Below this window and left projecting from the floor when the guardroom was excavated out of the rock, is a block on which the guard stood to peer down into the gloom of the cell below him. On the opposite side of the guardroom is the whipping block. Here, tied up by the wrists with leather thongs through staples at the top, a belt round his waist secured to a staple at each side, the prisoner would be stretched up taut and helpless. At his feet were two bowls carved in the rock, one for salt to disinfect his wounds, one for vinegar to revive him. Here, the apostles of the early Church received the legal number of forty stripes save one, thirteen on each shoulder from the back and thirteen on the chest from the front, were commanded not to preach Jesus as Christ, then sent home. Yet they returned daily to the Temple to teach and to preach this very thing.

Within the cell below this, on yet a fourth level within this one building, the walls bear the marks of devotion of many Christian pilgrims. Black and red crosses are still to be seen and deeply carved Byzantine crosses within the bottle-neck. Here Jesus spent what was left of the night of his trial and no doubt the eighty-eighth Psalm expressed his feelings well: 'I am counted with them that go down into the pit ... free among the dead. Shall thy loving kindness be declared in the grave? I am ready to die, lover and friend hast thou put far from me. I am in the darkness!'

Very early in the morning, prisoner and escort set out from the high priest's palace, on the western hill, for the Praetorium. It was the morning of the first Good Friday, and the procurator, Pontius Pilate, had been warned to expect them.

Gallicantus to Antonia

There were two great fortresses protecting the north wall of the city, called by Josephus the 'Second Wall'. At the north-east corner was the Antonia Fortress. At the north-west was Herod's Palace, on the site of what is now called the 'Citadel' or 'David's Tower'. The Roman procurators resided in the vast city-port of Caesarea, but when visiting Jerusalem they took up temporary residence in either of these two great fortress-palaces. Pilate certainly is known to have resided in both on different occasions, according to Josephus. We cannot, therefore, be completely certain from any documentary evidence, which one was occupied on this occasion. Scholars, even among the Dominicans of the École Biblique, agree to differ. Once again, however, recent excavations carried out under the supervision of the much-respected Jerusalem archaeologist/historian, Père Vincent, O.P., from 1857 to 1870, have convinced many of the identification of the gospel story with events which took place within the Antonia Fortress, rather than Herod's Palace. And certainly today it is the former that is recognised as a 'primary' Holy Place, from which, since the sixteenth century, Christian pilgrims have begun their devotions along the Via Dolorosa.

It will be as well first to outline the history and function of the Antonia, then to offer some documentary references, and finally to present the main features of the excavations, together with any light they throw on the gospel story. The term 'Praetorium' may need some preliminary explanation. It is the name of the judicial seat of the Roman governor or praetor at any given moment. He established his Praetorium simply by hanging his shield at the gate and posting his tribune on guard, whether in Jerusalem or Caesarea, at Herod's Palace or at the Antonia.

A Hasmonaean fort once stood to the west of the Temple Area to protect it from assault. Here Herod built a vast fortress with the triple purpose, not of protecting the Temple so much as suppressing riots, preserving order within the Temple courtyards and securing the external defence of the city at its most vulnerable point. The fact that he called it after Mark Antony, the Roman conqueror of Syria and Palestine, indicates his true purpose – that the Antonia and its western counterpart, the Tower of David, should successfully muzzle Jerusalem and her Jewish life. The 'Tower of David', as Crusaders and Muslims came to call it, was a vast palace containing halls, dormitories, barracks, aviaries, gardens and fountains, sumptuous as well as securely protected by its three great towers of Mariamne, Hippicus and Phasael.

Josephus describes the Antonia

Josephus' description of the Antonia makes it sound equally forbidding, though less luxurious and more functional:

> The inwards parts had the largeness and form of a palace, it being parted into all kinds of rooms and other conveniences, such as courts, and places for bathing, and broad spaces for a camp; insomuch that, by having all conveniences that cities wanted, it might seem to be composed of several cities, but by its magnificence it seemed a palace; and as the entire structure resembled that of a tower, it contained also four other distinct towers at its four corners; whereof the others were but 50 cubits high; whereas that which lay upon the south-east corner was 70 cubits high, that from thence the whole temple might be viewed; but on the corner where it joined to the two cloisters of the temple, it had passages down to them both, through which the guard (for there always lay in this tower a Roman legion) went several ways among the cloisters, with their arms, on the Jewish festivals, in order to watch the people, that they might not there attempt to make any innovations.

As Josephus wrote elsewhere, 'The city was dominated by the Temple and the Temple by the Antonia'.

The Antonia was well suited as a place for the suppression of disturbances because it was only in the north of the Temple that the city was overlooked by higher ground. Elsewhere the city stood at the head of a precipice and those who wished to assault it would have to do so uphill. Hence it was from this northern direction that Pompey had captured the city in 63 BC and that Herod the Great had himself made his final assault on the city. Herod was, therefore, well aware of the strategic importance

155

of this site, which was later to prove its worth as the place where the Jews made their last stand against Titus' assault (17 Tammuz). Sometime in June or July, AD 70, the Antonia was destroyed and its famous central pavement or Gabbatha, referred to in St John's gospel, was buried by the rubble for the next eighteen hundred years.

The Praetorium figures only very vaguely in Byzantine tradition. The Bordeaux Pilgrim in 333 describes some walls 'below in the valley, where was the house or Praetorium of Pontius Pilate'. Cyril of Jerusalem confirms the desolation of this site. Vincent comments on the proximity of the Justinian basilica of St Sophia, built in 543, to the site of the Praetorium and quotes Theodosius as referring to this as the place 'where the Wisdom of God was judged and condemned to death by the wisdom of earth'.

The Praetorium

Crusader perplexity about the site is reflected by the author of 'Gesta Francorum' in 1109: 'As to the scourging of Jesus, the crowning with thorns, the derision and other tortures that he endured for us, it is not easy to discern today where they happened, since the city has been subsequently so often sacked and destroyed.' Theodoric, in 1172, refers to ruins west of the Church of St Anne, which Abel would identify as the eastern towers of the Antonia. Marino Sanuto, in 1310, shows on a map of the city the Praetorium at the north-west corner of the Temple Area. With the establishment of the Franciscans in the sixteenth century, the Stations of the Cross began to be used along the Via Dolorosa, beginning from a point on what is now known to be the site of the Antonia.

Having discussed the history of the Antonia, let us now return to the first century, and from the excavations reconstruct a picture of the fortress and the events of the morning of Friday, the eve of the '15 of Nisan, of the year 30'. Vincent describes it thus:

A model of the Antonia Fortress within the Convent of the Sisters of Zion. Called by Herod the Antonia, after his friend Mark Antony, its purpose was to protect the city from the north-east, and particularly to maintain order within the Temple Area.

> This gigantic quadrilateral, cut almost entirely out of the rocky hill, covered an area of 150 metres east to west, by 80 metres north to south. It was protected by powerful corner towers and enclosed installations as complex and diverse as a palace and camp. The outstanding but characteristic feature of this complex was, without doubt, the courtyard, about 2,500 metres square, serving as a place of meeting between the city and the Antonia. Extending over deep water cisterns, covered with a massive polished pavement, surrounded by tall cloisters, this courtyard was really the heart of the fortress whose activity it regulated ... Pilate had his tribunal set up within the courtyard, transformed for the occasion into the Praetorium, called indeed the 'Pavement' *par excellence*. Where could one find more explicit evidence, more expressive and appropriate a setting for the place where Pilate pronounced the sentence which sent Jesus on his way to Calvary?

Leaving the high priest's palace, prisoner and escort, followed by the crowd, must have passed on over the great viaducts across the Tyropoean Valley. They must have left the city by the 'Fish Gate' and climbed the steep slope which ran alongside the ramparts of the north wall, to appear before the great double gate of the Antonia. This vast fortress, defended by a moat and scarp from the open country beyond, had its main gate

outside the city wall, as though fearing less from without than within the city walls. And with good reason too, for though it dominated the Temple Area, it was from here that trouble could be expected. Within the four great corners of the fortress, crammed with thousands of troops at such a time as Passover, Pilate had his own procurator's quarters in a little central tower facing down on to the Pavement. To water tens of thousands in a fortress often under siege must have demanded a phenomenal supply. This was yet another function of the Pavement, whose water runnels still lead down into the cavernous vaults below, where cistern tops yet bear the marks of lock and chain, and whose counter-weights and pulleys are still to be seen.

The Pavement   On to this Pavement prisoner and escort proceeded, while the crowd, for fear of defilement before Passover, crammed by the thousand into the great double gateway. Pilate, seated in his curial chair at the head of his private stairway, must have gazed down upon the Pavement in disgust. Having blotted his colonial copybook more than once, knowing himself to be outwitted by Caiaphas, he sought in desperation the sympathy of the people for the man and had him scourged. This scourging was even worse than that received at the palace whipping block. No salt and vinegar here, but crude pellets of lead and bone on the end of a 'cat-o-nine-tails'. This was the weapon with which the cowardly cohort was decimated on the field of battle. It could cut a man to death in moments. To use it was too degrading a task for Romans and was reserved for foreign auxiliaries. The place of the scourging cannot now be known, but it probably took place in view of the people on the Pavement and at a column or post designed and used for the purpose. The Pavement extends over a considerable area in the basement of the Convent of the Sisters of Zion, and runs through into the Chapel of the Condemnation, owned by the Franciscans, as is also the Chapel of the Flagellation.

This last is to be found at the east end of the Franciscan compound. On the west wall are carved, over the entrance, all the 'implements' of the Passion; within the church the modern stained-glass windows are particularly evocative, illustrating the scourging, Pilate's washing of his hands, and the triumphant release of Barabbas; over the sanctuary is a fine mosaic of the crown of thorns.

After the scourging, St John describes how the soldiers took him to their guardroom or quarters, before returning him to Pilate. It was in the guardroom that they had their opportunity to vent their detestation, as occupation forces, upon this representative of a subject race who had called himself a king. Just how they did so is well illustrated by carvings in the Pavement at the foot of the troops' stairways. Among a variety of knuckle boards and hopscotch designs covering several flagstones, there are the following signs: the 'B' for 'Basilicus', meaning 'King', a rough and prickly crown, and finally a sabre. This is evidence of a game called 'King', described by Plautus as derived from the Saturnalia, in which a burlesque king is chosen, mockingly honoured and saluted, before being killed. So, in the crucifixion squad, each soldier would adopt as his stake one of the condemned prisoners. The winner in the game of bones would

crown his own 'stake' with a crown of thorns in a mocking guardroom ceremony. The king, thus crowned, would receive his soldiers' homage. his swagger-cane as sceptre and his military cloak as a royal robe. All the guardroom would hail him 'Basilicus Judaiorum!' This indeed gives meaning to the gospel account of the mocking.

When the prisoner was returned to Pilate in a condition to draw pity from the crowd, Pilate presented him with the words 'Ecce Homo!' – 'Behold the Man!' The crowd continued to call for his crucifixion; Pilate pronounced his parody of judgment, washed his hands and returned to his quarters. After the necessary preparations, three prisoners and their judicial escort formed up on the Pavement and passed out along the chariot way, through the great double gate with its two guardrooms on each side, the three prisoners dragging their huge crosses up the Via Dolorosa to Calvary.

A final word needs to be said of the archaeological evidence: within the Convent of the Sisters of Zion, the Pavement is down in the enormous basement, which is about two metres below street level. The thickness of the flagstones is about twenty centimetres and they are mounted on about a metre of hard core and concrete above the solid rock platform. Running right across the Pavement and continuing in the neighbouring Franciscan chapel is the chariot way of grooved corrugated flagstones, designed to assist the chariot horses. This chariot way must have left the courtyard eastwards, down a ramp, passing near the procurator's staircase and between the two great towers in which the troops were accommodated.

The gaming boards of Roman soldiers carved in the pavement or 'gab-batha' at the foot of the staircase leading to the troops' quarters. On one side of the gaming board is the sword symbolising execution, on the other a crown of thorns.

Westwards it is still to be seen passing out through the northern arch of the double gateway.

Within this gateway are the two guardrooms on the north side, their door-stops, hinge-holes and bolt-sockets still to be seen in their entrances. These guardrooms are themselves cut out of the solid rock of the gateway to a height of at least three and a half metres. The easternmost guardroom has a chimney cut right up through the full height of solid rock, some ten metres high. The guardrooms face out on to a pavement some two metres wide, which drops down on to the chariot way. The corrugated flagstones do not rise to another pavement in the centre of the gateway, but continue until the central masonry of the gateway covers them. The southern side of the gateway is buried beneath the street. The sheer size and height of this enormous gateway, carved in the solid rock of the Bezetha hill, is astounding. If three of the corner towers were twenty-three metres high, the south-east corner one thirty metres high, and the southern front of the Antonia facing down on the Temple Area 120 metres long, what would be the height of the gateway to such a fortress?

It is small wonder that when the excavators discovered three Hadrianic arches on the same orientation that they expected to find the gateway, they should have jumped to the wrong conclusion and called them the 'Ecce Homo'. Very soon they were to discover the immense scale of the actual gateway. The triple Hadrianic gate formed the entrance to Hadrian's new city of Aelia Capitolina in 130. He purposefully left the Temple outside the walls, hence the entrance gate just north of the Temple Area. The central arch still spans the street, while the northern arch is above the altar in the basilica of the Sisters of Zion. At the back of which rises the rock of the real gateway and beneath runs the chariot way.

If, indeed, Pilate did 'stand to' with his troops on the Antonia and hold court on the morning of 15 Nisan in the year 30, then the Christian pilgrim follows in the steps of his master, here at this site, with an accuracy not possible elsewhere in Jerusalem.

The Way of the Cross The last journey of the road to the cross is the Via Dolorosa to Calvary. The Via Dolorosa is not so much a sequence of Holy Places with any historical association, but rather a traditional devotional exercise along an approximate route taken by Jesus on the first Good Friday. Aetheria described how pilgrims used to go to Gethsemane on Maundy Thursday night and walk the route of Jesus to arrive at dawn at Calvary. There the gospel of the trial and crucifixion would be read. By the eighth century, the pilgrim route from the Praetorium took in the high priest's palace on the way to Calvary. In Crusader times both direct and indirect routes were followed, sometimes with the object of walking in procession through as much of the city as possible. At the close of the Middle Ages, the direct route had established itself and certain devotional stations, or stands, had crystallised. By 1550, this was called the Via Dolorosa and the stations have remained more or less constant until the present day. In a sense, it is not the accuracy of the route but the centuries of devotion which have saturated it, that can justify the inclusion of the Via Dolorosa

among the Holy Places. Most of the stations are marked by chapels; a
number of these are of recent construction, and not very attractive to
western eyes. They do, however, remind pilgrims of the event, either
scriptural or legendary, to be commemorated at each point on their journey of prayer.

Archaeologically, the Via Dolorosa today follows surprisingly closely *The pilgrim*
the route that Jesus must have taken, if he went from the Antonia to *route today*
Calvary in the year 30. In the topography of the city and the Second
Wall, it was clear that from the Antonia Gateway the procession would
enter the city by the Fish Gate, pass along within the city walls and leave
the city again at the Judgment Gate, opposite the mound of Calvary.
Just how the present Via Dolorosa does this can well be seen from the
observation point on the roof of the Convent of the Sisters of Zion. The
road descends to the valley, turns left and continues again to the right,
up the opposite side of the valley. At a certain point it must pass through
the line of the Second Wall and out of the city to the site of Calvary, seen
clearly over the rooftops today as the black and white domes of the
Church of the Holy Sepulchre. Also, from this observation point, the relative positions of the Palace of Herod and the Antonia, with the line of the
Second Wall running between them, are very clear. The Garden, or
Gennath area, in which were both Calvary and the Tomb, is clearly
visible outside the line of the Second Wall, which included perhaps two
'dog-leg' turns on its way across the north of the city. The Via Dolorosa
today appears to follow those turns, within the line of the Second Wall,
before going out to Calvary. The threshold of the gateway and a sizeable *Out of the*
section of the Second Wall is still to be seen within the basement of the *city gate*
Russian hospice. It is believed that at this point the wall was adapted as
the facade, or east wall, of the first great Constantinian basilica of the
Holy Sepulchre. The triple entrance to this, set within the Second Wall,
is also to be seen in Coptic, Russian and Muslim properties behind the
Arab market or 'suq'.

The actual pilgrim route today cannot penetrate the maze of buildings
surrounding the sepulchre, and the processions must divert along to the
suq after the eighth station. They enter the Holy Sepulchre Church by
the main door and follow the remaining stations inside the church. Nor
can the route start from a point at which the pilgrim can see any of the
actual Pavement. For purely practical reasons, the assembly point needs
to be off the main road and large enough to enclose a considerable crowd.
So, of the fourteen stations, the First Station is in the courtyard of the old
Turkish barracks, now a school, opposite the Convent of the Sisters of
Zion. From here there is a magnificent view of the Temple area, such as
the ramparts of the Antonia Fortress afforded to the sentry on guard when
he saw St Paul about to be lynched by the mob (as related in the twenty-
first chapter of the Acts of the Apostles). When he had turned out the
guard to rescue Paul, they had to carry their man 'up the steps of the
castle because of the violence of the people'. This was the starting point
of St Paul's Way of Sorrows, as it had been that of his master, Jesus. At
this First Station the theme of devotion is 'Jesus is condemned to death'.

Within the actual gateway of the Antonia Fortress from front to back is seen the serrated chariot way, the troops' pavement and the guardroom, where a figure of Jesus scourged has been placed.

He is supposed to have come down a stairway following his condemnation; this stairway is supposed to have been removed at the order of St Helena and sent to Rome, where it is reputed to form the Scala Sancta, opposite the Church of St John Lateran. Despite the destruction of Jerusalem by Titus and Hadrian, it is just possible that some fragments of the original stairway may be within the one in Rome today.

The Second Station, whose pilgrim theme is 'Jesus receives the cross', is fortuitously at the bottom of another stairway leading down to the present street level. This is some two metres above the Pavement of the Praetorium. At the feet of the pilgrims taking part in the procession are the basement windows of the convent; if they were to be opened, the chariot way would be seen from the street outside. The Via Dolorosa now continues west, under Hadrian's Arch, along the axis of the chariot way, passing out of the great double gateway, where the road passes the external doorway to the back of the convent basilica. Next to this is a small Greek shrine of the 'Prison of Christ', of a very much more recent tradition. The Via reaches the bottom of the valley and turns left, as if at this point entering the Fish Gate in the Second Wall. Here on the left is the Third Station, whose legendary theme is 'Jesus falls the first time'. It is the site of a small Polish chapel with a high-relief presenting the fall of Jesus against a mural of wondering angels. Travelling south within the valley for a few metres only, the Via reaches the Fourth Station, whose theme is

'Jesus meets his mother'. Here on the site of another chapel is the Armenian Catholic church commemorating their legendary but possible meeting as Jesus dragged his cross through the crowded street. The lunette over the chapel doorway, of Jesus and his mother, is by the same Polish sculptor as the relief at the Third Station.

The Fifth Station, whose theme, mentioned in St Mark's gospel, is 'Simon of Cyrene helps Jesus carry his cross', is to be found only a few metres away on the corner, where the Via turns west again along the line of the Second Wall. Simon was presumably an African Passover pilgrim, whom the Roman soldiers seized and compelled to carry the cross. It is not surprising that after the events of the night before, and the scourging and mocking at the Praetorium, Jesus was no longer physically able to carry the cross alone. Legend has it that Simon became a disciple after this experience. Certainly, St Mark and the early Christians knew his family, and the names of his sons, Alexander and Rufus, come down to us in the gospel story.

The story of Veronica

The Sixth Station is eighty metres up the cobbled street, westwards, climbing out of the valley. Here the legendary theme is 'Veronica wipes the face of Jesus'. The name Veronica may be derived from the words 'Vera' and 'Icon', meaning together 'The True Image' traditionally left by the face of Jesus on her napkin. At this station, up some steps, is a Greek Catholic chapel. There is also the residence of the Little Sisters of Charles Foucauld, who live among and literally wipe the faces of the poor of Jerusalem. Their chapel at street level is lively, simple and evocative; behind it are the remains of an earlier, perhaps Crusader, chapel.

The Seventh Station is at the top of this street, where it joins the Khan-ez-Zeit. It has another legendary theme, 'Jesus falls the second time'. A Franciscan chapel of two storeys marks the site. In this area traditionally was the Judgment Gate, on the way out to Calvary. This gate we now know to be a little further south and its threshold is to be seen within the Russian excavations, though the Second Wall must have turned southwards very near the site of the Seventh Station. In fact, a little to the north is a ridge of rock more than thirty metres in length, which probably supported the Second Wall at this point.

The Eighth Station is on the left up Francis Street, marked by a stone plaque in the wall of the Greek Orthodox Convent of St Charalambos. The theme of this station is scriptural: 'Jesus speaks to the daughters of Jerusalem'. They were probably members of a philanthropic guild who were dedicated to comforting criminals on the way to execution, giving them myrrh to drug their pain before they reached the mount of punishment. The gospel tells us that Jesus bade them weep for themselves and that he refused the offer of drugged wine. Here the Greek convent intercepts the Via Dolorosa and the pilgrim procession must pass through the suq. This street was appropriately called by the Crusaders the 'Street of Bad Cookery' and the name is still appropriate today. Mounting a wide flight of steps, which incidentally lead at this point over the top of the Second Wall, we come to the Ninth Station at the entrance to the Coptic church. Tradition records that here 'Jesus falls for the third time'.

The remaining five stations are to be found within the Church of the Holy Sepulchre. Within its entrance, a flight of steps leads up to the Chapel of Calvary, on a level with the rocky knoll at the foot of which the Tenth Station reminds us: 'Jesus is stripped of his clothes'. The Chapel of Calvary is divided into two. The Latin altar on the right hand forms the Eleventh Station where 'Jesus is nailed to the cross'. The Greek altar on the left hand forms the Twelfth Station where 'Jesus dies on the cross'. Below and to the right of this altar the Rock of the Knoll of Calvary can still be seen; it is the top of the shaft of rock to be seen in the Chapel of Adam immediately below Calvary, but otherwise hidden within the masonry of the church. Both above and below, the Rock of the Knoll reveals an earthquake fissure, a strange reflection on St Matthew's statement that at the death of Jesus 'the earth did quake and the rocks rent'.

The Thirteenth Station is marked by a Latin altar of the 'Stabat Mater', between the Eleventh and Twelfth Stations, and its theme is, 'The body of Jesus is taken down from the cross'. The Fourteenth Station is within the Tomb, in the rotunda, its theme, 'Jesus is laid in the sepulchre'. In order to reach the tomb we descend from the Knoll of Calvary, at the foot of which is the Stone of the Anointing where, according to Crusader tradition, the body of Jesus was prepared for burial by Joseph of Arimathea and Nicodemus. Passing through the rotunda we are faced with the edicule, which is a vast and ornate model of the once simple, rock-hewn sepulchre. The archaeology and history of this formidable and at first sight forbidding complex of buildings which constitutes the present Church of the Holy Sepulchre is the subject of the next chapter; let us take now a final look at the Via Dolorosa.

Every Friday at 15.00 hours, the time of Jesus' death upon the cross, Christians of many denominations, colours and nationalities meet to make pilgrimage along the Way of Sorrows. (On Good Friday, they meet in the morning.) No one would deny their sincerity and devotion, or the sanctity of this road, hallowed by centuries of such prayer and love. The European visitors may be a little scandalised by the lack of inhibition of the oriental Christians, most of whom in Jerusalem are likely to be Arabs of an indigenous Christian community in the Holy Land. It is often to the courage and tenacity of these oriental Christians that the Christian Church as a whole owes the preservation of the Holy Places. When the western pilgrim on the Via Dolorosa longs for a moment of quiet in which he can shut out the clamour and clatter of the orient, he will do well to remind himself that the streets of Jerusalem were no less noisy on that first Good Friday, nor were the street traders likely to have paid any more attention to the crucifixion procession. The early Christians were given to a tumultuous and overflowing expression of their faith and joy, as were the pagans before them, and as are the oriental Jews and Muslims today. In many ways the Asians, whether they be Jewish, Christian or Muslim, have more in common with one another than with their European co-religionists. Christians, no less than Jews and Muslims, do well to remember that their faith was born and their creeds were formed not in Europe, but in Asia.

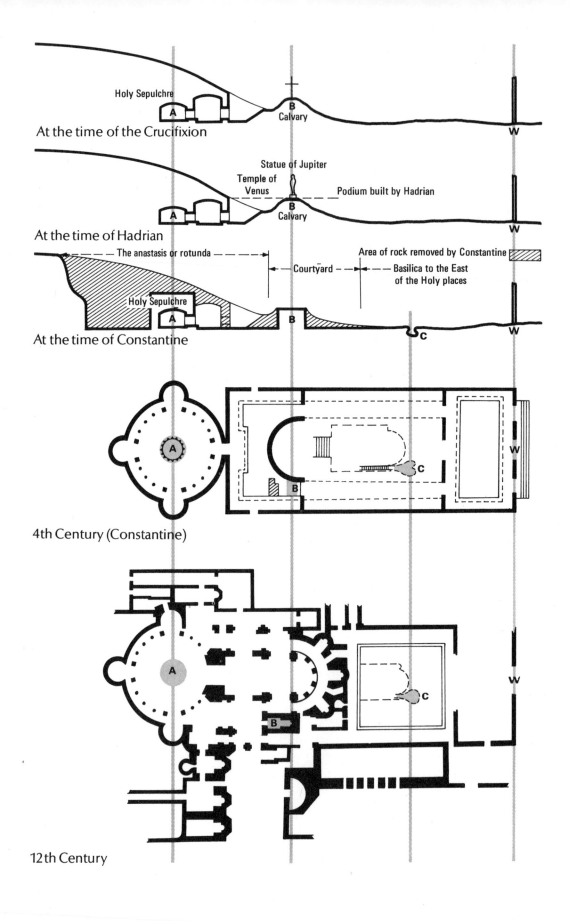

Holy Sepulchre

A

B
Calvary

W

At the time of the Crucifixion

Statue of Jupiter

Temple of
Venus

Podium built by Hadrian

A

B
Calvary

W

At the time of Hadrian

The anastasis or rotunda

Area of rock removed by Constantine

Courtyard

Basilica to the East
of the Holy places

Holy Sepulchre

A

B

C

W

At the time of Constantine

A

B

C

W

4th Century (Constantine)

A

B

C

W

12th Century

11 The Empty Tomb

'NOW, IN THE PLACE WHERE HE WAS CRUCIFIED, THERE WAS A GAR-den; and in the garden a new sepulchre wherein was never yet man laid. There they laid Jesus, therefore, because of the Jews' preparation day, for the sepulchre was nigh at hand'. The Passion of Jesus is fully described in St John's gospel: 'Nigh to the city' – 'Outside the gate'. The first followers of Jesus must have known exactly where the events took place.

If the sepulchre was in a garden, the tomb was that of a very well-known member of the Sanhedrin, Joseph of Arimathea. He had hewn it out of the rock himself. This garden was presumably his own private property. Even when Herod Agrippa, in extending the city, enclosed it within the walls, the garden would not have been built on. Because it had been a burial place, it was unclean land. If it had remained in Christian hands, how easy it would have been to point out to future generations where these great events had happened! There is a natural instinct in all men to remember the sites of great historical happenings; surely this site would have been preserved by early Christians. They would point out to their children the sacred places so carefully described in the gospels.

In AD 66 began the revolt of the Jews against the power of Rome, which ended in the destruction of Jerusalem, under Titus, in the year AD 70. From the crucifixion to AD 70 was forty years at most, too short a time for anyone to believe that these sacred places could be 'lost'. We come now to a sad period in the history of Jerusalem, from AD 70 to 135, a period of sixty-five years. The city was traditionally sacked and razed to the ground. But conquerors tend to exaggerate the damage they inflict upon their enemies. At any rate, repopulation and reconstruction began at once, on a modest scale. Although the city had lost all its old splendour, life began to return to normal.

The Christian community in the city, however small, continued to exist, for we have records of every single bishop of Jerusalem during this period. Although Titus is said to have destroyed the city, the sites of the crucifixion and resurrection, never having been built over, must have been comparatively unaffected by the rubble of destruction. There they remained for Christians to see. The bishops of Jerusalem must have pointed them out. And it may safely be said that the tradition of these Holy Places continued down through those unhappy years.

left: Sections and ground plans at different periods showing the development of the City Wall, the Mound of Calvary and the Holy Sepulchre.
A = Tomb of Jesus;
B = Knoll of Calvary;
C = Cistern of the Cross;
W = City Wall.

overleaf: On the way down to the Chapel of the Finding of the Cross: the walls are covered by the crosses of Byzantine and Crusader pilgrims.

Once again, revolt broke out in the year 135, under Bar Kochbar. Once again, the city suffered defeat and demolition. Hadrian captured and entirely rebuilt it on the lines of a Roman colonial city. He renamed it Aelia Capitolina. He again moved the city northwards and even excluded the Temple Area. He constructed a main road north and south through the city. Halfway along this were the forum and capitol, not far from the site of Calvary. He exiled the Jewish inhabitants of the city. Considering the Christian religion a Jewish sect, he tried to erase or desecrate the Christian sites. Hadrian built a great concrete terrace over the two sites of the crucifixion and resurrection. On this he erected a statue of Jupiter over Calvary and a temple of Venus over the tomb. (Part of the terrace is still to be seen in the Russian excavations.) Hadrian's action, however, had exactly the opposite result to what he had planned. For, under the providence of God, that mass of concrete served to mark indelibly the site of both the crucifixion and resurrection.

For the next two hundred years, Aelia Capitolina remained a Roman colony. Christians of Jewish race were exiled, but Christians of Greco-Roman origin were allowed to stay. The Church in Jerusalem grew and prospered as a Gentile Church, but kept in communion with the exiled Judaeo-Christians outside. We have again a record of all the Greco-Roman bishops of Aelia. There begins at this time a record of pilgrimage and of interest in the Holy Places, although they were still hidden and covered by Hadrian's concrete.

Although the crucial events of Christian history happened in Jerusalem, from the day of Pentecost onwards and even before the destruction by Titus, Jerusalem soon ceased to play, even in those early years, the leading part in the life of the Christian Church. The Book of Acts tells us, it is true, of the Council of Jerusalem, but the main resolution of that council was to establish that the Gentile Christian was not fully committed to the Jewish law. The Christians in Jerusalem were at times in considerable economic distress and required help from elsewhere. From the very earliest days of Christianity, as St Paul found in Damascus, Christian communities were established outside Jerusalem and indeed outside Palestine altogether. Even in Asia, it was in these early years Antioch rather than Jerusalem which was the centre of Christian life. After Pentecost, the Christian thought it his duty to carry the gospel over all the world; Christendom, in so far as it had a headquarters, had it in Rome rather than in Jerusalem. Even in the life of the Palestinian Christian Church, the bishop of Jerusalem was to become only a suffragan to the bishop of Caesarea. It was not until 451 that the Council of Chalcedon made Jerusalem a patriarchate independent of Caesarea. Despite persecution, by the time of Constantine Christianity was well established in Syria and Palestine and there is good reason to believe that the exact location of the Holy Places was known from a tradition going back to apostolic times.

Perhaps Constantine, like us, was surprised to find these sites inside the then city walls. If he had just intended to found a place of pilgrimage in honour of Jesus, would not he have chosen a site outside the walls? Macarius was bishop of Jerusalem at that time and pointed out the sites

to Constantine, within the city. Then began the destruction of one emperor's temple of the imperial state religion by another emperor, and this for the sole purpose of erecting the central shrine of Christendom! In a letter to Bishop Macarius, Constantine wrote: 'No words can express how good the Saviour has been to us. That the monument of his Holy Passion, hidden for so many years, has now at last been restored to the faithful is indeed a miracle. My great wish is, after freeing the site of impious idols, to adorn it with splendid buildings.'

Constantine planned to make these holy places an object of Christian pilgrimage and devotion. So he set about the task in this order: (1) Demolition of pagan shrines. (2) Excavation of concrete podium. (3) Discovery of the Knoll of Calvary and of the Tomb below. (4) Levelling off to form a floor-level for his church. (5) Excavation into the hillside to build a rotunda for the Anastasis, a circular ambulatory round the Tomb of Jesus. (6) Leaving the shell of the tomb in a circular space, or rotunda. (7) He left a symbolic cuboid of the Rock of Calvary. (Of the shell of the tomb Eusebius wrote: 'Is it not astonishing to see this rock standing isolated in the middle of a levelled space and with a cave inside it?')

Of the cuboid of rock Eusebius describes how the token 'mound' stood with a single cross on top, in an open colonnaded court.

The cathedral or 'martyrium' was beyond this open court. It was entered through an atrium or courtyard from the open street, which ran at right angles to the axis of the church (east to west). We can see in the Madeba Mosaic the magnificent setting of the basilica within the Byzantine city; to the north was the Damascus Gate, at which there was a single colossal column. Indeed the Arabic name for the Damascus Gate is still 'Bag-el-Amoud', Gate of the Column. From this column ran a colonnaded street, all through the city, to the great facade of the basilica.

If the reproduction of the Madeba Mosaic is turned upside down, the following will be clearly seen, front to back, east to west: (1) A broad frontage ascending in five steps. (2) A triple doorway of a central large and smaller side doors. (3) A huge building, orientated east to west, with a pitched roof. (4) A section with no roof, indicating an open courtyard. (5) Finally, at the west end, a separate domed building.

The details of the facade cannot be clearly shown, but it included part of the city wall from the time of Christ, adapted and faced with white marble, against which there was an imposing line of black basalt columns. The three entrances into the basilica are still to be seen behind the Arab market or suq – one in a café, one in a Russian convent, one under the Coptic convent, complete with their hinge-holes and bolt-sockets. The crypt of the Constantinian basilica, also still to be seen today, was the cistern in which were found three crosses. One of these was 'identified' as the true cross.

Constantine built a sloping staircase leading down to the Chapel of St Helena (now in the possession of the Armenians). The massive pillars which support its cupola are Byzantine work of the seventh century. From the Chapel of St Helena is a flight of thirteen steps which leads down to the Chapel of the Finding of the Cross. The walls of the stairway are covered

with graffiti of medieval pilgrims. The chapel, which looks like an old
disused cistern, is served now by the Latins and the Greeks. It was here,
of course, the story says, that the true cross was found on the initiative of
St Helena. There is no evidence dating back any earlier than seventy
years after her death of Helena's claim to have discovered the cross, nor
has the Church ever made any pronouncement about the story. There
are obvious and apparent improbabilities about the story, but when all
is said, wood is not quickly destroyed except by fire. It can survive for many
years in water and it is not difficult to think that the Romans carelessly
threw away their crosses when they had served their purpose, and that
there were plenty of used crosses lying about in neighbouring cisterns.
But such general arguments clearly cut both ways. If there were plenty of
crosses lying about, what reason was there for believing that they were
the three crosses in question? The Romans must have crucified hundreds
of people during those years.

*The finding of
the Cross*

Within the Church of St Pudenziana in Rome, there is a contemporary
fourth-century mosaic of Constantine's buildings in the apse and there,
in the centre of the mosaic, is the Rock of Calvary with its grille, above
which stands a large decorative cross. Although the scene of the mosaic
is very conventionalised, it does coincide rather remarkably with the remains in Jerusalem and with the ancient descriptions.

Here, Père Couasnon, able to excavate now for the first time in eight
hundred years, lately found that the Rock of Calvary was still four and a

The fourth-century mosaic within the Church of St Pudenziana in Rome includes a representation of the Church of the Holy Sepulchre built by Constantine. The colonnading and tiled roofing and the rotunda are clearly indicated.

half metres wide by four and a half metres long – with a height of at least ten metres! It is not for nothing that the endless stream of pilgrims – some with bare feet – some with dripping swords – some who see it all through the range-finders of their cameras – it is not for nothing that this stream has flowed past this traditional Rock of Calvary and the Tomb of Jesus.

Constantine was able and willing to command, for the building of his Christian churches, every financial resource of the empire. It was a deliberate part of imperial policy to establish majestic basilicas on the sites that had so important a part in Christian history. Craftsmen from every country, from both the East and the West, were unsparingly directed to the task. Constantine's buildings stood for some three hundred years, until in 614 the Persians captured Jerusalem, destroyed the basilica and took away the cross. The Persian occupation did not last long and when they withdrew, the patriarch Modestus attempted, in 628, to restore the basilica, substantially on the lines of Constantine. His financial resources, however, were far more limited. Then in 630 the Emperor Heraclius sent an expedition which defeated the Persians and recaptured the cross.

Muslim conquest   Eighteen years later, Jerusalem fell into Muslim hands and the financial condition of the Christians became even more difficult. There is an interesting account, however, of how the conqueror Khalif Omar spared the church for the Christians by refusing to enter the building. Spreading his prayer mat before the eastern doors he prayed outside, for where the khalif prayed his people would pray likewise; had he entered, the church would have become a mosque and have been lost to the Christians. The khalif in fact behaved most mercifully to the Christians, in accordance with the Muslim tradition of reverence for Jesus, and allowed them to enter for services and prayer.

A great earthquake in 746 brought further destruction. What with the burden of Muslim taxation, the destruction wrought by the earthquake and the generally distressed condition of Europe, it looked as if the Christians might well not be able to find sufficient resources to keep the basilica standing at all. However, after an unhappy period the basilica was rescued in the ninth century by Charlemagne. He made an arrangement with the Khalif of Baghdad, under whose political control Jerusalem then was, by which the basilica was taken under Charlemagne's protection. He sent sums of money and workmen from abroad and under him Palestine enjoyed prosperity such as it had never known since the time of Justinian. The basilica was substantially restored with the aid of money from Europe.

In the tenth century things again took a turn for the worse. The power of the Abbasid Khalifs of Baghdad, who had recognised the sepulchre as a place holy to Muslims as well as to Christians, and had accepted responsibility for its proper care, declined. A rival khalifate was established by the Fatimids of Africa and the Muslim world fell into disruption. The followers of a Turkish general, who called himself the Ilshid, or prince, led raids into Palestine. Their marauding also made the pilgrim route to Mecca difficult and dangerous, so pious Muslims performed their obligation by making a pilgrimage to Jerusalem instead. Thus the Muslim population of Jerusalem increased; generally they were less tolerant and cultured than had been the rulers of the Abassid Khalifate, and relations between Christians and Muslims, previously cordial, became bitterly hostile. In 938, on Palm Sunday, rioting broke out; the Holy Sepulchre was damaged and the basilica pillaged. Later in the century, the Emperor Nicephorus Phocas succeeded in augmenting the prestige of the Byzantine empire and made an alliance with the Fatimid Khalif against the Turks, who were then the masters of Egypt and who also held Syria and Palestine. The effect of this alliance was greatly to increase the unpopularity of the Christians in Jerusalem. In 967, Muslims and Jews joined together to set light to the basilica, at the same time burning the patriarch. Early in the next century, in 1009, the fanatical and eccentric Khalif Hakim, whose policy was the destruction of all non-Muslim buildings, finally destroyed virtually all that remained of the basilica.

This destruction was of a very serious nature. The Holy Places were devastated. The Rock of the Holy Sepulchre was almost hammered to pieces and all that was left was the shelf of the tomb upon which the body of Jesus rested. We have a description of the devastation by a writer of the time who witnessed the desecration. For a period of thirty years the area lay waste and unoccupied. Pilgrims still came to the holy sites of Jerusalem and there are preserved writings of pilgrims of the time, which tell of the devastation and profanation to which the Holy Places were exposed; they

Devastation of the Tomb of Jesus

Within the Church of the Holy Sepulchre: up steps to the right in a first-floor chapel is the place of crucifixion on a level with the top of the mound, whose natural rock is to be seen below the altar.

tell also of the wretched conditions of their brother Christians. The Byzantine emperors, however, reacted to these outrages and succeeded in re-establishing a protectorate over Jerusalem.

In 1048 the Emperor Constantine Monomachus rebuilt the basilica. The restoration was on a far more modest scale than that of Constantine or even Modestus. The rotunda over the Holy Sepulchre was rebuilt with an apsed presbyterium towards the east so that the altar faced the sepulchre, and for the first time a chapel was erected on Golgotha. It was the Chapel of Adam, where the Rock of the Cross stood 'about a lance' high, above the surrounding floor. Above the vault of the present Calvary chapel there is a vault of Byzantine character, possibly from this restoration. This vault was once decorated with mosaics, of which there remains a very fine panel representing Christ in his glory. In the court to the east of the presbyterium apse was the Omphalos, or stone, which was supposed to mark the centre of the world. The place is still marked in the present basilica. Under the ruins, as they now were of Constantine's basilica, the crypt of St Helena still remained in spite of the destruction of the basilicas of Constantine and Modestus above it.

It was the basilica of Monomachus that the Crusaders found when they captured Jerusalem in 1099. The Crusaders built their own basilica, which in spite of eight hundred years of alternate neglect and pillage is still the basilica of today. A staircase connects the basilica with St Helena's Chapel beneath, and a triumphal arch connects it with the rotunda to the west. It was the Crusaders' design to bring together under a single roof the Rock of Calvary, the Tomb and the Place of the Finding of the Cross. The rotunda and the basilica, called the Chorus Dominorum, together formed a cathedral church. The rotunda to the west occupied the place of the nave, and the basilica the choir. Immediately to the east of the rotunda, or nave, a transept was built, in the south end of which was the main entrance. Immediately to the east of the rotunda was the crossing between the north and south transepts which carried the dome. Beyond the crossing and through the triumphal arch was the basilica, with aisles to the north and south of it. The Rock of the Cross was in a chapel immediately to the south of the south aisle, and immediately to the east of the main entrance. On the whole, the Crusaders preserved what they could from the Byzantine basilicas, repairing the Chapel of St Helena, and retaining a Byzantine dome and a row of columns. They tried to make allowance for the effect of earthquakes, of which they recorded six during the building of their church between 1099 and 1149. Despite subsequent damage by earthquakes, fire, neglect and bad repairs, the architecture, construction and workmanship of the Crusader church can still be admired, particularly following the recent and current restorations.

In that period of the Middle Ages it is interesting to notice a certain change in the relative importance attached by pilgrims to the two Holy Places, the Tomb and Calvary. From the first it was the Tomb which had been considered the more important, and a building was erected over it, whereas Calvary, while given emphasis, was a rock in an open court. It was only at this stage that a building came to be erected over Calvary. The place of the death of Jesus now seemed to become of equal or even greater importance than the place of his entombment, and it is now that we have the legend of the finding of the cross by St Helena assuming greater proportions. It is the crucifixion, rather than the resurrection, which at this time seems to have the greater emphasis. In the West the Church has always been known as the Church of the Holy Sepulchre, that is, where the dead Christ lay, whereas in the East it is known to this day as the Church of the Resurrection, the place of the empty tomb.

The Crusaders' rule did not long survive the completion of their church. It was dedicated in 1149. In 1187 the Crusaders were disastrously defeated at the Battle of Hattin and their kingdom was destroyed. The Christian authorities in desperation stripped the silver off the Shrine of the Tomb, in order to coin money with which to pay their troops, who were threatening to desert. They were defeated, however, and Saladin captured Jerusalem. Saladin accepted the high reverence for Jesus which the Muslim religion inculcated. He sternly forbade any desecration of the basilica, only stipulating that Christians should not be allowed to make pilgrimage. The Emperor Frederick II signed a truce with Saladin and Frederick crowned himself in the basilica, in 1229.

In 1244 there was a Tartar invasion. The Tartars had none of Saladin's respect for Christians or Christian Holy Places. They massacred the Christians and damaged the church. Fortunately they were not able to maintain themselves in Jerusalem. There followed a hundred years of neglect. In 1335, the basilica was in the charge of only three Greek monks. The Franciscans arrived in 1345 to share its custody. The keys of the basilica were held by Muslims and entrusted to the head of a single Muslim family, and the Muslims agreed to allow Christian pilgrimages, but reserved to themselves the right to regulate them and also to arbitrate between the rival claims of different Christian denominations. By 1400, not only Greeks and Latins but also Georgians, Armenians, Syrians, Copts and Abyssinians all had holdings in the church. The Procession of Palm Sunday and the ceremony of the Holy Fire were celebrated by all the denominations in common, and the church was open to all local Christians.

During the fifteenth century the dukes of Burgundy succeeded in winning for the Latins a privileged position, especially in regard to the edicule of the Holy Sepulchre, while the Greeks, Georgians, Armenians and Syrians had to be content with lesser allotments.

In 1555 a new edicule was erected over the Holy Sepulchre by the Latins, and in the last quarter of the sixteenth century most of the repairs were carried out by them. In the seventeenth century, the Greeks and the Armenians succeeded in somewhat strengthening their positions. In 1664, the Georgians were evicted from their chapels, being too poor to pay the necessary dues, and in 1668 the same fate befell the Abyssinians. In 1698 a French traveller, Canon Morison, recorded that the Coptic community

The Latin procession arrives at the entrance to the Tomb. A priest stands within the ante-chamber, next to the stone which symbolizes the Rolling Stone, that once closed the Sepulchre.

had been reduced to one priest. The Latins were, by the beginning of the eighteenth century, in a slightly better position than they are now. Substantially the various sanctuaries were then distributed as they still are today.

The dome over the sepulchre had been erected by the Emperor Monomachus in the middle of the eleventh century and its timber dated from that time. By the end of the seventeenth century it was in an entirely insecure condition. In 1719 it was agreed that the Greek patriarch Chrysanthos should be allowed to reduce the height of the bell tower, whose condition was endangering all the neighbouring structure, and to repair the parts under his control. The Latins, by a special firman obtained from the sultan by the French ambassador at Constantinople, got the right to repair the dome and some other structures under their control. In return for this concession the French released a hundred and fifty Turkish prisoners, whom they happened at the moment to be holding. Yet the very idea of repairs was unpopular with some of the inhabitants of Jerusalem and the governor of Jerusalem had to set a guard of three hundred Turkish soldiers over the men who were do the repair work so that, protected by their bayonets, the work might be completed. The timber was found to be in such an appalling condition that the pious held it to be a miracle that the dome had not come through the roof long ago. Belgian pine was imported and used as the timber for the repair, which followed the line of Monomachus' dome. It was covered by lead sheeting. The Turkish authorities insisted on an opening thirty feet in diameter and covered by a wire netting at the top of the dome. Plaster was put up where the mosaics had fallen down, or had been removed, or where the marble linings had been taken away by the Turks. In 1728, the edicule over the sepulchre was repaired. It was in 1757 that the Turks decided to solve certain disputes by imposing the code of the *Status Quo*, settling who had the right to do repairs, exactly how many lamps each denomination might hang at each particular place, and on how many feet of ground they might worship. This principle, of course, gave the Anglicans no technical status, but ever since the closing years of the last century the Greek patriarch, as an act of grace, has allowed them to hold services in the chapel of Abraham, which is above the site of Calvary.

In October 1808 a fire broke out in the Armenian chapel in the southern part of the upper gallery of the rotunda. It spread until the whole dome of the rotunda was destroyed and much damage was done, both to the marble floor and to the edicule of the sepulchre, as well as to the Greek choir and other masonry. The sepulchre itself, however, suffered no damage. The year 1808 was in the middle of the Napoleonic wars and western Europeans were, therefore, too busily engaged in fighting one another to have much leisure to devote to architectural restoration in Jerusalem. This gave the Greeks an opportunity to regain some of their privileges. In 1809 they obtained a firman from the Sultan Mahmoud II to repair the church. The work was entrusted to an architect from Mitylene, named Comnenos. New entrance doors were substituted for the old. The old steps of the apse were removed and the apse was largely rebuilt. Walls

Under Turkish rule

174.

Within the Tomb of Christ, there is a single loculus or slab (on the right). Each reconstruction follows the description of Bishop Eusebius of Caesarea, who was present at the original excavation and building of the Constantinian basilica.

were put up, cutting the transepts off from the basilica. The columns of the rotunda, which were badly calcined, were set in plaster. The ambulatory of the rotunda was blocked by a number af storerooms. A new edicule was built over the sepulchre, a new Stone of Unction was laid down and the tombs of the Latin kings were destroyed. Three arches were erected under the triumphal arch, which indeed did something to prevent the danger of collapse but were themselves a disfigurement (though of course the modern methods for reinforcing structures were not then known). These repairs saved the church from complete collapse, but the work was far from satisfactory. After fifty years the new dome which had been erected over the rotunda showed signs of collapse, and from 1863 to 1868 the work of reconstruction which saved it was carried out at the joint expense of France, Russia and Turkey.

Survey under the British Mandate In 1927 there was an exceptionally severe earthquake which left many of the walls cracked. The stone twelfth-century dome over the crossing of the basilica and transepts had to be demolished. The work of reconstruction showed that the whole church was in an insecure condition and that it was necessary to carry out a total investigation. This task was entrusted by the British mandatory government to Mr William Harvey. An

exhaustive and detailed report confirmed the security of the foundations, but indicated the poor quality of mortar used in the twelfth century which had almost everywhere decayed, leaving dangerous cavities and allowing stone to sink. Such faults, of course, greatly increased the dangers likely to be caused by earthquake or fire. The original builder had used no true buttresses. The main cause of movement arose from the weight of the dome over the basilica and from the roof of the rotunda. As a result, however, of the inter-denominational friction, the coming of the war and the political situation after the war, very little was done. When, after the Jordanian occupation of the old city of Jerusalem, there was a further fire, King Abdullah of Jordan carried through the necessary repairs himself. During the Jordanian rule, King Hussein also threatened to carry out further repairs himself, saying that his only concern would be to obtain the agreement of the Christian denominations for what he was doing. The difficulties of doing this, however, proved too formidable and in 1955 he abandoned the policy and threw back the responsibility once more upon the Christian denominations. Whether it was the awakening of an ecumenical spirit, or shame that a Muslim monarch should have to threaten to save the first church of Christendom, the Christian denominations have at last united to produce and implement a scheme of extensive repairs and restoration.

The last ten years, in spite of the political difficulties, have been years of exploration and progress. New excavations have brought to light new discoveries. Some traces of the walls of Hadrian's old pre-Christian temple have been found in the south transept. An eleventh-century courtyard or colonnade has been revealed. It has been found that the north transept wall was not quite parallel with the south transept wall, and this has led to the speculation that, from the earliest building, it was believed that the so-called Prison of Christ was a place to be preserved. The intermixture

The Greek Orthodox ceremony of the feet-washing is conducted within the courtyard of the Holy Sepulchre. Here the Patriarch is surrounded by his clergy.

Repairs initiated by the Jordanian government

of Constantinian and Crusader pillar work has been shown. The work of restoration is now going forward according to plan and we can look forward to a day, when the scaffolding will all at last be gone, and the great Church of the Holy Sepulchre will be visible in all the magnificence for which its makers intended it.

This chapter would not be complete without reference to the respective Eastern and Western Calendars in Jerusalem, as well as some mention of the more colourful Easter ceremonies which take place today within the Church of the Holy Sepulchre.

Eastern liturgies in Holy Week The old Julian Calendar, once universal in the Christian Church, is used by the Orthodox Churches today. In the sixteenth century, at the order of Pope Gregory XIII, a new system of reckoning was adopted. This Gregorian Calendar has found acceptance within the Western Churches.

Both East and West observe as Easter the first Sunday after the full moon falling on or after 21 March. As their calendars differ, however, so their dates of 21 March differ and even sometimes, therefore, the moon by which they place their festival. The Eastern Churches still observe the rule of the Council of Nicaea that Easter may never precede or coincide with the Jewish Passover. The West has abandoned this rule a long time ago.

On their Good Friday, the Greeks enact the ceremony of the Entombment of Jesus within the Holy Sepulchre on the actual sites concerned, going in procession first to Calvary, then on to the Stone of Anointing and finally into the Tomb of Christ. The Armenian entombment at St James' begins at 3 pm, the Syrian entombment in the sepulchre at 4 pm. All these services are vivid portrayals of the burial of Christ.

On Holy Saturday the central ceremony is the 'Holy Fire', in which the Greek and Armenian patriarchs take part in procession with their Syrian and Coptic equivalents. The service symbolises the resurrection when Christ, the Light of the World, emerged from his tomb. Although the service begins at noon, most of the people will have spent the night in the Holy Sepulchre. All branches of the Eastern Churches mingle in a deafening din, penetrated by the ululation of the women and the shouts of the men dancing. The lights are extinguished, the tomb sealed and guarded. At last, after endless processions, the Orthodox patriarch enters the tomb with an Armenian monk, while outside a breathless suspense holds the crowded multitude. Inside, they pray and then thrust out through a 'port-hole' on the south side a lighted torch, from which the first candles are lit. Within seconds the whole rotunda is a blaze of moving and waving fire.

Another unique ceremony on the Saturday night, at 8 pm, is the Abyssinian 'Searching for the Body of Christ' on the roof of St Helena's Chapel. Here all the colour of the Ethiopians is to be seen in the vestments, umbrellas, symbols and drums of this primitive rite.

The Eastern liturgies then begin, before the Tomb of Christ, the Greeks from 11.30 pm that night to 2 am, the Armenians from 4 am to 7 am, while the Russians in their own cathedral have processions, matins and finally liturgy from 1 am to 5 am. The visitor will do well to begin in the sepulchre with the Greeks, then go on to the Russian cathedral if he can get there, before returning to the Armenians in the sepulchre. He should not fail to enjoy the wonderful music of the Russians and the atmosphere of expectancy and triumph within the crowded sepulchre. Only those who have spent Holy Week in Jerusalem can know the unforgettable thrill of the experience.

It is at night, however, that the strange and true life of the basilica is discovered. At sundown, the church is shut to the outside world. The Muslim doorkeeper locks the door from the outside, passes a ladder through a square trap to a priest who receives it and locks the church from the inside. As the night begins, there is no light in all the church except for the candles that continually shine before Calvary, the sepulchre and the Stone of Unction. Then, a little before eleven o'clock, lights begin to flicker up. The priests of the various denominations, who have been sleeping about the building in curious dormitories, are coming out for their evening devotions. The Greeks appear on a balcony above the Rock of Calvary; the Franciscans emerge from a tunnel beyond the Latin chapel; the Armenians down an iron staircase above the Stabat Mater. Three bearded sacristans appear and begin to trim the lamps. A sound of door-banging and electric bells is heard. At 11.30 as the ceremonies begin, two vested thurifers appear and proceed around the church incensing every one of the altars.

At midnight the night offices begin, the Latin severe and restrained, the Armenian exuberant and musical. The Latin office is the shortest and when it is completed the Franciscans file off to their tunnel; the Greeks and Armenians sing on. Then begins to permeate through the building the smell of newly baked bread, as the priests of the Eastern rites cook the bread for their morning masses. The Latins, the Greeks and the Armenians say mass every day. The Copts say it on certain days at an altar against the outer wall. The Syrians have a service on Sundays. The Abyssinians perform their liturgy in their homely little church on the roof. The Greeks and Armenians say their masses first. After the Armenians have finished, the Latins say their mass at about 3.30. There is no room within the tomb for more than one priest and his server. Other worshippers kneel outside this claustrophobic little chamber with its single luculus and its antechamber, called the Chapel of the Angels, containing a token of the rolling stone, on which the Angel sat on the first Easter morning.

When all is finished, the ladder is passed out again through the trap-door, the key handed out to the Muslim doorkeeper and the doors thrown open. The public congregation can come in, for the Latin mass in the sepulchre at 4.30, and other masses follow at all the various altars of Calvary, the Chapel of the Franks and the Latin chapel. At dawn, the worshipper steps out into the street, to be greeted by the cry from the near-by Muslim mosque, 'There is no God but Allah and Muhammad is His Prophet!'

At the Eastern Ceremony of the Holy Fire on Holy Saturday, the light of Christ emerges from the tomb to be passed round to every worshipper from candle to candle amid tumultuous excitement.

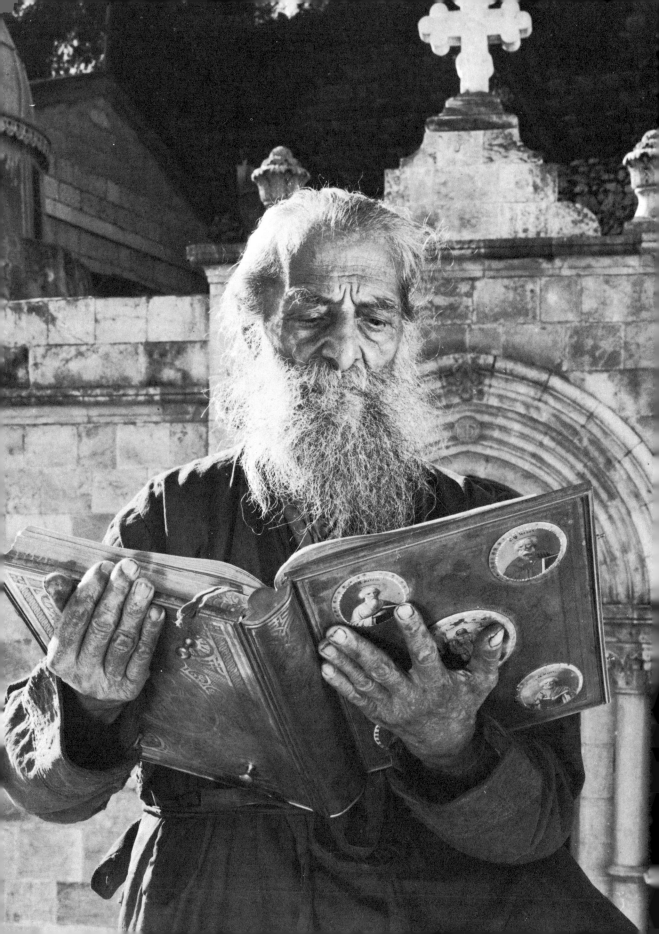

12 The Apostolic Tradition in Jerusalem

THE MOUNT OF OLIVES IS THE NATURAL STARTING POINT AMONG those Holy Places sanctified by the apostolic tradition and linked with the lives of Mary, the Mother of Jesus, and the Apostles. St Luke tells us, in both his gospel and in the Acts of the Apostles, that it was here that Jesus took leave of his followers and commissioned them, his Apostles, to the world. It is not surprising, therefore, that many Christian pilgrims today begin and end their visit to Jerusalem with a glimpse of the magnificent panorama of the Holy City from the Mount of Olives. Indeed, the very first goal of all early Christian pilgrimages was the Mount of Olives. To Graeco-Roman Christian pilgrims, the Jewish Temple destroyed in the year 70 was not of primary interest. The sites of the crucifixion and of the resurrection had been desecrated and covered by the pagan shrines to Venus and Jupiter, erected at the order of the Emperor Hadrian, and the sites of the Upper Room on the western hill, and of the Ascension on the Mount of Olives, were more easily approached and venerated.

> All believers in Christ flock together from all quarters of the earth [wrote Eusebius], not, as of old, to behold the beauty of Jerusalem, but that they may abide there and both hear the story of Jerusalem and also worship at the Mount of Olives over against Jerusalem, whither the glory of the Lord removed itself, leaving the earlier city. There also, according to the published record, the feet of Our Lord and Saviour, who was Himself the Word and through it took upon Himself human form, stood upon the Mount of Olives near the cave which is now pointed out there.

The pre-Constantinian Christian paid this honour to the Mount of Olives because Jerusalem, Aelia Capitolina, was not a holy, but a pagan and desecrated city. After the building of the Basilica of the Sepulchre and the Resurrection, all was changed and the Mount of Olives no longer had the place of honour. Yet it was still a popular place of pilgrimage.

Emperor Constantine, in the course of the fourth century, fulfilling the wishes of his mother St Helena, enshrined the Christian Holy Places in Palestine within three magnificent basilicas: the grotto where Christ was born, in the basilica at Bethlehem; Calvary and the Tomb of Christ, in

A priest of the Orthodox Church at the Holy Sepulchre.

the basilica of the Holy Sepulchre in Jerusalem; the cave where Christ foretold the end of the world and his return, in the basilica of Eleona on Mount Olivet, close to the scene of his ascension.

We have traced in chapters five and eleven the history of both the basilica at Bethlehem and that of the Holy Sepulchre. The Eleona basilica was destroyed by the Persians in 614, partly restored by the Crusaders in the twelfth century, and thereafter lost until the early years of this century. The gospel of St Matthew describes Jesus revealing his vision of the end of the world to his Apostles, on the Mount of Olives, on the Tuesday in Holy Week.

Constantinian basilica on the Mount of Olives

> When he was sitting on the Mount of Olives, the disciples came to speak to him privately. 'Tell us,' they said, 'when will this happen? And what will be the signal for your coming and the end of the age?' Jesus answered: 'Then will appear in heaven the sign that heralds the Son of Man. All the peoples of the world will make lamentation, and they will see the Son of Man coming on the clouds of heaven with great power and glory. With a trumpet blast he will send out his angels, and they will gather his chosen from the four winds, from the farthest bounds of heaven on every side'.

The sheikh of the Mosque of the Ascension, on the Mount of Olives, with the Crusader edicule, topped by the dome, behind which rises the Russian Tower of the Ascension.

As the gospels mention the summit of the Mount of Olives as the place where Jesus gave these teachings, the first generations of Christians held for certain that it was in the natural cave we find there still. It is, therefore, obvious why Constantine chose this site to build the third great basilica in the Holy Land: the Eleona, so called from a colloquial Greek word for 'Olive', over the traditional cave mentioned by Eusebius.

Today, Brunot describes the scale of this Constantinian basilica, which resembled those at Bethlehem and Calvary in that it enclosed atrium, nave, choir and cave-crypt:

> Going up Mount Olivet, on coming from Gethsemane, the fourth-century pilgrim reached an imposing staircase leading to a vast platform; there, rising eastwards, was the basilica. As at Bethlehem and the Anastasis, here was a fine atrium, approximately thirty metres by twenty-five metres, with covered galleries along the sides and a large underground cistern in the middle. Three doors gave access to the church. This measured thirty metres long and twenty metres wide inside; with walls one and a half metres thick at the base and as much as two metres in the apse. It surrounded and enshrined the memorable cave which, like that of Bethlehem, lay beneath the choir, reached from the north by steps which the excavators found intact. Altogether the building had an overall length of over seventy metres and covered an area of seventeen hundred metres. Knowing how gorgeously decorated were both the basilicas of the Nativity and the Anastasis, we can imagine what this third one must have been. Eusebius tells us that 'the Emperor had adorned it with his usual lavishness, decking it in resplendent ornamentation'.

Brunot further describes the magnificent liturgy within this basilica:

182

On Tuesday in Holy Week, the Christian community in Jerusalem gathered there to commemorate the mystery of the Coming of the Lord. The bishop entered the holy grotto, carrying the gospels, and read out the Master's eschatological discourse. They returned in the evening of Maundy Thursday to read again the last Words of Jesus, and to commemorate the ascension which had taken place close by. Again during the octaves of Easter and that of the Epiphany they reassembled, in order to call to mind those manifestations of Christ which foreshadowed his last manifestation.

The early Maundy Thursday processions to the Garden of Gethsemane, to the Cave of the Arrest and the Rock of the Agony, began from the Eleona basilica.

It was in 1910 that the White Fathers, excavating on a property purchased by the Princesse de la Tour d'Auvergne in 1868, revealed the entire foundations of the Byzantine basilica. In 1920 the foundation stone of a new basilica, on the same foundations, was laid by the French Cardinal Dubois. Under the supervision of Père Vincent, plans were drawn up for as close a reproduction of the first basilica as possible, but these still remain to be completed.

In 380, Aetheria differentiated clearly between the 'Church in Eleona' and the shrine 'on the Hill', where solemn services were also held. According to another pilgrim, Peter the Iberian, a round open courtyard had been built on the very hill-top by a Roman lady called Pomenia in about 378, on the traditional site of the ascension of Jesus. Arculf describes it as 'having in its circuit three vaulted porticos roofed over' and surrounding an open space. The Crusaders built, over the ruins of the Byzantine shrine, an octagon whose remains still encircle the site. Within the Crusader court an edicule was built to enclose a rock in the very centre of the octagon which was long linked with the place of ascension.

In 1187 the Muslims transformed the shrine of the ascension into a mosque, themselves venerating the place of the ascension of Jesus. Today, Christians are allowed to celebrate within the courtyard and there are Greek, Latin, Armenian, Coptic and Syrian altars round the walls, besides a small central domed shrine.

The Mount of Olives was, so far as is known, not built upon in the time of Jesus. In Byzantine times it became the site of many monasteries and nunneries. Melania built two convents for religious to pray night and day 'in the Church of the Ascension and in the cave where the Lord had talked with his disciples about the end of the world'; that is the crypt of the Eleona basilica. By 570, the pilgrim Placenza saw the mountain covered with convents, all of which were destroyed by the Persians in 614, when 1,207 Christians were killed. Modestus restored the hill-top shrine of the ascension in the seventh century and convents were rebuilt around it.

Today, also, many branches of the Christian Church own properties near the crest of the Mount of Olives. Both the Greek and Latin patriarchates look down on the city from different points along the ridge. The Latin Carmelite convent and Church of the Pater Noster have already been mentioned (see p. 145). One of the most imposing properties is the Russian compound, east of the Byzantine site of the ascension. The Russian tower of six storeys can be seen from the Dead Sea and sometimes from the Mountains of Gilead. There are two fine churches within this compound, one of which encloses a Byzantine mosaic and an ancient Armenian inscription. To the north-west of the Russian compound is the 'Vineyard of the Hunter'. Here is the Greek patriarchate and the chapel of Viri Galilaei which is supposed to mark the spot on which the two men in white apparel stood and told the Apostles, as 'men of Galilee', that they would see Jesus descending again, in his day of glory, from the clouds into which he had just ascended.

There is every reason to believe that Mary the Mother of Jesus shared with the Apostles the events of Pentecost. Mary occupies a unique place in the affection and devotion of the more catholic branches of the Christian Church, both of the East and the West. Mary is to them what Abraham is to both Jews and Muslims: the person whose obedience to and acceptance of God's call and commission brought blessing to his people. To Christians also, Mary was the ark by which God became present among his people, in the person of Jesus. Consequently, the place of her birth, traditionally the Church of St Anne her mother, the place of her 'falling asleep' or Dormition, on the western hill, and the tomb in which she rested in the Kedron ravine before her assumption into heaven, are greatly venerated in Jerusalem.

The history of the Church of St Anne is closely linked with that of the Pool of Bethesda. The church is traditionally built over the home of Joachim and Anna, the parents of Mary. Both in Aramaic and Hebrew the word 'Bethesda' means 'House of Mercy'. St Jerome and Bishop Eusebius interpreted it as 'House of Effusion', which is also the meaning of the word 'Anna'. A large Byzantine basilica appears on the Madeba Mosaic at the site of the present church.

The Church of St Anne

St John says that the pool was by the Sheep Gate. Some suggest that the Greek word for Sheep Gate is itself the corruption of an Aramaic word for 'baths'. Of many suggested sites for the Pool of Bethesda, that under the present Church of St Anne is the most interesting. Excavations show that twin pools, separated by and surrounded by cloisters, were built over by a large church, in about AD 530. Both pools and church fell into ruins following the Persian invasion of 614, but were restored by the Crusaders, who shortened and covered in the pools, building a church of 'St Mary in the Sheep Market' over the top. Then the pools and church were destroyed and lost, until discovered by the French after the Crimean War. The neighbouring Crusader Church of St Anne was offered to and declined by Queen Victoria in favour of the island of Cyprus!

The present Crusader Church of St Anne, though showing signs of some reconstruction, survived the Saracen occupation. It was requisitioned by order of Saladin for a Muslim school of theology. It was restored by the French and in 1878 handed over to the care of the White Fathers of Cardinal Lavigerie. They have continued with the excavations to this

The deep excavations of the Church of St Mary in the Sheep Market and the twin Pools of Bethesda reveal a mass of Byzantine and Crusader ruins below the magnificent Crusader church of St Anne.

day. Beneath their Crusader church are a series of crypt-caves, recalling the house and living conditions of the family of Mary, the Mother of Jesus.

The great modern church and convent of the Dormition stand on the traditional site of the house of St John, where Mary the Mother of Jesus 'fell asleep'. The German Emperor Wilhelm II laid the foundation stone, on his visit to Jerusalem in 1898, and the consecration took place ten years later.

Beneath the magnificent Romanesque tower, dome and choir, where the German Benedictines at their offices are a constant inspiration to Christian pilgrims, is the dark 'Crypt of Mary's Sleep'. Here, the statue of the Virgin recumbent is looked down upon by the heroines of the Old Testament.

East of the viaduct on which the Jericho road crosses the Kedron is an ancient church, now almost buried by the accumulation of centuries of rubble in the bottom of the ravine. A fourth-century tradition records how the body of Mary, the Mother of Jesus, was brought here from the house of St John on Mount Zion, for burial. A slightly later tradition records how from here she was assumed soul and body into heaven, three days after burial. As in the case of the Holy Sepulchre, her rock tomb was

The medieval tiling in the Armenian patriarchal Cathedral of St James, with which the whole cathedral is surrounded to a height of four feet.

excavated and its shell left standing within a basilica, about AD 440. It is perhaps this basilica that is also to be seen on the Madeba Mosaic, outside the eastern wall, in the Kedron. '

The present church, in the form of a Latin cross, has a Crusader porch, the gift of Millicent, Queen of Fulke the eighth king of Jerusalem. She was also buried here in 1161. The Franciscans were entrusted with the care of this shrine until 1757, when it was ceded to the Eastern Churches. Today the tomb of Mary is a tiny rock chamber surrounded by Armenian, Greek and Syrian altars – besides also a Muslim prayer niche in honour of Mary, the Mother of Jesus.

Among the Apostles of Jesus were James and John, the sons of the Galilean fisherman Zebedee. It is this John, the youngest of the Apostles, who cared for Mary the Mother of Jesus and who is reputed to have lived on the western hill. Another tradition links John with the early Christian Church in Ephesus, from which he is said to have been exiled to the lonely, rocky island of Patmos. There he reputedly spent years as a convict in a chain gang at work in the stone quarries, having been deported as a Christian agitator from the pagan city of Ephesus, the 'Benares' of the Mediterranean world of the first century. His brother, James, was the first of the Apostles to die, executed by Herod as recorded in the Acts of the Apostles. James, the 'brother' of Jesus, became the first bishop of the early Christian Church, at its headquarters on the western hill, and presided at its first council, whose minutes are recorded in the fifteenth chapter of the Acts.

On the western hill today, and just within the present city wall, is the Armenian quarter, whose inhabitants belong to an ancient and distinctive race coming from the southern Caucasus. There is a style about all things Armenian, from their architecture to the conical head-dress of their clergy, representing, it is said, the cone of Mount Ararat in their native Armenia. The Armenian Church and the Armenian nation are co-terminous and have been established in Palestine since the fourth century. Their cathedral church is dedicated to the two St James's and dates from the twelfth century. Their magnificent patriarchate looks out on to a garden of pine trees, on the site of Herod's citadel gardens.

Within the cathedral porch are two ancient knockers or gongs, with which the community was summoned to prayer when the Christians were forbidden the use of bells by the Muslims. One of these knockers, or enormous planks suspended on chains, was of iron, the other of wood. The lofty cathedral is decorated with glorious blue tiling. On the north side is the Shrine of St James, the brother of John. It is an exquisite little chapel of tortoiseshell inlaid with mother-of-pearl, below whose altar is said to be preserved the head of St James, the first Apostle-martyr. Before the high altar of the cathedral is the traditional throne of St James, but the patriarchs, as a mark of humility, always take the chair beside it. There is another ancient chapel on the north side, which is used as a sacristy. The treasure of the Armenian convent is reputed to be a fabulous collection of gold and silver plate, jewelled vestments and priceless manuscripts, among which is the royal insignia of the last Armenian king, Haytun, of the thirteenth century. The Armenian Church and culture are a strange blend of antiquity and modernity, a blend which is reflected in the beauty of its Church's Gregorian music and ceremonial and the remarkable business acumen of its people.

The first martyr of the early Christian Church was not the Apostle James, but the Deacon Stephen, who was stoned outside the city wall by men who put down their coats at the feet of Saul of Tarsus, later to become the Apostle Paul. There are two conflicting traditions of the place of the stoning of Stephen. The earlier locates it to the north of the present city wall in the neighbourhood of the Beth ha-Sekelah, mentioned in the Mishnah. In the year 415 his tomb was 'identified' in the area of Geth Gemal, thirty-five kilometres south-west of Jerusalem, by the priest Lucian. In 460, the Empress Eudocia built a basilica on the traditional stoning place, to the north of the city, to which his relics were transferred and where the empress herself was buried, near her patron Stephen. The basilica was destroyed in 637, rebuilt two centuries later, restored by the Crusaders, but later demolished deliberately in order that it should not serve Saladin as a fortress from which to attack the Damascus Gate. In 1881 the Dominicans acquired the site and excavated the ruins of the fifth-century basilica, on which they built their present church, consecrated in 1900. Here, today, is the renowned École Biblique.

Sites linked with St Stephen

The later tradition locating the stoning of Stephen in the Kedron ravine, where the Jericho road crosses the valley on a low viaduct, dates from Crusader times. This tradition, however, accounts for the association with St Stephen of the only gate opening into the east wall of the Old City today. The Arabic name for this gate is 'The Gate of the Lady Mary', linking that immediate area with the birth of Mary at St Anne's, and her assumption, from the tomb in the Kedron ravine. Today a Greek Orthodox oratory stands on the Crusader-traditional site of the stoning of St Stephen.

The last words of Jesus to his followers, recorded in the Acts of the Apostles, are: 'You will bear witness for me in Jerusalem, all over Judaea and Samaria, and away to the ends of the earth.' St Matthew adds: 'Be assured, I am with you always, to the end of time.' So it was that with this sense of the presence of their risen and ascended Lord, Jesus, the Apostles went out into the world. Beginning from Jerusalem on the day of Pentecost, they burst – like seeds from a pod – Philip to Samaria and Gaza, Peter to Lydda, Jaffa, Caesarea and later to Rome, John to Ephesus, Andrew to Achaia, Bartholomew to Armenia, Thaddaeus to Egypt, Thomas to India. With the conversion of St Paul, the gospel reached round the Mediterranean to Antioch, Athens and Rome – literally, throughout the known world, 'to the ends of the earth'. All but one of the Apostles died as martyrs. Their monuments are not so much hewn stones as human hearts. As St Peter, their leader, put it, they are 'living stones, built up into a spiritual temple, a holy priesthood, to offer spiritual sacrifices acceptable to God'.

The Greek Orthodox Patriarch on his throne in the Catholicos, or Cathedral, within the Church of the Holy Sepulchre at Jerusalem.

13 The Prophet in the Land of the Bible

PALESTINE IS ONLY A LITTLE TO THE NORTH OF ARABIA AND FOLLOW-ing the fall of Samaria in 721 and Jerusalem in 587 BC, it is highly likely that Jewish merchants travelled to the Arabian peninsula. There, the Ishmaelites and the descendants of Abraham, through Keturah, had journeyed long since, as commercial pioneers, and had retained a memory of the God of their father Abraham.

The tribes of Arabia were really nature worshippers, in a world peopled with spirits good and bad. Following their great dispersion in the year 70, some Jews again moved southwards and founded colonies in the towns of Arabia. In the sixth century there were three or four Jewish tribes around the city of Medina, but they kept their own religion of the one God, their Law and Prophets, to themselves. The Arabs respected the Jews for their sacred books and their prophet Moses, but it never ocurred to the Arabs that they should leave their tribal customs to obey the law of Moses. It did not occur to the Jews to ask their pagan brothers to do so.

The Christians took the gospel of Jesus to the Aramaic-speaking tribes in the north of the peninsula, but do not appear to have translated the gospel into Arabic. There is considerable evidence, however, of early Christian initiative in Arabia: five bishoprics in the province of Najtan, the attendance of Arab bishops at the Council of Nicaea in 325, three Christian kingdoms and the Arabic gospel of the Infancy. It was a Christian bishop, Quss ibn Sa'ada, who originated the Arabic script. Muhammad himself learned much from the Christian Waraqa ibn Naufal. The Arabs respected the Christians, as also having a book from the great God, whom they worshipped at the ordained times throughout the twenty-four hours. Christian tribes even fought alongside Muslims in the early days of Arab expansion.

The eastern doorway of the Dome of the Rock within the Temple Area. The magnificent blue tiles were brought at the command of Suleiman the Second in the sixteenth century from Kasham in Persia.

The Quran bears witness to the strength of Hebrew traditions and the respect for the Hebrew prophets, among the Arabs. The Quranic testimony to Jesus, Son of Mary, means that Jesus was an important historical figure on both sides of the Red Sea. The fact remains, however, that for nearly six hundred years after the coming of Jesus, the greater part of Arabia remained pagan, without book, without vision, without prophet, without single ruler or plan to unite the tribes. This was not from a failure of Christian apostolic fervour, so much as from the later weakness and

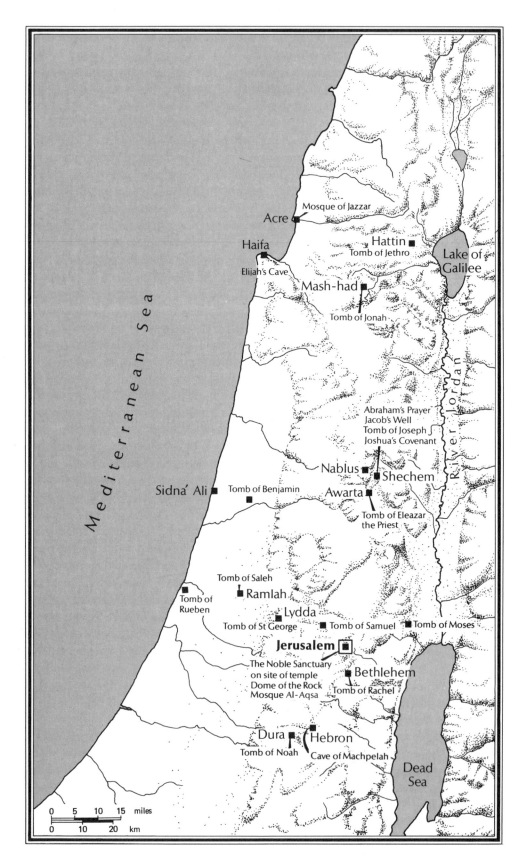

Mediterranean Sea

Mosque of Jazzar
Acre

Haifa
Elijah's Cave

Hattin
Tomb of Jethro

Lake of
Galilee

Mash-had

Tomb of Jonah

River Jordan

Abraham's Prayer
Jacob's Well
Tomb of Joseph
Joshua's Covenant

Nablus
Shechem

Sidna' Ali
Tomb of Benjamin

Awarta

Tomb of Eleazar
the Priest

Tomb of Saleh

Tomb of
Rueben

Ramlah

Lydda

Tomb of St George
Tomb of Samuel
Tomb of Moses

Jerusalem

The Noble Sanctuary
on site of temple
Dome of the Rock
Mosque Al-Aqsa

Bethlehem

Tomb of Rachel

Dura
Tomb of Noah

Hebron

Cave of Machpelah

Dead
Sea

0   5   10   15   miles
0   10   20   km

divisions of Christian witness all round the Mediterranean world. It was, then, in the city of Mecca that Muhammad was born to be the prophet and ruler of his people. His followers became Muslim, submitting to Allah, a brotherhood bound together by another sacred book, the Quran.

> The people of Moses and the people of Jesus were given revelations,
> But alas! they played false with their own lights, and in their selfishness, made narrow God's universal message.
> To them it seemed incredible that His light should illumine Arabia and reform the world.
> But his ways are wondrous, and they are clear to those who have Faith.
> If the People of the Book rely upon Abraham, let them study his history. His posterity included both Israel and Ismail.
> Abraham was a righteous man of God, a Muslim, and so were his children. For God is the God of all Peoples.   (Sura 2. 47 and 48)

Judaism and Islam

The chief task of the early Hebrew prophets was to combat syncretism, the dilution of the worship of the one, Yahweh, with the fertility cults of the many, Baalim. Following conquest by Joshua, the nomadic Hebrew tribesmen adapted themselves to an agricultural mode of life, reverting to a settled pattern by which the tent was replaced by the house and the tent circle became the walled town. To a certain extent, the pagan Canaanite religion and worship on the high places was absorbed into the worship of Yahweh. It was the genius of the Hebrews to link their agricultural festivals with their national historical commemorations, thus sanctifying the former and celebrating fully the latter.

By contrast, it has been said that the genius of Islam was precisely in its gift of syncretism. Islam's veneer of monotheism, upon those of Judaism and Christianity, covers a Canaanite paganism, successfully proclaiming the oneness of God among many primitive peoples in a way that both convinces and satisfies: 'There is no god but Allah – [*the* God]: Muhammad is the Apostle of Allah!' As one who broke away from the primitive animism and idolatry of Arabia, Muhammad was inspired or possessed by the spirit of Abraham, who himself broke away from the idolatry of Mesopotamia. The word 'muslim', 'submitted' or 'dedicated', seemed to Muhammad a highly appropriate term for his ancestor, Abraham. Indeed, it was from the six sons by his wife Keturah (Genesis 25), that Abraham is said to have fathered the desert tribes, as well as by their cousins, the Ishmaelites.

Folklore and local traditions

Today, when the primitive features of Palestinian life are disappearing so quickly and so much folklore is being lost, the innumerable Muslim shrines in the villages, on the hills, in the valleys and fields, are not easily found. There is hardly a village that does not honour at least one local saint. The village of Anata, north of Jerusalem, possesses seven shrines, and Awarta, south of Nablus, fourteen, to mention but two villages. Today these shrines of holy Muslims are often to be found in cemeteries, surrounded by the bodies of those who valued their protection even in death. Sometimes there is no building, only a 'maqam', the site or station of an event in the life of a 'wali' or saint. It may be a single tree, a large rock or

Map showing the Muslim Holy Places.

a heap of stones, a watercourse, a spring or even a cistern, which local tradition over the centuries has led people to venerate. Where there is a building, it may be a rectangular shrine, with or without a tomb; it may be a tomb within an enclosure or even without any protection; it may be a simple cave. If it is a tomb, it will be likely to be covered by a 'qubba', or dome. The word suggests a pavilion, tent or tabernacle in which to shelter. The 'cupola' comes to us from the Arabic, through the Italian. The functional use of the 'qubba' is to run water off a flat roof for conservation in a hot climate; the Arabic word 'qubba' means rain-drop!

The rites and practices at such shrines are of an infinite variety, from the most simple prayers and offerings in money or kind, to animal sacrifice, the taking of religious vows and circumcision. The saints commemorated will in all likelihood have been good, trustworthy elders of their local community, who by their spiritual lives and devotional practices deserve respect as possible mediators between the simple people and Allah, the Holy One.

In Arabic, the word for a building for public worship, 'masjid', suggests a place of kneeling and prostration; it develops from the same root as the word for 'prayer-carpet'. The Psalmist says: 'O come, let us worship and *fall down* and *kneel* before the Lord, our Maker'. The same word is used for the bowing, kneeling and subjection of the camel for the mounting of

The Tomb of Joseph at Shechem near to Jacob's Well, where by tradition his bones were brought from Egypt for burial.

Mosques,
sanctuaries,
and shrines

194

its rider. It is not dificult to see how the Arabic 'masjid' has come through the Spanish 'mesquito' to reach us as 'mosque'. The focal point within the mosque is the 'mihrab', or prayer niche, which indicates the 'qibla', or direction to be faced when praying. The last and most important holy place is the 'haram', or sanctuary, in Hebrew 'herem'. The word is equivalent to the Latin 'sacer' and the Greek 'hieros', implying 'consecrated to God', or 'forbidden ground'. The sacrifice of Jericho by Joshua had to be complete because Jericho was 'herem', consecrated to Yahweh. Similarly, Moses at the burning bush had to remove his shoes, for he was standing on 'holy ground'. Hence, too, the women's apartments in the Muslim household are 'harīm', forbidden ground.

The Night Journey To the Muslims Jerusalem is known as 'Al Quds', 'the Holy'. Quite apart from its associations with the Old Testament figures, Abraham, David, Solomon and others whom they venerate, the Muslims cherish a strong traditional connection between Jerusalem and the Prophet Muhammad. The tradition of the Prophet's Night Journey is alluded to in the Quran thus: 'I declare the glory of Him who transported His servant by night from the Masjid al-Haram (the mosque at Mecca) to the Masjid al-Aqsa (the further mosque) at Jerusalem.' Here is meant the whole area of 'the Noble Sanctuary', not just the main building of the Aqsa which, in the Prophet's days, did not exist.

According to the received account, Muhammad was on this occasion mounted on the winged steed called Al-Burak – 'the Lightning' – and, with the Angel Gabriel for escort, was carried from Mecca, first to Sinai and then to Bethlehem, after which they came to Jerusalem. 'And when we reached Bait al-Makdis, the Holy City', so runs the tradition mentioned in the Chronicle of Ibu Al-Attir, 'we came to the gate of the mosque and here Jibrail caused me to dismount. And he tied up Al-Burak to a ring, to which the prophets of old had also tied their steeds.'

Entering the Haram Area by the gateway, afterwards known as the Gate of the Prophet, Muhammad and Gabriel went up to the Sacred Rock, which from ancient times had stood in the centre of Solomon's Temple; meeting there a group of prophets, Muhammad proceeded to perform his prayer-prostrations before this assembly of his predecessors – Abraham, Moses, Jesus, and other of God's apostles. From the Sacred Rock, Muhammad, accompanied by Gabriel, next ascended by a ladder of light up into heaven; here, in anticipation, he was vouchsafed a vision of the delights of Paradise. Passing through the seven heavens, Muhammad at last stood in the presence of Allah, from whom he received injunctions on the prayers his followers were to perform. Thence, after a while, he descended again to earth; and alighting from the ladder of light stood again on the Sacred Rock at Jerusalem. The return homeward was made after the same fashion – on the back of the steed Al-Burak – and the Prophet reached Mecca again before the night had waned. Such is the tradition which sanctifies Jerusalem, the Rock and the Haram, or Sanctuary area, in the sight of all Muslims. After the capitulation of Jerusalem to Omar in 635, that khalif caused a mosque to be built on what was considered to be the ancient site of the Temple of David.

In the early days of Islam – that is, under Omar and his successors – mosques were constructed of wood and sun-dried bricks and other such perishable materials, so that of the building erected in Omar's days, probably very little remained even half a century later to be incorporated into the magnificent stone mosque erected by the orders of the Omayyad khalif, 'Abd al-Malik, in about the year 690. It seems probable, also, that this latter khalif, when he began to rebuild the Aqsa, made use of the materials which lay to hand in the ruins of the great St Mary's Church of Justinian, which must originally have stood on approximately the same site on which the Aqsa Mosque was raised.

The Aqsa Mosque within the Haram

The Chronicles make no mention of the date or fact of 'Adb al-Malik's rebuilding of the Aqsa Mosque, and the earliest detailed description of this mosque is that given by Muqaddasi in 985, some three centuries after 'Abd al-Malik's days. Of the Dome of the Rock, on the other hand, we possess detailed accounts in the older authorities, describing both the foundation in 691 and its general appearance. It would appear that the Arab chroniclers and the travellers who visited the Haram Area during this period were more impressed by the magnificence of the Dome of the Rock than by the main buildings of the Aqsa Mosque, of which the Dome of the Rock was in fact but an adjunct.

Jamal ad-Din Ahmad describes in 1351 how, in 746, the Aqsa was destroyed by earthquake and rebuilt by the Khalif Al-Mansur. This restoration by Al-Mansur was probably completed by 771, for in that year the Chronicles of Tabari and of Ibn al-Athir inform us that Al-Mansur visited Jerusalem and prayed in the mosque. A further earthquake reduced Al-Mansur's building to ruins; later, the Khalif Al-Mahdi, his successor, rebuilt the Aqsa a second time, making it on this occasion broader and shorter.

When referring to the Arab descriptions of the Haram Area at Jerusalem, an important point to remember is that the term *Masjid* applies not to the Aqsa alone but to the whole of the Haram Area, with the Dome of the Rock in the middle and all the other minor domes, chapels and colonnades. The Dome of the Rock (misnamed by the Franks the 'Mosque of Omar'), is not itself a mosque or place for public prayer, but merely the largest of the many cupolas in the Court of the Mosque, in this instance built to cover and do honour to the Holy Rock which lies beneath it.

In 985, during the rule of the Fatimid Khalif Al-Aziz, Muqaddasi, a native of Jerusalem, described the Aqsa thus:

> The Masjid al-Aqsa lies at the south-eastern corner of the Holy City. The stones of the foundations of the Haram Area wall, which were laid by David, are ten ells, or a little less, in length. They are chiselled, finely faced, and jointed, and of hardest material. On these Khalif 'Abd al-Malik subsequently built, using smaller but well-shaped stones, and battlements are added above. This mosque is even more beautiful than that of Damascus, for during the building of it they had for a rival and as a comparison the great Church [of the Holy Sepulchre] belonging to

View, from the Tomb of
Samuel, of the Crusader's
Mont Joie, their first
sight of Jerusalem after
the long climb from the
coast. Once a Crusader
church, the building is
now in use as a mosque.

the Christians at Jerusalem, and they built this to be even more magnificent than that other. But in the days of the Abbasids occurred the
earthquakes, which threw down most of the main building; all, in fact,
except that portion which is round the Mihrab. Now when the khalif
of that day obtained news of this, he inquired and learned that the sum
at that time in the treasury would in no wise suffice to restore the
mosque. So he wrote to the governors of the provinces, and to all the
commanders, that each should undertake the building of a colonnade.
The order was carried out, and the edifice rose firmer and more subs-
tantial than ever it had been in former times. The more ancient portion
remained, even like a beauty spot, in the midst of the new, and it extends as far as the limit of the marble columns; for beyond, where the
columns are of concrete, the later building commences.

The main building of the Aqsa Mosque has six doors. The door
opposite to the Mihrab is called the Great Brazen Gate; it is plated
with brass gilt, and is so heavy that only a man strong of shoulder and
of arm can turn it on its hinges. To the right of this [Great Gate] are
seven large doors, the midmost covered with gilt plates; and after the
same manner there are seven doors to the left. And further, on the
eastern side [of the Aqsa] are eleven doors unornamented. Over the

Within the Mosque Al-Aqsa, the magnificent minbar or pulpit, built at the order of Saladin for Aleppo but later brought to Jerusalem.

first-mentioned doors, fifteen in number, is a colonnade supported on marble pillars, lately erected by 'Abd Allah ibn Tahir.

On the right-hand side of the court [that is, along the west wall of the Haram Area] are colonnades supported by marble pillars and pilasters; and on the back [or north wall of the Haram Area] are colonnades vaulted in stone. The centre part of the main building [of the Aqsa] is covered by a mighty roof, high-pitched and gable-wise, over which rises a magnificent dome.

The description of the Aqsa in 985 by Muqaddasi is, in the main, identical with that given by Nasir, who visited Jerusalem sixty years later, and the two accounts taken together give us an exact idea of the appearance of the Great Mosque before the arrival of the Crusaders.

On 14 July 1099, the Crusaders, under Godfrey de Bouillon, captured the Holy City. The Haram Area was given over to the Knights of the recently established Order of the Temple, who derived their name from the Dome of the Rock, which the Crusaders imagined to be the Temple of the days of Christ and named *Templum Domini*. The Aqsa Mosque, on the other hand, was known as the *Palatium* or *Templum Solomonis*. The Templars made considerable alterations to the Aqsa Mosque and the adjoining portions of the Haram Area, but left the Dome of the Rock untouched. On the west of the Aqsa, along the south wall of the Haram Area, they built their armoury. In the substructures of the south-east angle of the Haram Area, to the west of the Cradle of Jesus, they stabled their horses, using probably either the ancient 'Triple Gate' or the 'Single Gate' as an exit from these vaults. The Latins considered the Aqsa Mosque to hold a very secondary place (while the Dome of the Rock was in their eyes the true *Templum Domini*); hence the Knights Templars felt no compunction in remodelling probably the whole building, when they turned part of the Aqsa into a church for the Order and established their main-guard and armoury in the outlying quarters of this great Mosque.

Crusander and Saracen   After Saladin's reconquest of the Holy City in 1187, the whole of the Haram Area and its various buildings underwent a complete restoration. The account given in the Chronicle of Ibn al-Athir of what was done in the Aqsa Mosque is as follows:

> When Saladin had taken possession of the city and driven out the infidels, he commanded that the buildings should be put back to their ancient usage. Now the Templars had built to the west of the Aqsa a building for their habitation, and constructed there all that they needed of granaries, and also latrines, with other such places, and they had even enclosed a part of the Aqsa in their new building. Saladin commanded that all this should be set back to its former state, and he ordered that the Masjid should be cleansed, as also the Rock, from all the filth and the impurities that were there. All this was executed as he commanded.

Over the Great Mihrab, in the Aqsa Mosque, may still be read the inscription set here by Saladin after this restoration was completed:

> In the name of Allah the Compassionate, the Merciful! Hath ordered the repair of this holy Mihrab, and the restoration of the Aqsa Mosque – which was founded in piety – the servant of Allah, and His regent, Yusuf ibn Ayyub Abu-l Mudhaffar, the victorious king, Salah ad-Dunya wa'ad-Din [Saladin], after that Allah had conquered [the City] by his hand during the month of the year 583. And he asked of Allah to inspire him with thankfulness for this favour, and to make him a partaker of the remission [of sins], through His mercy and forgiveness.

After Saladin's time there is no detailed description of the dimensions and appearance of the Aqsa Mosque until we come to that written by Mujir ad-Din in 1496; in his day the Mosque was evidently identical in form with the one we now see. The present Mosque (exactly like that described in 1496) has seven gates to the north, and only one to the east. Two other gates, on the western side, lead into the court, and one into what was, in Crusading days, the Templars' Armoury.

The Mosque we see today was entirely renovated between 1938 and 1943. During this period all the long walls and arcades were demolished to the foundations, with the exception of the two western aisles and the arcades flanking the dome. The nave and eastern aisles were reconstructed on arches carried by monolithic marble columns. The upper part of the north wall was also reconstructed and the whole refaced. The central doors and porch were also repaired. The work was supervised by the Director of the Department for the Preservation of Arab Monuments, in the Egyptian Government, which presented the magnificent gilded ceiling. At the southern end of the Mosque are the only surviving Fatimid mosaics and construction in Jerusalem; here is also a fine rose-window and mihrab in the place of the Forty Martyrs, and a very beautiful pulpit and mihrab installed by order of Saladin. Perhaps the most impressive sight of all, however, is that of some four thousand men, line after line in perfect order and action, covering every square metre of carpet in this vast mosque – the brotherhood of Islam at worship.

In remarkable contrast with the little that is known of the early architectural history of the Aqsa Mosque, is the very full account of the date and the historical incidents connected with the foundation of the Dome over the Sacred Rock. From the earliest times, also, there are extant such detailed descriptions of this beautiful building that it may be affirmed with almost complete certainty that the edifice as it now stands is (with regard to ground-plan and elevation) substantially identical with that which the Khalif 'Abd al-Malik erected in the year 691. The cupola, it is true, has on many occasions been shattered by earthquakes, and the walls have been damaged and repaired, but the octagonal ground-plan and the system of concentric colonnades have remained unaltered through all the restorations; even down to the number of the windows, the Dome of the Rock, as described in 903 by Ibn al-Fakih, is almost exactly similar to the Dome of the Rock of the present day. *The Dome of the Rock*

The Dome of the Rock for Muslims ranks in sanctity only after the Ka'ba in Mecca, according to Muslim tradition erected by Abraham and Ishmael, and the Tomb of the Prophet in Medina. This Rock on Mount Moriah was already held sacred, even before the Dome was built upon it, as the site of Abraham's offering of Isaac, and also as the ancient 'Qibla' of Moses, for Muslims hold that the Ark of the Covenant was placed on this Rock. As the direction of prayer of Moses, it was adopted as the first 'Qibla' of Islam. It was also the very spot from which Muhammad made his famous Night-Journey to heaven. It was, however, a political situation nearly a century later that resulted in the erection of a sanctuary on this site and in its becoming a place of pilgrimage.

Professor E. H. Palmer gives us the condition of the Omayyad khalifate at the period when the Dome of the Rock was built:

In AD 684, in the reign of 'Abd al-Malik, the ninth successor of Muhammad, and the fifth khalif of the house of Omayyad, events happened which once more turned people's attention to the City of David. For eight years the Muslim Empire had been distracted by factions and party quarrels. The inhabitants of the two Holy Cities, Mecca and

200

The interior of the Mosque Al-Aqsa showing the roofing, clerestory windows and arches, beautifully restored and renovated between 1938 and 1943.

Medina, had risen against the authority of the legitimate khalifs, and had proclaimed 'Abd Allah ibn Zubayr their spiritual and temporal head. The Khalif Yazid abd M'awiyah had in vain attempted to suppress the insurrection; the usurper had contrived to make his authority acknowledged throughout Arabia and the African provinces, and had established the seat of his government at Mecca itself. 'Abd al-Malik trembled for his own rule; year after year crowds of pilgrims would visit the Ka'ba, and Ibn Zubair's religious and political influence would thus become disseminated throughout the whole of Islam. In order to avoid these consequences, and at the same time to weaken his rival's prestige, 'Abd al-Malik conceived the plan of diverting men's minds from the pilgrimage to Mecca, and inducing them to make the pilgrimage to Jerusalem instead.

Political and religious policy of 'Abd al-Malik

The history of this political move, which was doomed to failure, is told by Ya'qubi, one of the earliest (AD 874) Arabic historians:

Then 'Abd al-Malik forbade the people of Syria to make the pilgrimage [to Mecca]; and this by reason that 'Abd Allah ibn az Zubayr was wont to seize on them during the time of the pilgrimage, and force them to

201

pay him allegiance – which, 'Abd al-Malik having knowledge of, forbade the people to journey forth to Mecca. But the people murmured thereat, saying, 'How dost thou forbid us to make the pilgrimage to Allah's house, seeing that the same is a commandment of Allah upon us?' But the khalif answered them, 'Hath not Ibn Shihab az-Zuhri told you how the Apostle of Allah did say: *Men shall journey to but three Masjids, Al-Masjid Haram [at Mecca], my Masjid [at Medina], and the Masjid of the Holy City [which is Jerusalem]*? So this last is now appointed for you in lieu of the Masjid al-Haram. And this Rock, of which it is reported that upon it the Apostle of Allah set his foot when he ascended into Heaven, shall be unto you in the place of the Ka'ba. Then Abd al-Malik built above the Sakhra a Dome, and hung it around with curtains of brocade, and he instituted doorkeepers for the same, and the people took the custom of circumambulating the Rock, even as they had paced round the Ka'ba, and the usage continued thus all the days of the dynasty of the Omayyads.

This story has a precedent in that of Jeroboam setting up golden calves at Dan and Bethel to divert Israelite pilgrims of the Northern Kingdom from pilgrimage to Jerusalem.

Muqaddasi, who wrote in 985, or nearly a century later, gives another reason, which may have been a factor in the case, although Ya'qub's reason must have been the principal one as it so perfectly fits the political situation at the time. Muqaddasi says:

Verily Al-Walid was right, and he was prompted to a worthy work. For he beheld Syria to be a country that had long been occupied by the Christians, and he noted herein the beautiful churches still belonging to them, so enchantingly fair, and so renowned for their splendour, even as are the Kumamah [the Church of the Holy Sepulchre at Jerusalem], and the churches of Lydda and Edessa. So he sought to build for the Muslims a mosque that should prevent their regarding these, and that should be unique and a wonder to the world. And in like manner is it not evident how the Khalif 'Adb al-Malik, noting the greatness of the Dome of Al-Kumamah and its magnificence, was moved lest it should dazzle the minds of the Muslims, and hence erected above the Rock, the Dome which is now seen there?

Had 'Abd al-Malik's attempt succeeded, it is a question whether Jerusalem might not then have become the capital of the Omayyads, in place of Damascus. As events turned out, the khalif failed to divert the Muslim pilgrimage to the Holy City of Palestine, and Mecca did not lose its pre-eminence as the religious centre of Islam.

That the Khalif 'Abd al-Malik was the builder of the Dome of the Rock is further confirmed by the well-known inscription which may still be read above the cornice of the octagonal colonnade supporting the cupola. Running round this is a magnificent Cufic script, in yellow on blue tiles, which must have been placed here by 'Abd al-Malik when the building was finally completed. It is dated 691.

The Dome of the Rock from the south-east, showing the southernmost Mawazin, or scales, upon which the legendary weighing of the souls of men will take place on the Day of Judgement. The Dome of the Chain is just to be seen on the right.

HATH BUILT THIS DOME THE SERVANT OF ALLAH 'AB DALLAH THE IMĀM AL MĀMŪN COMMANDER OF THE FAITHFUL DAL MALIK
IN THE YEAR TWO AND SEVENTY –
ALLAH ACCEPT OF HIM!

It will be observed that the date, 691, falls in the reign of 'Abd al-Malik, and therefore supports the texts, but that the name of al-Ma'mun has been fraudulently substituted. That there has been a clumsy forgery is evident owing (1) to the omission of the forger to alter the date, and (2) to the crowding together of the letters of the Abbasid khalif's name and title. In addition to this the tint of the newer mosaic, being darker, does not match that of the rest of the band. This forgery probably took place in 831, following restoration and repairs to the Dome.

The architecture of the shrine is well described by Creswell:

The Qubbat as-Sakhra, the earliest existing monument of Muslim architecture, is an annular building, and consists in its ultimate analysis of

203

a wooden dome on a high drum, pierced with sixteen windows and resting on four piers and twelve columns, placed in a circle and so arranged that three columns come between each pier. This circle of supports is placed in the centre of a large octagon measuring about twenty-one metres a side, formed by eight walls, each pierced with five windows in their upper half. The space between the circle and the octagon being too great to be conveniently spanned by single beams, an intermediate octagon, consisting of arches borne by eight piers and sixteen columns, so arranged that two columns come between each pier, has been placed between the two to provide the necessary support for the roof. The two concentric ambulatories thus formed are covered by a slightly sloping roof of wood covered with lead. There is a door in each of the four alternate sides of the octagon which face the four cardinal points.

The diameter and proportions of the Dome of the Rock were taken from those of the Church of the Holy Sepulchre. The dimensions of the octagonal exterior were almost certainly modelled, as their similarity shows, on the Church of the Ascension on the Mount of Olives.

The Shrine within the Sanctuary

One of the early accounts shows the setting of the Dome of the Rock within the Haram or Sanctuary Area. In the 978 Ibn Haukal abd Istakhti writes:

The Holy City is nearly as large as Ar-Ramlah [the capital of the province of Filastin]. It is a city perched high on the hills, and you have to go up to it from all sides. There is here a mosque, a greater than which does not exist in all Islam. The Main-building [which is the Aqsa Mosque] occupies the south-eastern angle of the mosque [Area, or Noble Sanctuary], and covers about half the breadth of the same. The remainder of the Haram Area is left free, and is nowhere built over, except in the part around the Rock. At this place there has been raised a stone [terrace] like a platform, of great unhewn blocks, in the centre of which, covering the Rock, is a magnificent Dome. The Rock itself is about breast-high above the ground, its length and breadth being almost equal, that is to say, some ten ells and odd, by the same across. You may descend below it by steps, as though going down to a cellar, passing through a door measuring some five ells by ten. The chamber below the Rock is neither square nor round, and is above a man's stature in height.

Within the Dome, the Holy Rock or Sakhra is associated with Abraham and Isaac, Araunah the Jebusite, the Shrine of David and the Altar of Sacrifice within Solomon's Temple, and also with the Ascension of the Prophet Muhammad on his Night Journey.

A hundred years later in 985, Muqaddasi of Jerusalem gives a more detailed description:

The Court [of the Haram Area] is paved in all parts; in its centre rises a Platform, like that in the Mosque at Medina, to which from all four sides ascend broad flights of steps. On this Platform stand four Domes. Of these, the Dome of the Chain, the Dome of the Ascension, and the Dome of the Prophet are of small size. Their domes are covered with sheet-lead, and are supported on marble pillars, being without walls. In the centre of the Platform is the Dome of the Rock, which rises above an octagonal building having four gates, one opposite to each of the flights of steps leading up from the Court. All these are adorned with gold, and closing each of them is a beautiful door of cedar-wood finely worked in patterns. Over each of the gates is a porch of marble, wrought with cedar-wood, with brasswork without; and in this porch, likewise, are doors, but these are unornamented.

Within the building are three concentric colonnades, with columns of the most beautiful marble, polished, that can be seen, and above is a low vaulting. Inside these [colonnades] is the central hall over the Rock; it is circular, not octagonal, and is surrounded by columns of polished marble supporting circular arches. Built above these, and rising high into the air, is the drum, in which are large windows; and over the drum is the Dome. The Dome, from the floor up to the pinnacle, which rises into the air, is in height one hundred ells. From afar off you may perceive on the summit of the Dome the beautiful pinnacle [set thereon], the size of which is a fathom and a span. The Dome, externally, is completely covered with brass plates gilt, while the building itself, its floor, and its walls, and the drum, both within and without, are ornamented with marble and mosaics.

The Cupola of the Dome is built in three sections: the inner is of ornamental panels. Next come iron beams interlaced, set in free, so that the wind may not cause the Cupola to shift; and the third casing is of wood, on which are fixed the outer plates. Up through the middle of the Cupola goes a passage-way, by which a workman may ascend to the pinnacle for aught that may be wanting, or in order to repair the structure. At the dawn, when the light of the sun first strikes on the Cupola, and the Drum reflects his rays, then is this edifice a marvellous sight to behold, and one such that in all Islam I have never seen the equal; neither have I heard tell of aught built in pagan times that could rival in grace this Dome of the Rock.

The city suffered several severe earthquake shocks between the time of Muqaddasi and the arrival of the Crusaders. In the year 1016, the Dome fell in and restorations were undertaken in 1022 and 1027. The last account before the Crusaders is that of Nasir-i-Khusran, in which occurs a description of the Rock itself together with its place in Muslim tradition.

The Rock itself rises out of the floor to the height of a man, and a balustrade of marble goes round about it, in order that none may lay his hand thereon. The Rock inclines on the side that is towards the Qiblah [or south], and there is an appearance as though a person had walked heavily on the stone when it was soft like clay, whereby the imprint of his toes had remained thereon. There are on the Rock seven such footmarks, and I heard it stated that Abraham – peace be upon him! – was once here with Isaac – upon him be peace! – when he was a boy, and that he walked over this place, and that the footmarks were his.

In the house of the Dome of the Rock men are always congregated – pilgrims and worshippers. The place is laid with fine carpets of silk and other stuffs. In the middle of the Dome, and over the Rock, there hangs

The Mosque of Ahmed al-Jazzar, 'The Butcher', an Albanian soldier of fortune who became Governor of Acre, capital of the Ottoman Province of Sidon, in the eighteenth century.

from a silver chain a silver lamp; and there are in other parts of the building great numbers of silver lamps.

In 1099 the Crusaders took Jerusalem, and the Dome of the Rock, considered by them to be the *Templum Domini*, passed to the Knights Templar. Holding this building to be the veritable Temple of the Lord, its outline was emblazoned by the knights on their armorial bearings, and in both plan and elevation the edifice came to be reproduced by the Templars in the various Temple churches which the order caused to be built in London, Cambridge, Laôn, Metz and other cities throughout Europe. Godfrey de Bouillon established a house of Augustinian Canons to which he entrusted the care of the building. An altar was erected on the Rock and a golden cross upon the Dome.

In 1187 Jerusalem was, as we have already mentioned, retaken by Saladin, who effected a complete restoration of the Haram Area to its pristine condition. The state into which the Rock had come through the zeal of the Franks for the acquisition of relics, is described in the Chronicle of Ibn al-Athir. Saladin removed the marble pavement with which the Christians had covered the Rock in order to prevent pilgrims from chipping off pieces of it.

Medieval restorations
After Saladin had completed his restoration, he set up inside the cupola of the Dome, above the Rock, a beautiful inscription in tile-work on a series of bands and medallions, which may still be seen *in situ*.

In the year 1448, the roof of the Dome was destroyed by fire and restored by Sultan al-Malik ibn Dhabir, 'so as to be more beautiful even that it had been aforetimes'. Suleiman II carried out extensive repairs early in the sixteenth century. It was Suleiman who transformed the exterior of the Mosque from a Byzantine into a Persian style, putting on tiles which had been fetched from Kasham in Persia and introducing the windows as they still are. He also restored the north, south and west doors, leaving only the simple and splendid east door as it originally was. He brought in some Indian artists to restore the roof. Suleiman died in the middle years of the sixteenth century, and after him Ottoman rule fell into a decline. Practically nothing was done, and what little was done, was ill done during the remaining years of Ottoman rule. Up until 1855, non-Muslims were not allowed to enter the Dome. Under the mandate, the British government handed over responsibility for Muslim buildings to the Supreme Muslim Council, and after the earthquake of 1927 this Council set about their task with refreshing vigour. In the fighting of 1948 the Dome was slightly damaged and one worshipper was killed. Partition left the Mosque in Jordanian hands and it was a matter of great pride to King Hussein that, as a Muslim, he should prove himself worthy of the high privilege with which he found himself possessed. The last of these restorations was carried out by Egyptian engineers between 1958 and 1962. The old foundations were exposed and reinforced with concrete. Certain columns were replaced within the drum of the Dome, and the old lead sheeting on the Dome was replaced with a special aluminium bronze alloy that shines like gold in the sun.

The Mihrab, or prayer niche, in the Mosque of Abraham at Hebron.

A few paces east of the Dome of the Rock stands a small cupola, supported on pillars but without any enclosing wall, except at the Qibla point, south, where two of the pillars have a piece of wall, forming the Mihrab, which was built up in between them. This is called Qubbat as-Silsilah – 'the Dome of the Chain'. As early as 913 it is mentioned by Ibn 'Abd Rabbih as 'the Dome where, during the times of the children of Israel, there hung down the chain that gave judgement [of truth and lying] between them'. Yakut, describing this Dome, mentions that it was here that was 'hung the chain which allowed itself to be grasped by him who spoke the truth, but could not be touched by him who gave false witness, until he had renounced his craft, and repented him of his sin'. Besides the Great Dome of the Rock and the smaller Dome of the Chain to the east of it, there have at all times stood on the Platform at least two other smaller domes, built to commemorate the incidents of the Prophet's Night-Journey. Muqaddasi, writing in 985, lists the minor shrines as follows:

Subsidiary shrines within the Sanctuary

> Of the holy places within [the Haram Area] are the Mihrab Maryam [the Oratory of Mary], Zakariyyah [of Zachariah], Ya'kûb [of Jacob], and Al-Khadr [of Elias, or St George], the Station of the Prophet [Makam an Nabi], and of Jibrâil [Gabriel], the Place of the Ant, and of the Fire, and of the Ka'ba, and also of the Bridge As-Sirât, which shall divide Heaven and Hell.

An up-to-date list of the qubbas within the Haram is given by Aref el-Aref in his *Dome of the Rock*.

A few metres only from the Dome of the Rock north-west is Qubbat al-Mi'raj, or the Dome of Ascension, because it is thought that on this spot Muhammad prayed before he ascended to heaven. No one knows when the original dome was made, but an inscription on the inner wall says that it was torn down and rebuilt in its present form in 1220 by Prince Asphah Salar 'Iz-ud-Din Said as Sa'ad Abu 'Omar 'Uthman Ibn 'Ali az-Zanjeeli. It is a small, attractive building standing on sixteen marble pillars. Near the above and north-west of the Dome of the Rock is Mihrâb an-Nabi, the Prayer Recess of the Prophet. It is a small dome but the mihrab is beautiful. It was built by the Governor of Jerusalem, Muhammad Bey, in 1538.

About one hundred metres from the Dome of the Rock to the south stands the Qubbat Yoûsef. It is an open rectangular building two metres square and was built by Asphah Salar Sayf-ud-Din 'Ali Ibn Ahmad in the time of Saladin, in 1191.

Still another Qubba, An-Nahawia, is situated on the south-west end of the Dome of the Rock elevation. This one was built in the reign of Al-Malik al-Mu'azzam 'Isa by Prince Hussam-ud-Din Abu Sa'id 'Uthman Ibn 'Abdullah, in 1207. It is small and was originally the place where literature and grammar were taught, hence its name. In recent years it has been used as a library by the Supreme Muslim Council.

Qubbat al-Khaleeli, Dome of the Hebronite, is a few metres to the north-west of the Dome of the Rock and is of comparatively recent con-

The Gate of the Chain leading from the Tyropoean Valley into the Temple Area.

struction, having been erected during the nineteenth century by Sheikh al-Khaleeli as a special place for prayer.

Still on the same elevation at the very north-west side is Qubbat Al-Khadr, Dome of St George. It is a very small qubba lifted on six small but very fine pillars made of marble. Beneath it is a small chapel for prayer and a room where building material belonging to the Waqf and for the use of the Haram is stored. Qubbat Musa stands between the Gate of the Chain and Qubbat an-Nahawia. It is a medium-sized dome and was built by the Ayyubite king, Al-Malik as-Sâleh Najm-ud-Din Ayyub in 1251 as a place where late-comers could pray. Kursi Suleiman, Throne of Solomon, is a small mosque situated on the east side of the Haram on the wall not far from the Gate of the Tribes. It is

The great minaret to the north-west of the Temple Area. Once the site of the towering Fortress of the Antonia, the minaret resounds at regular intervals with the Muslim call to prayer.

believed that Solomon sat on this spot and watched the jinn who worked for him at the building of the Temple.

Another place associated with Solomon is Qubbat Suleimân, north of the Haram a few metres from the Dark Gate. According to Mujeer-ud-Din, Solomon used to sit here, and not at Kursi Suleimân, to watch the workmen. The building is a very fine dome supported by twenty-four marble pillars and is of the Omayyad period. South-west of the Haram, near the Wailing Wall is Jâmi' al-Maghâribah, Mosque of the Moroccans. Certain parts of it are clearly from the Omayyad period. It was renovated by the Turks in the reign of Sultan 'Abdul-'Azeez, in 1871. Minbar Burhan, a fine pulpit made of marble, stands on the elevation opposite the Dome of the Rock, to the south. It is believed that this was built in the time of Saladin and was renovated in 1843 by a Turkish Amir, Muhammad Rasheed.

The platform on which the Dome stands is some sixteen feet above the level of the main parvis, and eight flights of steps lead up from the parvis to the platform. At the head of each of these flights is an elegant arcade surmounted by pointed arches of a style which indicates that they are of Crusader introduction, though they were restored by Saladin's brother, Al-Malik al-Adel. These are the traditional Mawazin, or scales, upon which the legendary weighing of the souls of men will take place on the Day of Judgement.

All these minor features are like small islands in an ocean of space, from the centre of which the Dome of the Rock rises superb and triumphant in its beauty and proportions. The very height and isolation of the Haram are refreshing and invigorating after the clamour of the city. Few would deny that from the purely aesthetic point of view, the Dome is superior to any of the great Christian basilicas of the Holy Land. It has one great advantage over them. They are all hemmed in by crowded, busy, jostling streets. By contrast, as we pass through the Gate of the Chain into the Haram, in the centre of which the Dome stands, we pass out of the turmoil into an atmosphere of spaciousness and peace. There is room for everything. There is room to breathe and to listen to the silence.

Other shrines of Islam Among the remaining Muslim Holy Places, Hebron, El-Khalil, or the 'Friend of God' (meaning Abraham), and the Tomb of Rachel, Qubbat Rahil, have been mentioned at some length in the first chapter as Hebrew shrines. These indeed they were, long before the time of Muhammad, and were accepted as such by the Christians, St Jerome and Eusebius the historian. Long before Jerome and Eusebius, Herod built his sanctuary over the Cave of Machpelah and Josephus knew Rachel's Tomb near Bethlehem. Muslim veneration of these two and other early Hebrew shrines is, in a sense, retrospective and under Muslim rule apt to be protectively exclusive. Consequently the Muslim annexation of sites sacred to the Jews has not been popular; nor perhaps nowadays is the virtual control at the Haram El-Khalil and the Qubbat Rahil by the Orthodox Jews very popular with Muslims. Whereas in Ottoman times Jews were

The entrance to the Cave of Machpelah within the Mosque of Abraham at Hebron, the burial place of the Patriarchs.

excluded from the Harams in Jerusalem and Hebron, now there is limited freedom of access to both for all faiths.

Of Lydda, Muqaddasi writes: 'Lydda lies about a mile from Ar-Ramlah. There is here a great mosque, in which are wont to assemble large numbers of the people from the capital [Ar-Ramlah], and from the villages round. In Lydda, too, is that wonderful church [of St George] at the gate of which Christ will slay the Antichrist.' The Church of St George mentioned by Muqaddasi must have been the original church which the Crusaders restored, for the present ruins are those of a building of the Crusading epoch. According to local tradition, St George the Cappadocian martyr came from Lydda, and over his remains was built a church mentioned in the fifth century. On the approach of the Crusaders, the church was burnt, but was rebuilt and again destroyed in 1291. Today the white minaret, rebuilt after the 1927 earthquake, and the mosque occupy the site of the Byzantine church. The remainder of the Crusader church was acquired by the Greek Orthodox, who built the present church over a crypt in which is shown the Tomb of St George. St George is revered by the Muslims as Al-Khadr (the green and living one).

The thirteenth-century geographer, Yakut, tells this story of the mosque at Ar-Ramlah and the church at Ludd (Lydda);

> The immediate cause of the building of the mosque there was this. A certain scribe of the name of Ibn Batrik demanded of the people of Lydda that they should give him a certain house that stood near the Church [of Lydda], in order that he might turn it into an abode for himself. But the people refused it him. Then said he, 'By Allah, then will I pull down that other!' – meaning the church. And so it came about, for at this time Suleiman was saying to himself, 'Behold the Commander of the Faithful that was – namely, 'Abd al-Malik – did build in the Mosque [or Haram Area] of the Holy City a Dome over the Rock, and thereby obtained fame to himself, and, further, the khalif Al-Walid hath built a mosque in Damascus, and obtained fame thereby unto himself also – why should not I, too, build a mosque and a city, and transport the people thither? So he founded the city of Ar-Ramlah, and built the mosque there; and this was the cause of the ruin of the city of Ludd [and of the church there].

Ramlah Ramlah was the provincial capital from its foundation by Suleiman, son of 'Abd al-Malik, until the coming of the Crusaders. Then, the famous White Mosque stood in the centre of the city, but its shrine was that of Nebi Salih, a Muslim prophet mentioned in the Quran who was sent to the tribe of Tamud. The Tower of Ramlah is an interesting and outstanding monument of the fourteenth century, originally erected as the minaret of the mosque, and now six storeys and thirty metres high. In its basic features it is an imitation of a gothic belfry, perhaps that of the Holy Sepulchre, but the decorations are Moorish. It stands within the White Mosque enclosure which was itself built six centuries earlier. It is called by Christians the Tower of the Forty Martyrs and by Muslims that of the Forty Companions of the Prophet. The Tomb of Nebi Salih lies to the west of the tower. Ramlah is also the traditional site of Arimathea, the home of Joseph in whose tomb Jesus was buried.

Nablus Nablus was built in AD72 by Titus and named Neapolis. It was the see of a Christian bishopric and also a Samaritan stronghold. It was occupied by the Muslims in 636, until it fell to the Crusaders in 1100. Today Nablus is a centre of cultural and political thought as well as a centre of light industry. The two fine mosques were in origin Byzantine churches. Ali of Herat, in 1173, wrote:

> Outside the town is a mosque where they say Adam made his prostration in prayer ... the Samaritans are very numerous in this town. Nearby is the spring of Al-Khadr [Elijah] ... further, Joseph is buried at the foot of a tree at this place.

Of Nablus, the geographer Idris wrote:

> There is here the well that Jacob dug – peace be on him! – where also

the Lord Messiah sat, asking of water to drink from a Samaritan woman. There is at the present day a fine church built over it. The people of Jerusalem say that no Samaritans are found elsewhere but here.

Among the provincial cities of Muslim interest is Acre, ancient *Acre* Ptolemais, a naval base under the Omayyads second only to Alexandria, and a key port throughout the Crusader occupation. On the fall of Jerusalem, Acre became the capital of the Latin kingdom. Towards the end of the eighteenth century, Acre became the capital of the Ottoman province of Sidon, under the Albanian soldier of fortune Ahmed al-Jazzar, justly nicknamed 'The Butcher' for his indiscriminate cruelty towards all classes of his subjects. He has left behind a magnificent mosque, square in plan and roofed with a great dome. With its slender minaret it stands in the middle of a large rectangular court, which is surrounded on three sides by arcades resting on ancient columns with modern capitals. The columns, which are partly of granite and partly of marble, were brought from the ruins of Tyre and Caesarea. Along these arcaded walks or cloisters are domed cells for the servants of the mosque and the pilgrims who come to visit it. In the courtyard, near the north-west corner of the mosque, stands a small domed chamber containing the white marble tombs of Jazzar Pasha, the founder of the mosque, and of Suleiman Pasha his successor.

Although the Book of Numbers denies that anyone knows the Tomb of *Tomb of Moses* Moses, in 1269 the Mamluk Sultan Beybars built a mosque at a point on the old pilgrim road, from which pilgrims could view Mount Nebo, to enclose a representative Tomb of Moses. What began, perhaps, as pilgrimage provision soon developed into political expedient, to ensure that there was a large Muslim contingent in Jerusalem over the Christian Easter festival. Since the Middle Ages it has been the custom to make an annual pilgrimage to Moses' tomb and shrine. The villagers used to come from all over Palestine; after services in the Haram es-Sharif, they would proceed in a picturesque procession to the shrine of Nebi Musa. After festivities lasting about a week, there was a return procession to Jerusalem, the whole festival coinciding exactly with the Holy Week services of the Eastern Churches!

It is a solemn thought that if Jews and Christians had set out more purposefully to share their faith with the Arabic tribes in the early centuries of the Christian era, they might not now be confronted with the vast brotherhood of Islam throughout the world. This brotherhood is drilled to a pattern of prayer, from preliminaries to prostrations, which binds together its members of all colours and countries. Hardened by the burning fast of Ramadhan, united in its single focus of pilgrimage, this brotherhood has developed its own exclusiveness, without reference to the universal fatherhood of God. 'Only believers are brothers', says the Quran, in which the mercy and compassion of God are outweighed by his justice and judgement. Islam still remains in character a brotherhood, whose words of witness, 'There is no God but God: Muhammad is the Apostle of God' are of great power, both to the simple and the wise.

With the Mosque Al-Aqsa in the background and the women in the foreground, the Faithful gather for prayer on Friday morning. An impressive sight, a brotherhood of believers whose words of witness are: 'There is no God but God: Muhammad is the Apostle of God'.

Acknowledgements

The photographs for this book were taken by Alistair Duncan, Middle East Archive, with the following exceptions (the number refers to the page on which the illustration appears):

W. Braun, 10-11, 68, 69, 72, 73, 98, 112, 113, 114, 127 and 137; Ronald Brownrigg, 52, 102, 109, 118, 142, 144, 154, 156, 158 and 161; Georg Gerster, 8; David Harris, 53, 83 and 104; Ronald Sheridan, 30, 50 and 175.

The remaining pictures are reproduced by permission of: Dura-Europos Publications, 20; Israel Office of Information, 21; The Israel Museum, 57 and 63; The Mansell Collection, 169; The Maritime Museum, Haifa, 14; Reinisches Bildarchiv, 18, 39, 40 and 41; The State of Israel Government Press Division, 66; Y. Yadin, 56.

The maps were drawn by Design Practitioners Ltd: those on pages 12, 74 and 192 were based with permission on maps by Carta, Jerusalem, in the *New Israel Atlas*, published by the Israel Universities Press, Jerusalem, and those on pages 110 and 124 were also based on maps by Carta, Jerusalem, in the *Macmillan Bible Atlas* published by Macmillan, New York.

The authors wish to express their warm thanks to John Curtis of Weidenfeld and Nicolson for selecting the illustrations and seeing the book through the press.

Amid the mass of material written on this subject, they wish to acknowledge their indebtedness to the following: Aref el-Aref, O.B.E., *Dome of the Rock*; Martin Buber, *History of an Idea*; Taufik Canaan, *Mohammedan Saints and Sanctuaries*; G. Dalman, *Sacred Sites and Ways*; P. Lagrange, *Palestine under the Muslims*; E.W.G. Masterman, *Studies in Galilee*; J. W. Parkes, *Conflict of Church and Synagogue*, and other works; George Adam Smith, *Historical Geography of the Holy Land*; and Robert Alter for quotations from Chaim Nachman Bialik; K.A.C. Cresswell of the British School of Archaeology; Father Geoffrey Curtis C.R.; Darton, Longman and Todd, for permission to use material from *Come and See*, by Ronald Brownrigg; Laurence King, for his plans of the Church of the Holy Sepulchre; R. W. Hamilton and E. Tatham Richmond, directors of the Mandatory Department of Antiquities; the Palestinian Exploration Fund, for use of their Library; Stewart Perowne's works on the background of the New Testament; Soeur Marie Aline de Sion; Pères R. Vincent O.P., Eugene Hoade O.F. and Brunot O.P.

Finally the authors wish to thank all who helped and encouraged them in Jerusalem and the United Kingdom.

Index

Domus Obed-Edom

PARS

Kidron torrens

Lucus Maachah

Mons C...

Hortus

Sepulcrum Dot.

Vivat Rex Solomon

MONS GIHON

VI

Emaus
Nicopolis

Baal-perazim

VALLIS...

Domus Zachariae

Geba

REPHA=

Mori

IM

Sive

OCCIDENS

GIGANTUM

Zelzan

Sepulcric

Rahelis

Bethsur

TRIBUS

Ramath

PARS

Bezek

Cisterna Davidis

Arca Boaz

Ephrata
Bethlehem

Via tendens ad Hebronem

Geduth Cimham

Sepulcrum Asaelis

Silva